Contemporary

Also available from Bloomsbury Methuen Drama

Contemporary Scottish Plays

Contemporary Welsh Plays

Contemporary Irish Plays

Contemporary English Plays

Edited and Introduced by
Aleks Sierz

Eden's Empire
James Graham

Alaska
DC Moore

Shades
Alia Bano

A Day at the Racists
Anders Lustgarten

The Westbridge
Rachel De-lahay

Bloomsbury Methuen Drama
An imprint of Bloomsbury Publishing Plc

B L O O M S B U R Y
LONDON • NEW DELHI • NEW YORK • SYDNEY

Bloomsbury Methuen Drama
An imprint of Bloomsbury Publishing Plc

50 Bedford Square	1385 Broadway
London	New York
WC1B 3DP	NY 10018
UK	USA

www.bloomsbury.com

BLOOMSBURY, METHUEN DRAMA and the Diana logo are trademarks of Bloomsbury Publishing Plc

First published in 2015

Introduction copyright © Bloomsbury Methuen Drama 2015.

Eden's Empire first published in Great Britain in 2006 by Methuen Drama. Copyright © 2006 by James Graham.
Alaska first published in Great Britain in 2007 by Samuel French. Copyright © 2007 by DC Moore
Shades first published in Great Britain in 2009 by Bloomsbury Methuen Drama. Copyright © Alia Bano, 2009
A Day at the Racists first published in Great Britain in 2010 by Bloomsbury Methuen Drama. Copyright © Anders Lustgarten, 2010
The Westbridge first published in Great Britain in 2013 by Bloomsbury Methuen Drama. Copyright © Rachel De-lahay 2011.

The rights of the authors and editor to be identified as the authors and editor of these works have been asserted by them in accordance with the Copyright, Design and Patents Act, 1988

All rights reserved. No part of this publication may be reproduced or transmitted in any form or by any means, electronic or mechanical, including photocopying, recording, or any information storage or retrieval system, without prior permission in writing from the publishers.

No responsibility for loss caused to any individual or organization acting on or refraining from action as a result of the material in this publication can be accepted by Bloomsbury or the authors and/or editor.

All rights whatsoever in this play are strictly reserved and application for performance etc. before rehearsals begin should be made: for *Eden's Empire* by professionals to Curtis Brown Group Limited, Haymarket House, 28–29 Haymarket, London, SW1Y 4SP, and by amateurs to Methuen Drama (Rights), Bloomsbury Publishing Plc, 50 Bedford Square, London, WC1B 3DP (email: permissions@bloomsbury.com); for *Alaska* by professionals to Troika Agency, 10a Christina Street, London, EC2A 4PA; and by amateurs to Methuen Drama (Rights), Bloomsbury Publishing Plc, 50 Bedford Square, London, WC1B 3DP (email: permissions@bloomsbury.com); for *Shades* by professionals and amateurs to The Agency (London) Ltd, 24 Pottery Lane, Holland Park, London, W11 4LZ; for *A Day at the Racists* by professionals to Curtis Brown Group Limited, Haymarket House, 28–29 Haymarket, London, SW1Y 4SP, and by amateurs to Methuen Drama (Rights), Bloomsbury Publishing Plc, 50 Bedford Square, London, WC1B 3DP (email: permissions@bloomsbury.com); for *The Westbridge* by professionals and amateurs to Tavistock Wood, 45 Conduit Street, London, W1S 2YN.

No performance may be given unless a licence has been obtained.

No rights in incidental music or songs contained in the work are hereby granted and performance rights for any performance/presentation whatsoever must be obtained from the respective copyright owners.

British Library Cataloguing-in-Publication Data
A catalogue record for this book is available from the British Library.

ISBN: PB: 978-1-4725-8798-5
EPUB: 978-1-4725-8799-2
EPDF: 978-1-4725-8800-5

Library of Congress Cataloging-in-Publication Data
A catalog record for this book is available from the Library of Congress.

Typeset by Fakenham Prepress Solutions, Fakenham, Norfolk NR21 8NN
Printed and bound in India

Contents

Chronology vi

Introduction by Aleks Sierz xi

Eden's Empire by James Graham 1

Alaska by DC Moore 91

Shades by Alia Bano 161

A Day at the Racists by Anders Lustgarten 253

The Westbridge by Rachel De-lahay 339

Chronology

1996 8–30 June: England hosts the UEFA European Football Championship (Euro 96), with the slogan 'Football Comes Home'. For the first time, English football fans popularize the flag of St George, widely used by supporters all around the country. But the English team loses on penalties to Germany, whose team wins the competition.

1997 March: *Vanity Fair* magazine devotes issue to Cool Britannia, a moment of renewed cultural confidence which includes theatre as well as Britpop. 1 May: Tony Blair elected Prime Minister in a landslide General Election victory for the Labour Party, which under his leadership has been rebranded as New Labour. Labour wins 418 seats to the Conservative Party's 165. A record number of women, 120, are elected to parliament, of whom 101 are Labour MPs. Blair's government includes his ally, and rival, Gordon Brown as Chancellor of the Exchequer. 30 July: Blair, youngest Prime Minister of the twentieth century, hosts party at Number Ten Downing Street for Cool Britannia celebrities, such as rock musician Noel Gallagher. 31 August: Princess Diana is killed in a car crash in Paris; Blair salutes her as the 'People's Princess'.

1998 June: First meeting of the Campaign for an English Parliament, a pressure group campaigning for a devolved English Assembly, set up in response to the upcoming Scottish, Welsh and Northern Irish devolutionary processes. 31 July: Crime and Disorder Act introduces Anti-Social Behaviour Orders (ASBOs) as well as other ways of imposing discipline on unruly working-class youth. BBC journalist Jeremy Paxman publishes *The English: A Portrait of a People* (Penguin).

1999 1 January: The new Euro currency introduced in most European Union (EU) states, excluding the United Kingdom. 24 February: Macpherson Report into the racist murder of black London teenager Stephen Lawrence, stabbed to death in 1993, condemns London's police force as 'institutionally racist'. October: Nick Griffin becomes leader of the British National Party (BNP). His aim is to 'modernise' the party's image.

Chronology vii

2000 1 January: Millennium Dome opens. 7 June: During local elections, the BNP wins three seats on Burnley council. 27 November: Damilola Taylor, a ten-year-old schoolboy originally from Nigeria, is stabbed to death on his way home in Peckham, south London.

2001 25 June: A race riot in Burnley, Lancashire, with more than 200 white and Asian youths involved in fighting, vandalism and arson. Other disturbances in Bradford, West Yorkshire, and Brixton, south London follow in July. 11 September: Four American airplanes are hijacked by a group of Al-Qaeda militant Islamists, with two being flown into the World Trade Centre building in New York. More than 3,000 people are killed, including about 67 UK nationals, the largest loss of life from any nation other than the United States. 9/11 creates a climate of fear of terrorism and leads to US and UK invasions of Afghanistan and Iraq.

2002 29 April: Queen Elizabeth II, as part of her Golden Jubilee celebrations, dines at Number Ten Downing Street with five of the prime ministers that were in office during her reign, including the present incumbent Tony Blair. Another guest is Clarissa Eden, widow of former PM Anthony Eden.

2003 February: BBC Three, a new digital channel, launches. One of its comedy programmes is *Little Britain*, a sketch show which includes the character Vicky Pollard, a grotesque stereotype of a disadvantaged single mother. She soon becomes identified with 'chavs', a new name for anti-social urban youth. 20 March: The Iraq War begins, with US and UK troops invading Iraq, ruled by dictator Saddam Hussein. The war is quickly won, but peaceful reconstruction of the country proves to be very difficult. In London, this is Nicholas Hytner's first year as new artistic director of the National Theatre, and he begins to promote a more racially diverse picture of Britain by commissioning playwrights such as Kwame Kwei-Armah, who writes a trilogy of plays about the experience of Black Britons: *Elmina's Kitchen* (2003); *Fix Up* (2004); *Statement of Regret* (2007). Hytner's response to the Iraq War is a modern-dress production of Shakespeare's *Henry V*, in which the warrior king is played by Adrian Lester, a black actor. Also in 2003, Kumar

Krishan publishes his study, *The Making of English National Identity* (Cambridge University Press).

2004 1 May: The EU expands as eight new East European countries join, prompting fears of more immigration from countries such as Poland. On average, since 2004 some 170,000 EU citizens have migrated to the UK each year, compared to an average of about 300,000 from outside the EU. 12 June–4 July: Euro 2004 football competition; fans buy about 30 million flags of St George. 14 June: Results of the European Elections sees gains by the United Kingdom Independence Party (UKIP), up from three to twelve MEPs. 'Chav' designated Word of the Year by Susie Dent in her *Larpers and Shroomers: The Language Report* (Oxford University Press).

2005 7 July: London bombings. Four Islamist men, all born in the UK, perpetrate suicide attacks on the transport system in central London, killing 52 people. 22 October: Riot in Birmingham involving some 2,000 Afro-Caribbean youths after rumours that a 14-year-old Jamaican girl was sexually assaulted. November: A study conducted for the Commission for Racial Equality finds that, in England, the majority of ethnic minority participants identified themselves primarily as British, whereas white English participants identified as English first and British second.

2006 14 January: Gordon Brown, Chancellor of the Exchequer, gives a speech arguing that Britain should have a day to celebrate its national identity, and urges Labour supporters to 'embrace the Union flag' and recapture it from the far right BNP. 4 May: in local elections, the BNP more than double its members, and becomes the second largest party on Barking and Dagenham council. September: Nigel Farage becomes leader of UKIP. Also in 2006, the British Social Attitudes survey shows that between 1992 and 2005, the percentage of English people describing themselves as such is up from 31 per cent to 40 per cent.

2007 24 June: Gordon Brown becomes leader of the Labour Party, replacing Tony Blair. 14 September: Depositors withdraw about £1 billion from Northern Rock building society, the biggest run on a bank for more than a century, part of the global financial crisis.

Chronology ix

Also in 2007, the artistic directors of the main new writing theatres change: Dominic Cooke takes over from Ian Rickson at the Royal Court; Josie Rourke takes over from Mike Bradwell at the Bush Theatre; Lisa Goldman takes over from Abigail Morris at the Soho Theatre.

2008 22 February: Northern Rock nationalized. 14 June: Fires lit at the Campsfield immigration detention centre in Oxfordshire, which houses asylum seekers. 4 November: Barack Obama wins US presidential election, becoming the first African-American to hold this office. Also in 2008, David Edgar's play *Testing the Echo* examines national identity.

2009 4 June: In elections to the European Parliament, the BNP gets two seats while UKIP wins twelve seats and is the second largest party after the Conservatives. Both parties capitalize on widespread public anxiety over immigration. 22 October: BNP leader Nick Griffin appears for the first time on *Question Time*, the BBC political debate programme. Many commentators say he is humiliated. Also in 2009, Jez Butterworth's play *Jerusalem* and Richard Bean's play *England People Very Nice* examine English national identity.

2010 6 May: General Election results in a hung parliament, with a Coalition government made up of the Conservative Party (which wins the largest share of the vote but no overall majority) and the Liberal Democrat Party. David Cameron, leader of the Conservatives, becomes Prime Minister and Nick Clegg, leader of the Lib Dems, is his deputy. 9 December: Protests by university students against increased tuition fees and reduced public spending on higher education take place in Whitehall, central London. The Cenotaph war memorial and statue of Winston Churchill are vandalised, and a car carrying Prince Charles and his wife Camilla is attacked.

2011 Census of the UK: London is the most ethnically diverse area, and Wales the least. 91 per cent of the resident population identify with at least one UK national identity (English, Welsh, Scottish, Northern Irish, and British). Whites make up 86 per cent of the population, a decrease from 91.3 per cent in 2001 and 94.1

per cent in 1991. Indian is the next largest ethnic group with 1.4 million people (2.5 per cent) followed by Pakistani (2 per cent). This is consistent with census findings on migration, which say that South Asian countries (India, Pakistan and Bangladesh) are the most common non-UK countries of birth. Islam is the largest minority religion in London, with Muslims making up 12.4 per cent of the population, and more than 30 per cent in Newham and Tower Hamlets boroughs. 6–11 August: Riots break out across England after a protest over the police shooting of Mark Duggan in Tottenham, north London, gets out of control. Fuelled by the use of digital social media, these are the worst disturbances in living memory. By 15 August, about 3,100 people have been arrested, more than 1,000 of whom are charged for looting and other public order offences.

2012 10 January: Five Muslim men are tried in Derby for calling for gay men to be killed, the first prosecution under new hate crime legislation. 6 February: Diamond Jubilee of Queen Elizabeth II marks sixtieth anniversary of her accession to the throne. 27 July: Summer Olympics begin in London.

2013 22 May: Drummer Lee Rigby, a British soldier, is killed during the day in a street in Woolwich, south London, by two Muslim men. 7 July: Abu Qatada, a Muslim cleric, is deported to Jordan to face charges of terrorism. 17 July: The Marriage (Same Sex Couples) Bill is passed, enabling gay marriages to take place in England and Wales from the following year. Also in 2013, Vicky Featherstone, formerly artistic director of the National Theatre of Scotland (NTS), becomes new artistic director of the Royal Court.

2014 22 May: in elections to the European Parliament, UKIP wins the largest share of the vote (27.5 per cent); the BNP loses its seats. Also in 2014, the Royal Court announces that six playwrights and directors partner with six *Guardian* newspaper journalists to make short filmed theatrical events in response to the question 'Is there such a thing as English Identity?'

Introduction

Contemporary English Plays is an anthology of five plays which together offer a vivid snapshot of the country at the end of the first decade of the new millennium. The collection comprises outstanding and award-winning work from a group of young and emerging playwrights, namely James Graham, DC Moore, Alia Bano, Anders Lustgarten and Rachel De-lahay. Their subject matter and their sensibility is England and Englishness, and their work has clearly been moulded by 9/11, a global rift which separates then from now, and which led directly to the Iraq War, one of the defining issues of the 2000s. These playwrights grew up in the era of New Labour, when the idea of Englishness, and disputes about its definition, began to be heard more and more in the media as a hotly discussed subject (a debate joined by the Chancellor and then Prime Minister Gordon Brown). Following the positive experiences of devolution in Scotland, Wales and Northern Ireland, the question of what should happen in England became an increasingly contested one. What is Englishness? Should there be an English parliament? Do the English always appropriate Britishness (in a way that the Scots and Welsh don't)? With interventions by the ultra-right British National Party (BNP), its flags emblazoned with the cross of Saint George, and the anti-European United Kingdom Independence Party (UKIP), the temperature of these debates rose markedly throughout the decade. At the same time, increased globalisation and migration to the UK produced social strains, not only accelerating the creation of a multicultural society, but also fuelling resentment from the white working class, who often saw themselves as abandoned by New Labour. In this social context, these five plays together examine not only the current state of the nation, but also the heritage of Empire.

The plays were mostly conceived and written in the second half of the era of New Labour, when the party was losing popularity and the discourse of social problems associated with national identity and racial integration was at its height. They are all good examples of the strengths of what can be identified as an English playwriting tradition, as opposed to the more overt theatricality of Scottish,

Welsh and Irish theatre traditions. Its characteristics are those of a specific English idea of naturalism, which aims to show the nation to itself, articulating debates about social issues and priding itself on its overt realism. At its best, this work has an authentic and honest voice, is meticulously researched, usually linear in form but complex in its representation of character, and written in a passionate and gritty vernacular which is not afraid of exploring excruciating emotional states. As such, the five examples in this collection portray an instantly recognisable picture of multicultural London, and their content could be described, in historical terms, as the Empire writes back.[1]

One of the most popular genres of English playwriting is the history play and the first piece in this collection is James Graham's *Eden's Empire*, a play about the Suez Crisis of 1956, which even sixty years after it happened still retains its place as a pivotal historical moment. Graham wrote the play while he was Pearson Playwright-in-Residence at the Finborough Theatre, on the London fringe, and it won the Catherine Johnson Award for the Best Play in 2007. It was first staged at that theatre in September 2006, in a production directed by Gemma Fairlie, and is a state-of-the-nation drama that starts at the end of the Second World War, with Winston Churchill and his Foreign Secretary Anthony Eden walking through the ruins of Hitler's bunker. It then shows key moments in Eden's career, as he waits with increasing frustration for the superannuated Churchill to resign. Even after he becomes Prime Minister he remains in the shadow of the Churchill family because his second wife Clarissa is Churchill's niece. Eden's attempt to hang on to Empire and to punish the Egyptian leader, Gamal Abdel Nasser, whom he wrongly identifies with Hitler, leads to the ill-conceived and humiliating Suez Crisis, a typically English mix of muddle and mendacity. Eden is portrayed as an able Foreign Secretary who is out of his depth as Prime Minister. The play's theme is failure, a very English preoccupation.

Graham underlines the parallels between Eden and Blair, between Suez and the War in Iraq, when the Caricaturist comments: 'Looks like old Tony is taking the country to war' (61). For most of the play, Harold Macmillan, Eden's Chancellor and successor, waits, like Brown in Blair's administration, for his turn as Prime Minister.

But as well as being a history play, this is also a play about being English. It is a study of an Englishman — Clarissa remembers her first sight of Eden as 'Very English' (14) — and the text is full of references to English values, English virtues and English habits. At one point, Eden mentions the son he lost in the Second World War, who had a copy of Shakespeare's *Henry V* among his possessions. The cover of the original playtext shows a Union Jack flag in flames, an image that suggests the destructive nature of imperial adventures. At the time of the Suez debacle, eight years had passed since the first arrival in 1948 of the aptly named *Empire Windrush*, bringing some five hundred passengers from Jamaica, most of whom didn't expect to settle in England. This was a landmark in the history of contemporary Britain, the point when the story of postwar mass migration begins. As the Jamaican poet Louise Bennett-Coverley concludes in her 1966 poem, 'Colonization in Reverse', 'Wat a devilment a Englan!/ Dem face war an brave de worse,/ But me wonderin how dem gwine stan/ Colonizin in reverse.' It's a question explored in the next four plays of this collection.

DC Moore's debut play, *Alaska*, was first staged at the Royal Court in May 2007, directed by Maria Aberg, and won the Tom Erhardt Award for promising new playwright from the Peggy Ramsey Foundation the following year. It presents a picture of contemporary racial antagonism. It is also a play about such quintessentially English themes as failure and class. The central figure is twenty-four-year-old Frank, one of life's losers. As the first scene, which takes place at university, appears to show, he is out of his depth both educationally and socially. Exploited by middle-class students as a drug dealer, he is eventually told by Adam to 'crawl back to your little estate' (103). Emotionally damaged, Frank attracts bad stuff. He drops out of university, he gets a job working in a multiplex cinema, and he refuses promotion. In fact, when a new employee is given the job of supervisor, it comes as an unpleasant shock; she is a woman; she's younger, and she's Asian. To Frank, who is an unapologetic racist, this feels like a provocation. At the same time, despite his moodiness, he is sexually attractive to his work colleagues. Emma, another white loser, offers him sex as sympathy, while the new Asian supervisor, the up-and-coming Mamta, is initially also attracted to him.

What is striking about Moore's playwriting is his ability to explore the complex connections between sexism and racism with uncommon clarity. In one perfectly paced scene, Frank and Mamta share some chocolates. When he tells her that they have probably been nibbled by rats, she gags. Then she turns to him for affection and he rejects her because she's not white. It's a visceral, excruciating moment. In another scene Mamta meets Frank, who has developed his white supremacist theories through Bible study, on the steps of a church. When he argues for the superiority of the white race, and develops at length his ideas about the 'legacy of Empire' (143), she fights back with admirable logic and zest. Here Moore's most provocative suggestion is that Frank's racism is not dissimilar to the attitudes of Mamta's father, a Ugandan Asian who came to Britain in the early 1970s. Then, in a confrontation with Emma, Mamta shows that she can be as dictatorial as any other boss. This is a play as much about class as about race.

Having watched *Alaska*, what you remember are not just the dark passions and the violence, but also the lovely theatrical moments. When Frank teaches the young Chris, a fellow employee, how to smoke a cigarette, or when the two young men play a game of Dictators Top Trumps, in which the cards have details of the world's worst political rulers, or when Chris tends to Frank's wounds, after the latter has got into a fight, you immediately sense how perfectly pitched the tone of the writing is. There's something very English about the eccentricity of these scenes, and their self-deprecating humour. Moore confidently stages moments of great tenderness as well as incidents of abrupt violence. And then, in a quirky twist, he gives Chris, who at first appears to be a minor character, the motive and the opportunity not only to find out the truth about Frank's real identity, but also to provide the title of the play.

If much of the emotional fuel of *Alaska* comes from the frustrations of Frank, the characters in Alia Bano's debut *Shades* arrive on stage from a very different place. First staged in January 2009 at the Royal Court, in Nina Raine's production, the play secured Bano the title of Most Promising Playwright in the 2009 Evening Standard Awards. Once again, the setting is multiracial London, but this time everything is seen from the perspective of Muslim culture. The cast list is specific: Sabrina is Pathan, Zain Bengali, and Reza, Ali and Nazia Pakistani, while Mark is white English. The plot follows the single Sabrina's search for love. She gets a helping hand from Zain, who takes her to a Muslim speed-dating event. He is gay and, along with his boyfriend Mark, provides a lot of the play's humour and a counterpoint to her story. When she organizes an event – a fashion show – to raise money for the Palestinians in Gaza, she meets Reza. Although Sabrina is attracted to Reza, his strong Muslim beliefs turn the path of true love into a bumpy ride. Nazia, Reza's sister, represents his traditionally minded family, who don't approve of modern womanhood and who imagine that because Sabrina is sharing a flat with Zain she must be sleeping with him. Added to this, Reza is betrayed by his friend Ali, a hypocritical playboy, who makes his own pass at Sabrina. Bano ensures that Ali gets his comeuppance and ends the play on a qualified note of hope.

Like *Alaska*, *Shades* is set in a variety of unusual locations: a speed-dating event, a rented hall, a coffee shop, an Islamic talk, an office, rehearsals for a fashion show and behind the scenes at the event itself. Bano writes clearly and amusingly about the clash between traditionalists and liberals within London's Muslim community, questioning clichéd ideas about collective identity. What emerges is a vivid picture of the various contradictions between religious faith and the business of living in a highly secular and highly sexualised society. With a text that is energetic and often delightful, the play's issues come at you dressed in a garb that is partly humorous and partly serious. Bano skilfully avoids sentimentality and crassness, and her plea for mutual understanding features an engrossing group of well-rounded characters. Although much of the conflict is between tradition and modernity, with the question of what behaviour is 'appropriate' to good Muslims running through the show like a kind of religious Political Correctness. One other theme is national identity, with mentions of the England soccer team, and Reza at one point saying that after 9/11 he felt that he had to choose between being a Muslim or being British. He's English enough to side with the underdog so logically 'The underdog at the moment is a Muslim, and in an ironic way, by standing up for Muslims, I think I'm being very British' (196). But, near the end of the play, the romantic notion of Zain and Mark getting married

– despite some misunderstandings – casts a warm glow over a play that argues for tolerance and self-determination.

By contrast, the power behind Anders Lustgarten's *A Day at the Racists* is a barely suppressed fury. Written as part of the Pearson Residency Scheme by a playwright who is also a political activist, and first staged in Ryan McBryde's production at the Finborough in March 2010, the play won its author the inaugural Harold Pinter Playwright's Award as well as the Catherine Johnson Award for Best Play. The story focuses on Pete Case, once known as Head Case for his left-wing views while he was a union organiser working in a car factory. Now that the factories have closed, he works as a painter and decorator with his black friend Clint. But his son Mark, who has a young daughter, finds it difficult to get work and impossible to move up the waiting list for Council housing (he sleeps on his father's sofa). When Pete remonstrates with the local Labour MP he gets little sympathy. His complaints about immigrants getting preferential treatment in jobs and housing fall on deaf ears. He's also not impressed that his mixed-race granddaughter is being taught ethnic history at the expense of British history in her primary school. Then he meets Gina, a young mixed-race parliamentary candidate, and agrees to be her campaign manager. The twist is that she is standing for the racist BNP. The play then examines both the conflicts within the BNP and the effects of Pete's decision on his mate Clint and his son Mark (who falls for Zenobia, a young black teacher at his daughter's primary school).

Powerfully written, taut and emotionally true, the play's scenes burn and broil with a sense of political rage that is neither simplistic nor hectoring. It is rare for a piece of contemporary new writing to grasp a pressing political issue and give it such a strong story, one that engages both the mind and the emotions with such a firm grip. At its first outing, *A Day at the Racists* was timely, controversial and thought-provoking, set in the same Barking and Dagenham constituency that BNP leader Nick Griffin campaigned in for both local and national elections. In the play, Lustgarten explores the rise of the BNP and the reasons for it, especially engaging with the uncomfortable reality that many respectable people are drawn to the racist party, a result of their feelings of abandonment by New Labour and perhaps because of the success of the BNP's rebranding strategy. So Pete's initial revulsion from the BNP is beautifully balanced by his desire to do what's best for his son and granddaughter. Failed by the policies of New Labour, he is both an individual and a representative of the resentful English white working class, whose support for the BNP is one way of achieving better material conditions. As the play puts Pete under pressure, the various contradictions of his position are finely articulated. At the same time, the struggle within the BNP between traditional vulgar racists, here represented by McDonald, and a new breed of more manipulative strategists, such as Coleman, is acutely pictured. As the text's epigraph, by American black activist Malcolm X, says: 'Racism is like a Cadillac. There's a new model every year' (253). But not only is this a political tale, it is also the story of a pair of amorous relations: Pete and Gina; Mark and Zenobia.

Lustgarten's analysis of racism is both general and highly specific. When McDonald throws his beer over Gina's head, Coleman dabs the mess with his hanky, but she notices, in the words of the stage directions, 'Something in his fastidiousness, the care he takes not to touch her skin with his bare hand, says more about the way he sees her than any amount of rhetoric' (304). The writing is often visceral and gutsy, but it is also full of ideas. Lustgarten understands the ability of the BNP to vary its message depending on its audience, and in one scene Pete gains support from ordinary working people by leading a task force to clear up rubbish on a local estate. At the same time, Lustgarten doesn't shy away from the basic brutality of racist politics. McDonald's mission, for example, is based on a fantasy of pure blood: 'My job is to preserve the purity of England for generations yet unborn,' (328) he says. More subtly, Gina aims to campaign for the party on 'a positive line about England' (306). Her pride in her country is obvious, especially in the scene when she talks to Pete about its thousand-year history. By contrast, Clint articulates the precarious situation of first-generation migrants such as his parents. Amid the main arguments of the play, Lustgarten finds room for incidental cultural comments, such as Coleman's 'You can always rely on a little bit of violence to tickle the jaded palate of middle England' (329). The strength of the drama is that the four main characters – Pete, Mark, Gina and Zenobia – engage your sympathy and voice their arguments with a passionate intensity. They might struggle with ideas of national identity, and their psychological motivations are complex, but they all contribute to a play that is both richly funny and very moving.

A similar mix of passion and laughter animates Rachel De-lahay's *The Westbridge*. This was first produced by the Royal Court at the Bussey Building – a former cricket bat factory and now a cultural centre – in Peckham, south London, in November 2011 as part of the Court's Theatre Local initiative, which takes plays out of its posh Sloane Square base and stages them in more deprived areas. Energetically directed by Clint Dyer, its awards include joint winner of the 2010 Alfred Fagon award for playwrights of African and Caribbean descent, and Writers' Guild's Best Theatre Play in 2012. It was developed while De-lahay participated in the Royal Court's Unheard Voices Writers Programme, being part of a group comprising young Muslim writers. Set in Battersea, south-west London, it paints a picture of urban life that is sexually, emotionally and racially complex. The lynchpin of the story is one family: Saghir is a Pakistani man who runs a local convenience store. His wife is white, although the couple are now divorced, so their twenty-something kids, Ibi and Soriya, are mixed race. But while the older Ibi is a good Muslim and has had an arranged marriage with a young woman from Pakistan, Soriya makes a different choice. She flat-shares with George, a white British woman, and at the start of the play we see her lover, Marcus – mixed race with an African-Caribbean heritage – moving in with them. Marcus is also part mentor, part hero to the sixteen-year-old tearaway Andre, a black Briton whose Jamaican mum, Audrey, is a neighbour of Saghir's. Close by is the notorious, but fictional, Westbridge estate.

De-lahay confronts a living issue: the tensions between black and Asian people. The relationships of her characters are brought to crisis point when a rumour spreads that a fourteen-year-old Pakistani girl has been gang-raped by black teenagers on the Westbridge estate. Messages on Facebook and Twitter help circulate the news and a riot soon erupts, recalling similar disturbances in Birmingham in 2005, although the racial mixture was different, and the violence of the summer riots of 2011. In the play, Andre is accused of participating in the rape. At the same time, Soriya brings Marcus home to meet her father and brother, and the issue of how various ethnic groups relate to each other is discussed. The complications of the various relationships – Soriya is torn between Marcus and George; Ibi was once George's boyfriend – demonstrate some of the confusions of cultural identity in contemporary London. Even the fact that George uses a male form of her name – reminiscent surely of that most English of tomboys, Enid Blyton's George in her *Famous Five* novels of the 1940s and 1950s – raises a question about gender identity. The play's message is not only that traditional racial categories make little sense nowadays, but also that sexuality is more fluid than ever before.

De-lahay has a real talent for depicting vivid characters. Soriya is a smart Cambridge-educated young woman who works in PR; she likes clubbing, but her confidence in her choice of Marcus for a mate wobbles when a neighbour confronts her and when her father disapproves. Her white friend Georgina is a hilarious creation, with her sharp tongue, fashion sense and dreams of becoming a top model. The play is as much about female friendship as a snapshot of a community. On the male side, there's a nice contrast between the insecure Ibi and the more confident Marcus. This portrait of mixed-race, upwardly mobile twenty-somethings is both witty and engaging. Equally convincing is De-lahay's view of the grown-ups, from Audrey to Saghir. She has a knack for comic dialogue and writes the quick-fire banter of the youth, and the exasperation of their parents, with an acute ear and impressive emotional sensitivity.

The Westbridge is a play that sizzles with contemporary relevance: its discussions of Englishness range across topics which have become part of a nationwide debate. For example, if we are what we eat, then what is our national dish: fish and chips or chicken tikka masala? In this context, the suggestion voiced by Soriya – that Marcus would like to eat African-Caribbean food betrays her assumptions about his background. He soon puts her right: 'My mom's white and my dad left. She didn't cook this stuff' (383). So what did he eat at home? 'English stuff. Roasts, spaghetti … ' To which Soriya sarcastically replies: 'Spaghetti? Very English' (383). In miniature, this exchange shows the complexity of cultural and racial elements in today's London. Powerfully written, emotionally engaging and full of lively humorous chat, this is a fast-moving and vigorous debut.

What all the plays in this collection have in common is that they paint an instantly recognisable picture of English culture, whether the setting is contemporary London or 1950s England. Together, they tell the story of a country which loses its Empire and then, through migration, retains numerous links to its former colonies. Since they were premiered, not only have the individual playwrights gone on to achieve greater successes, but the political climate around the issue of immigration has intensified. In the European Union Parliamentary elections of May 2014 this issue has been raised by UKIP, which now receives more publicity, and much more electoral success, than the BNP. Yet despite being widely perceived as racist, UKIP is very successful in electoral terms, articulating the same kind of resentment as some of these plays so vividly outline. In the May 2014 elections UKIP won more votes than any of the mainstream parties, a result seen as a political earthquake. With its core policy of demanding a withdrawal of the UK from the European Union, UKIP represents a Little Englander mentality, and its popularity suggests increasing social tensions and yet more questions about the concept of national identity. Yet despite such problems, UKIP has been notably less successful in London – with its more youthful and diverse population – than in areas outside the capital. Indeed, as Londoners born and bred, most of the characters in these plays not only confront the complexities of the issues around Englishness with stout hearts, but also with a touch of hope.

Aleks Sierz, June 2014

Note

1 See Bill Ashcroft, Gareth Griffiths and Helen Tiffin, *The Empire Writes Back: Theory and Practice in Post-Colonial Literature* (Routledge, 1989).

Eden's Empire

James Graham

Eden's Empire was first performed at The Finborough Theatre, London on 6 September 2006, with the following cast (in order of appearance):

Anthony Eden	Jamie Newall
Winston Churchill	Ted Pleasance
Reporter	Michael Kirk
Byrnes	Nigel Pegram
Molotov	Hayward Morse
Caricaturist	Selva Rasalingam
Lady Clarissa Eden	Daisy Beaumont
Schuman	Nigel Pegram
Colonel Nasser	Selva Rasalingam
Dulles	Hayward Morse
Harold Macmillan	Kevin Quarmby
Butler	Hayward Morse
Swinton	Michael Kirk
Woolton	Nigel Pegram
Frederick Bishop	Nigel Pegram
Selwyn Lloyd	Michael Kirk
Anthony Nutting	Selva Rasalingam
Lord Mountbatten	Hayward Morse

All other parts were played by members of the company

Director	Gemma Fairlie
Designer	Alex Marker
Lighting	Matt Peel
Sound	Steve Mayo

Characters

Anthony Eden, *Prime Minister (1955–57), fifties*
Lady Clarissa Eden, *his wife, thirties*
Harold Macmillan, *Chancellor of the Exchequer (1955–57), fifties*
Winston Churchill, *Prime Minister (1940–45 and 1951–55), seventies*
Colonel Nasser, *President of Egypt (1954–70), thirties*

An ensemble cast of four can share the following roles, or alternatively one actor can take each part.

Selwyn Lloyd, *British Foreign Secretary (1955–62)*
Frederick Bishop, *Eden's Principal Private Secretary (1956–57)*
Anthony Nutting, *Minister of State, Foreign Office (1954–56)*
Earl Mountbatten, *First Sea Lord (1955–59)*
Molotov, *Russian Foreign Minister (1939–49 and 1953–56)*
Byrnes, *American Secretary of State (1945–47)*
Dulles, *American Secretary of State (1953–59)*
Schuman, *French Minister of Foreign Affairs (1948–53)*
Woolton, *Cabinet Minister*
Butler, *Cabinet Minister*
Viscount Swinton, *Cabinet Minister*
Dr Hume
Reporter
Caricaturist

A chorus of **Ministers**
Assembled **Figures** *(Potsdam)*

Act One

The Führerbunker, Hitler's former war rooms beneath the Reich Chancellery in Berlin, 1945. Complete darkness. There are shouts in Russian, off.

Eden (*off*)   Yes, yes thank you. We know. Through here.

A torchlight flashes around the stage. We catch glimpses of a desk, a map of the world on the wall, files. Footsteps in the room.

Right, according to ... Yes, these were ... well, his private quarters, I suppose. (*More flashes round of the torch.*) Oh. Mind, mind your step, Prime ... Here, let me ... find a –

The torchlight catches a red and white flag emblazoned with a Nazi swastika, and there is a pause where only this is seen. We hear a click, and overhead lighting in the room flickers on to reveal **Anthony Eden**, *standing by a light switch and holding a torch, and* **Winston Churchill**, *who stands, back turned to us, smoking a cigar, motionless, and taking in his surroundings of the cold concrete bunker.*

Eden (*looking around, barely audible*) Winston ...

A long silence. **Churchill** *shuffles around. He looks at the floor, at the map on the wall.* **Eden** *also takes an apprehensive glance around, anxious, expecting to discover something unpleasant.* **Churchill** *picks up a Bible from the desk, and shows it to* **Eden**, *who nods.* **Churchill** *replaces it, and stands for a moment in thought.*

Churchill   My chair was comfier than his.

Eden   Ours was warmer, too.

Churchill (*pause, then gesturing around, half-laughing, tragically*) Anthony. Did you ever imagine? (*Beat.*) Berlin looks worse than I feared. I am surprised they have welcomed us with such warmth.

Eden   We have set them free.

Churchill No. No, they must do that for themselves.

Churchill *faces the map on the wall. He brushes his fingers across Britain. Pause.*

Churchill Still! On to Potsdam, what?! To begin rebuilding.

Eden Hear, hear.

Churchill We must stay close to the Americans now that Truman is in charge. Roosevelt and Stalin were all over each other at Yalta like young lovers.

Eden I'm keen to push for quick justice against those Nazis being held. We're working with the Americans on devising a trial. It's a little tricky, of course. Nothing like this has ever … Our chaps are playing with a charge of … 'crimes against humanity'.

Churchill 'Crimes against humanity' ? What a thing to be guilty of.

He brushes his hand across the chair again.

Eden Uh, through there, I believe … like yourself, he had a bedroom and … that's where he … though they warned of some blood still evident, so you might not want to –

Churchill *exits in the direction indicated by* **Eden**. *Pause.* **Churchill** *returns, nods and exits.* **Eden** *flicks off the light and the bunker descends into darkness once more.*

The **Reporter** *appears, reading from his notepad, making alterations as he reads.*

Reporter The much heralded … (*Scribbles.*) No, the much lauded … (*Scribbles.*) The great! – that's it – the great tripartite conference between allies Britain, Russia and America begins in Potsdam, near Berlin, today, following the German surrender. The 'bulldog', the 'bear' and, uh … (*Scribbles out.*) Misters Churchill, Stalin and Truman, in attendance with their foreign secretaries Mr Eden, Mr Byrnes and Mr Molotov …

Potsdam. A map of the world lit up on the floor. The room is dimly lit.

The tango theme creeps in as **Eden**, **Byrnes** *and* **Molotov** *enter. They embrace each other individually in dance holds and stride, stomp and turn into their seats, positioned as a semicircle in a pool of light, as chairs and other* **Figures** *assemble behind them.*

In the surrounding darkness are the shapes of other seated **Figures**, *with smoke billowing from cigarettes and cigars. Behind* **Eden**, *perhaps only his legs visible in the light, is* **Churchill**. *His hand extends frequently into the light, holding a note, and tapping* **Eden** *on the shoulder. Without a break in the dialogue,* **Eden** *always takes the note from over his shoulder, reads it, and then passes it back into the darkness. This happens frequently throughout. The equivalent happens between* **Byrnes** *and* **Molotov** *with the figures behind them.* **Eden**, **Byrnes** *and* **Molotov** *have notes on their laps that they refer to. Amongst the other* **Figures** *seated, barely visible in the dark, perpetual note-passing occurs and continues ritualistically throughout.*

Eden So we are agreed on the draft ultimatum for Japan?

Byrnes Of course agreed. Our boys are still engaged there and we need a resolution fast.

Molotov We would also suggest the United States do not keep this new weapon of theirs under their hat. Rather they use it as a bargaining point.

Eden Very well. Japan must surrender to the Allied forces immediately. (*Copying from a sheet.*) 'The alternative … is prompt and utter … destruction.' (*Pause.*) Right.

They tick something off on a sheet. A common occurrence, even when not mentioned.

Establishing a Council of Foreign Ministers to deliver peace treaties to those who've surrendered and answer outstanding territorial questions. We three shall act as chief representatives, but to ensure a lasting peace, Britain wishes to submit France as well.

Byrnes Agreed.

Molotov Agreed, if China may join also.

Byrnes I'm afraid my government simply cannot acknowledge China as a power, Mr Molotov. It would make this Council's policies unenforceable.

Molotov They will be unenforceable if the world's fifth great power is missing.

Eden Perhaps additions can be negotiated later. Can we at least agree to London being the permanent seat of the joint secretariat?

Molotov Can it move to other capitals from time to time? Just as a change?

Byrnes Yeah. That would be nice.

Eden (*beat*) Agreed. Next.

Byrnes Regarding the peace treaties, we would like Italy to be the first of the fallen Axis Powers to receive theirs, as they were first to sever ties with Hitler.

Eden We won't have a problem with that.

Molotov *shrugs.*

Eden On to Germany. The Yalta agreement dictates each occupying force shall govern the zones their troops currently occupy. (*Opens a map.*) To clarify, Russia shall be in charge from here in the east, Britain here, America here and there, and we'll give France that.

Byrnes The Soviets have submitted their application to extend their authority across the whole of Austria. Mr Eden, my recommendation is we allow this once our troops are stationed there. Perhaps Vienna?

Molotov Why? Our troops are already stationed there. (*Receives note from behind.*) Fine.

Byrnes Poland, and what territories should return to the provisional government.

Eden (*opens the map*) The new proposal would see the Soviet-occupied territories east of this line, running from the Baltic, west of Swinemuende, along the Oder to the Czech frontier, returning to Poland and not withheld by the Soviets.

Molotov Wait. This has barely changed from the first draft, if at all.

Byrnes This isn't a war anyone can gain from, Mr Molotov. The land belonged to Poland.

Molotov So after my countrymen died to save this land, are dying in occupation, we are to walk out and leave us with no barrier of defences? We cannot accept this proposal until representatives visit the area.

Byrnes We should wait until the peace treaty has been signed anyway.

Molotov No, no more delays. If no good alternative is produced, we shall not withdraw.

Eden (*receiving a note over his shoulder. Pause*) What if we gave you Czechoslovakia?

Molotov (*pause*) Czechoslovakia is no good to us. It cannot protect us.

Byrnes Maybe we could negotiate over Danzig.

Eden No. That would mean the new Poland is completely landlocked.

Molotov (*with the map*) Well … (*Sighs.*) What about Koenigsberg?

Byrnes (*beat*) We'd be willing to negotiate Koenigsberg.

Molotov With the transfer of all existing residents back to Poland?

Byrnes (*beat*) Agreed.

Eden (*beat*) Agreed.

Byrnes As for the future, it is the job of the Allied Control Council and the responsibility of the German people to redirect their lives to a peaceful democratic basis and retake their place amongst the free people of the world.

Molotov (*with his notes*) Guidelines include the full disarmament of Germany and the annihilation of the National Socialist Party. The Allied Council also assumes the authority to reverse every law passed by the Party.

Eden Additionally, the destruction of all arms and decommissioning of the armed forces.

Molotov (*laughing*) I think you'll find my forces have already done that for you, Mr Eden.

Byrnes Should we maybe consider delegating some of the arms between us?

Molotov It does seem a waste.

Eden Perhaps. Let us maybe establish what has survived first? With regard to the economy, an emphasis on shifting it from arms production, metals and chemicals, to things such as … (*Writing.*) agriculture, farming and … (*Thinks.*) fishing?

Molotov (*pause, then shrugs*) Mm-hmm. Fishing.

Byrnes (*overlaps, mumbling*) Yeah, fishing sounds fine.

Eden Very well. The war crimes trial for those captured prisoners.

Byrnes Right. Now, the arrests are still continuing. Needless to say, we still have some pretty big catches in our net. Including Speer and Goering, of course.

Eden And we are as adamant as the Americans that a fair and just trial be given to them.

Molotov You won't seriously let them defend themselves. We should just execute them.

Eden They must be tried under the international law of the new

United Nations body. We must not resort to the injustices they did. This is a message to the world. We are now all accountable for every wrong we commit on this planet. Inside or outside of war. Only then can we hope neither our predecessors nor we ever again find ourselves sitting where we are today. The object is peace, gentlemen. Let us continue.

Potsdam begins to fade into darkness amidst a frenzied exchange of handshakes between parties. The **Reporter** *appears, independent of this action, holding a newspaper. Next to him, the* **Caricaturist**, *who scribbles frantically on a pad of paper.*

Reporter Results are in, Fred. State of the parties: Conservatives 180, Labour 364! It's a veritable landslide!

Caricaturist Blimey. Well … that's it, then. He's out.

Reporter So it'll be Attlee and Bevin wrapping up Potsdam then. Word is, the old boy's taking it personally, Fred.

Caricaturist Well you would, Bill, wouldn't you? I mean, you just would.

Reporter Yeah. Shame. In a way.

Caricaturist 'Tis a shame.

Reporter Some might even say ungrateful.

Caricaturist Yeah. They might.

Churchill's *quarters.* **Eden** *and* **Churchill** *flick on a couple of dim desk lamps.*

Churchill (*solemnly*) Was it really as bad as all that?

Eden I'm afraid it rather was, yes. Even Wimbledon went Labour.

Churchill Heavens. The game is really up. (*Pause.*) Though I suppose this is the democracy we have been fighting and dying for. And it has been exercised with vigour. I cannot judge them poorly, Anthony. For poorly is what they are. We have bestowed upon them nothing bar hardship and pain.

Eden This doesn't mean they do not love you, Winston. All they want is change.

Churchill The next few years protesting from the shadows. Perhaps this is an ideal time for you to take over, Anthony. And me to step down. It feels like the end.

Eden Or a new beginning. Perhaps.

Churchill (*smiles*) My Anthony. What will you do? I hate to think of you all alone now.

Eden Well, there's still my Warwick and Leamington seat, of course.

Churchill Well, you are always welcome with me. (*Beat.*) I know my niece, Clarissa, is … very fond of your visits …

He disappears as **Clarissa** *appears.* **Eden** *bows. Waltz music swells. They embrace in a dance hold and begin to turn, slowly.*

Clarissa I remember when you first came round. All those years ago.

Eden You were ever so shy.

Clarissa I was sixteen! And you were this … *man.* (*Laughs.*) Your tweed jacket and pinstriped trousers!

Eden What's wrong with my tweed jacket and pinstriped trousers?

Clarissa No, nothing. Very English and … what's the – debonair.

Eden Yes, I forget I'm conversing with a professional fashion expert. Must watch what I wear more carefully from now on.

Clarissa Well, these things are important. Especially in politics.

Eden They didn't used to be.

Clarissa (*pause*) I was … ever so sorry to hear about your son.

Eden Well … thank … (*Pause.*) War, it … Everybody lost somebody.

Clarissa (*beat. Smiles*)   I thought you were an actor, actually. The first time we met.

Eden   Really?

Clarissa   You have that look. Like Errol Flynn.

Eden   Is that a good thing?

Clarissa   I think so. (*Pause.*) So they say one day you may be Prime Minister.

Eden   Well. That's ... Hmm. (*Pause.*) You know I, uh ... have recently ... divorced ...

Clarissa   Yes, I did know that. Though I hardly see why it matters.

Eden   It does to some.

Clarissa   Well, they're silly.

Eden   You *are* a Roman Catholic.

Clarissa   I'm also a woman. (*Pause.*) Why did she ... leave?

Eden   Uh, it all got a little ... much. Politics wasn't in her blood. Alas. I ... well. Don't blame her. (*Pause.*) Would it bother you?

Clarissa   I'm a Churchill, Anthony. It *is* my blood.

They smile as they dance into a racier jitterbug, opening out to become less formal, more sensual and fun.

They disappear as **Reporter** *and* **Caricaturist** *appear.*

Reporter   Course, that one's getting in with the old boy's niece, now. That won't do him any harm in the long run, will it?

Caricaturist   No. So long as he doesn't stray this time.

Reporter   Stray, Fred?

Caricaturist   Well, you know. Good-looking. Powerful. He's uh ... well. Made good use of his talents, Bill, is all.

Clarissa's *home.*

Eden Here. Uh, as a present, you know.

Clarissa Oh, lovely. How kind. We're having fish, if that's all right. Busy day?

Eden Uh, yes. So-so. Met with the Shadow Cabinet. At the Savoy, no less. And you?

Clarissa Oh, just in the garden. And how was Uncle? His usual self?

Eden 'Fraid so. Though at least we've managed to get him out of bed now. (*Sighs.*) I'm sorry, I know he's family, but –

Clarissa Gosh, you needn't fret. I know more than most how difficult he can be.

Eden It's just all so gloomy and, worse, reactionary. I mean look what Labour are doing? A 'National Health Service'. State education for all. Us? There's no vision, no drive. Just moaning about the pettiest things. If it's not about those 'young Labour scallywags' coming onto our side of the Commons dining hall, it's how the opposition offices aren't as clean, or whatever, before Winston starts grumbling into his cream tea with a torrent of inconsequential ramblings, and then, lo!, we're back on the War again! (*Taking his glass of wine.*) It's a pain in the neck, it really is.

Clarissa Anthony, calm down. You just need to be stronger. Firmer. Take off your shoes.

Eden And they just go on and on, it's so tiresome. Seems all Tories have this irksome habit of starting a conversation without a point, hoping to find one along the way. And to keep jabbering on until one finds one! God!

Clarissa Anthony. (*Taking his glass.*) Stop it. I will not waste good wine on a bad mood.

Eden It's my wine.

Clarissa No, it's not, you said it was a present. Now buck up, all right?

Eden All right. Sorry. (*Taking the glass of wine.*) Sometimes I just despair of the whole wretched thing. As much as Rab, Harold and I try to push us forward, it's no good until we get rid of all these old dinosaurs on our front bench.

Clarissa One in particular.

Eden *pauses.*

Clarissa Does he mention it often?

Eden Others do. I don't know. Wish he'd never labelled me as next in line. Crown Prince is hardly an enviable position. And he talks continually as though he is anointed by God. The time he was walking through London during the blitz, and a bomb hits a building nearby. Everyone but Winston hits the ground. Asked why he wasn't afraid, he points up and says, 'He has not done with me yet.' How can you argue with that?

Clarissa Well, your support in the party is unanimous.

Eden How do you know?

Clarissa Being a former Prime Minister's niece, you'd be surprised how many conversations one can find oneself within earshot of.

Eden (*pause*) You know he first mentioned my succession back in '42. That long ago. A secret between us. Now everyone knows and it's just unbearable. I could take the party forward, and the country, I know it, I *know* it. But every time we broach the subject we end up rowing. We really are turning into father and son!

Clarissa And when we're married, he really will be family.

Eden God, don't remind me! His control over me will be final. (*Pause.*) 'Uncle Winston'.

They laugh.

Clarissa You know, for the honeymoon I was thinking Portugal or France? Any thoughts?

Eden Well, it rather depends what happens here. With the election.

Clarissa I don't see how. We will be going on a honeymoon, Anthony.

Eden I know.

Clarissa We will.

Eden Yes, I know. (*Pause.*) Speaking of the election. Played around with a new name today. Can you believe?

Clarissa For what? The Conservatives?

Eden Yes. The 'New Democrats'.

Clarissa Ha! And what did Uncle say to that?

Eden Said it sounded (*Mock-Winston voice.*) 'Nazi'. So there you go.

Clarissa Oh, you're no Hitler, darling. Your moustache is much more charming. (*Kisses him.*) I don't know how that Eva Braun put up with the wretched thing tickling her.

Eden (*serious*) Don't joke, darling.

Clarissa (*pause*) Well, you know if you need help on the campaign trail …

Eden Thank you. That's awfully kind.

Clarissa It's what Beatrice did for you. Last time. Wasn't it?

Eden (*pause*) Yes. Though that's by the by. You shouldn't … shouldn't feel you must –

Clarissa I know. I'm only doing it for a place in the Cabinet once you're PM.

Eden Certainly. How does Minister of Fish and Wine grab you?

Clarissa Perfect.

They kiss.

An explosion of sound as lights pick up **Churchill** *at a podium, cheering and waving, giving the V-sign to his adoring public. Cheering and clapping. Red white and blue ticker tape falls around him, as 'Jerusalem' plays, and we move into* **Churchill**'s *quarters. He is with* **Eden**.

Churchill We're back, Anthony! Back!

Eden Congratulations, Winston.

Churchill And now to the matter in hand. As to who goes where and what and why. So, I must formally ask you, Mr Eden, if you would do me the honour of taking over ... at the Foreign Office again.

Eden (*pause, then visibly deflated*) Right.

Churchill My Anthony. Your time will come, I promise you that. I shall hand over power before the end of this parliament.

Eden (*still dejected*) Right.

Churchill The world is still weak and the cure slow. The War left Britain skinny and poor and in the pockets of those who had not fought for so long or so hard. I need the best Foreign Secretary I have. And you are the finest international negotiator there is. So go and join the leaders of this world. For Britain, Anthony. And be strong ...

He disappears.

Three independent places appear in pools of light:

PARIS *Two armchairs.* **Schuman** *reclines in one. A small table with two glasses of wine. Cigar smoke. The French flag flies.*

CAIRO *Two armchairs.* **Nasser** *reclines in one. On the table are two cups of Moroccan tea. Cigar smoke. The Egyptian flag flies.*

WASHINGTON *Two armchairs.* **Dulles** *reclines in one. On the table are two cups of coffee. Cigar smoke. The American flag flies.*

The tango theme sounds as **Eden** *enters Paris, greeting* **Schuman** *in a dance hold, spinning into a seated position. The music fades down but remains in the background.*

Schuman Well, what a welcome back for you, Mr Eden. A standing ovation from the United Nations Assembly!

Eden The polite reception was most welcome, thank you.

Schuman So. Mr Churchill was not available?

Eden I am trusted with all foreign affairs, Monsieur Schuman. And I trust we can make steady progress today. So. You're not happy.

Schuman I'm a politician.

Eden You want Britain to go further. Be more committed to Europe publicly. I can understand that. But I'm afraid we cannot cast our net that far out as yet.

Schuman I'm under pressure, you see. To show them something ... real. What we are trying to create is a Community. You know, the geographical position of nations is something we cannot help. This is where we have been put, next to each other, and nothing we can do. Like the family you are born into. You cannot choose the sisters and the brothers that share your house. But you must do all that you can to live with them in a manner that is ... mutually beneficial. Europe? Europe is not a land mass, a piece of earth. Europe is a state of mind. An idea, existing nowhere but in our head until ink lands on a dotted line. Until we have clear participants. Words, these words you offer, 'association', 'support'. They have no currency, nothing to hold in your hand and say 'there'. Britain is part of Europe's family, Mr Eden. We're just asking you to come and sit at the dinner table.

Eden Our position is that we support a European Defence Community, but that our support would rather be ... helping from the outside, rather than participating within.

Schuman Ha! And once again, Britain's political position in Europe is also its geographical one. Looking from the outside in.

Eden That is my position and the position of Her Majesty's Government. (*Standing.*) One moment, please.

Schuman Remember. The Channel is only large in terms of

psychology. In actual size, though, anyone who truly wanted to cross it could.

Schuman *and Paris fade slightly.*

Eden (*aside*)   You never managed it.

The tango theme rises as **Eden** *cross-steps over to Cairo and* **Nasser**. *They greet in a similar fashion, spinning to their seats as the tango fades again.*

Nasser   Where did you learn Arabic, Mr Eden?

Eden   At Oxford. Wonderful language. I find it has opened up a range of simply … uh, simply marvellous texts that would have otherwise been closed to me. The Koran, particularly, contains a great deal of wisdom. So. Have you made any decision on joining our Baghdad Pact? We have Iraq and Turkey now. Britain views Middle Eastern defence amongst its top priorities.

Nasser   And why is this?

Eden   Well. We have a … responsibility.

Nasser   We were pleased to finally settle the Base Agreement. The people of Egypt are looking forward with hope to the end of British occupation.

Eden   Occupation? Colonel Nasser, I hardly …

Nasser   Despite the declaration of independence, what, thirty years ago? We still find ourselves at British mercy.

Eden   No Egyptian citizen is at our mercy and I really must object to such a statement.

Nasser   I'm sorry. (*Smiles.*) My English is perhaps not translating as it should.

Eden   Yes, perhaps not. But this all seems rather academic now, anyway. The treaty has been signed. Our forces will be out within two years. Including the Suez Canal Zone.

Nasser (*pause*)   Where is Mr Churchill? I was hoping to meet with him.

Eden Well, he isn't here. You'll be dealing with me.

Nasser Hmm.

Pause. Cairo and **Nasser** *fade slightly. The tango theme rises.* **Eden** *crosses to Washington and greets* **Dulles** *with a similar flourish and sits. The tango quietens.*

Dulles I never really got a chance to, uh ... congratulate your negotiating prowess on Iran, Anthony. Seems you were right about Mussadeq after all. I think it's safe to say we'll all benefit now he's gone. And forty per cent of the oil revenue! Well done, you.

Eden Well. A victory for peace is a victory for all, Mr Dulles. And we all have a, uh ... a responsibility towards peace, now.

Dulles It was a shame we didn't quite see eye to eye when it mattered in Geneva, though. We feel it's important to keep a united front, especially when sitting across the table from the Russians and Chinese. Particularly when it comes to Germany and Europe.

Eden I've no doubt that we will only ever differ on the details, Foster. Britain's desired outcomes for peace and international security will always be the same as yours.

Churchill's *hand extends out from the darkness to tap* **Eden** *on the shoulder.*

Eden Would you excuse me, please?

Washington and **Dulles** *dim. The tango theme ceases completely.* **Churchill** *appears.*

Churchill Anthony. What is the worst thing that could happen to us? (*Pause.*) The King is dead. Princess Elizabeth is flying back from her tour to become our new Queen.

Eden Heavens. (*Beat. Laughs faintly, shrugging.*) God save the ... Queen.

Churchill Of course, I shouldn't think I could leave any time soon, now. Must get our new monarch settled in first, what? Then we'll talk about a transfer of power.

Eden Um. Yes. (*Sighs*.) Right ...

Churchill *disappears as the tango music sounds.* **Eden** *spins back to Washington.*

Dulles What is it with the English and tea? Personally, I think it tastes like dirty water. Have to put five sugars in it to get any goddamn taste. Now coffee is a real drink.

Eden Well. Tea will always be the choice of England.

Dulles We'll see. (*Sips*.) You know, the United States have their own issues too, Anthony. With Europe, frankly, we feel we've done all we can. And God knows we've given as much financial assistance as possible before we cripple ourselves. We're not a charity, Mr Eden. Didn't we come to your aid when you needed it?

Eden Of course. Of which we will be for ever in your debt. We were certainly worn out after fighting for so long. Alone. But we couldn't just allow tyranny to spread across the globe unchecked, now could we? Apathy and Evil go hand in hand.

Washington and **Dulles** *dim, the tango rises, as* **Eden** *crosses to Paris. Tango quietens.*

Eden You talk of family. That's nice. Our problem is we've so many responsibilities elsewhere. Commitments to the Commonwealth, they're our *immediate* family, now NATO, the UN. Our special relationship with the United States –

Schuman Uh-hum. *Entente Cordiale?*

Eden And with the French.

Schuman (*beat, then smiles and toasts*) Merci.

Eden We certainly wouldn't be prepared to commit to the EDC without the integration of Germany. They must be actively involved. At least one division in any federal army.

Schuman That would mean rearming them.

Eden We don't have a problem with that.

Schuman You don't live next door.

Eden We must learn from the mistakes of Versailles. We believe in second chances.

Schuman Yes. Well. This would be their third.

Eden One regiment can't start a war.

Schuman In 1939, one man did! (*Pause.*) Look, if we let everyone into this community then we won't need defending from anyone anyway.

Eden I rather thought that was the point.

Schuman We need signed confirmation of your assistance in the event of any aggression.

Eden Do you really think, Monsieur, that Britain would not come to the aid of France, or anyone, under attack? Have we not always, our fathers, grandfathers, our ... sons, defended those in need? Whether there is or is not a piece of paper saying we have to?

Paris and **Schuman** *dim, tango rises, as* **Eden** *crosses to Washington. Tango quietens.*

Dulles Say, where *is* Churchill?

Beat. **Eden** *grimaces as the tango rises and he crosses to Cairo, where it fades.*

Nasser And I would like to give congratulations on your new Queen. You do not mind being led by a lady? (*Laughs.*)

Eden In our history, the Queens have generally been more ferocious than the Kings. But, yes, it was a huge success. Watched on television by millions, no less.

Nasser Astonishing! This new thing of tele ... television. Still, it is not all so good for the people to see so much into the government working. In Egypt, I think we will not let them see so much. They might find things they do not like.

Eden Well, in Britain, all documents must eventually become public property. We're even looking into reducing the embargo to just fifty years before information is released.

Nasser What a thing!

Clarissa's *hand appears from the darkness to tap him on the shoulder.*

Eden Please, ex … one moment … *Cairo and* **Nasser** *dim. The tango theme ceases.* **Clarissa** *appears.*

Clarissa Winston's had a stroke. He's fine, but … well … taking it easy.

Eden Oh. Uh … heavens. Right. Well.

Clarissa Anthony, are you all right? You look exhausted. Maybe *you* should see someone.

Eden No, of course not. I'm fine. And busy. Excuse me.

Eden *returns to Cairo and* **Nasser** *with a brief burst of the tango theme.*

Nasser Yet, the Base Agreement allows you to reoccupy the Suez Canal when you please.

Eden Only in an emergency. Should the free passage of the Canal come under threat. As … as the nation that built it and owns it, Britain has a certain responsibility to ensure free passage for the entire world. And we don't take that role lightly.

Nasser The free passage is safeguarded by the 1888 convention. Egypt will always respect that. Except with Israel, of course! Another Western conquest, carved deep into the heart of Palestine. It seems wherever we find tension in the Middle East, Mr Eden, we find the British Empire.

Pause. **Eden** *leaves Cairo in a burst of tango music, crossing into Washington.*

Dulles Of course you're right, Anthony. Though Europe really needs to learn to stand on its own two feet. My people, we're … well, we're shifting our focus. To Asia. The Middle East. Keep that ticking over.

Eden (*mopping his brow*) And the oil flowing.

Dulles Foreign aid costs money, Anthony. And. Well. We now see ourselves as liberators. Heroes of the downtrodden and the oppressed. Fighters for those who want independence from Empire.

Eden Careful. You'll be taking *our* territories away next.

Dulles We've made no secret of our dislike for colonialism and your imperialist past, Mr Eden. Let's not forget that we were once in your grasp. We were, of course, happy to see you finally let India go. And that you're withdrawing from Palestine. Egypt.

Eden Yes, we were less pleased to hear of your arms package to Colonel Nasser. Do you really think that's wise? To a fast-becoming fiery, nationalist dictator?

Dulles Don't take offence, Anthony. Like you say, we are living in a different world. No longer can we afford to float around, oblivious to anything outside our own borders.

Eden We ... (*Holding his side and wincing.*) We never did.

Dulles Are you all right?

Clarissa's *hand appears from the darkness, tapping* **Eden** *on the shoulder.*

Eden Would you ... one second, please.

Washington and **Dulles** *dim. The tango ceases completely.*

Clarissa *appears.*

Clarissa Anthony, the doctors would like to do some tests. You're not well.

Eden You don't understand.

Clarissa You're working yourself into the grave, do *you* understand? You need a break!

Eden I can't stop now. Winston ... all that I've ... I'll lose my chance, damn it! I'm fine!

Clarissa *disappears as the tango bursts out.* **Eden** *crosses,*

Eden's Empire   27

holding his side, to Paris. The tango quietens. He appears to cover his pain quite well.

Schuman   We will have to settle with that for now, then. *Bien.* (*Drinks.*) I must congratulate you on your new wife. She is well?

Eden   Uh ... yes, yes she's – we're ... thank you, we're both well.

Schuman   And your boss? You must be getting really eager to take over now, yes?

Eden   You ... shouldn't pay attention to gossip, Monsieur Schuman. Our house is in order.

Schuman (*laughing*)   Things have not changed, have they? Since your Henry VIII or our Louis XIV. We still find ourselves at the mercy of the gossip and treachery of the court!

Paris and **Schuman** *disappear, a quick burst of tango as* **Eden** *stumbles to Cairo.*

Eden   President, I'm sure ... I'm sure you appreciate that the Canal is an international asset, vital for world trade. And, if you recall, the ... the 1936 treaty granted Her Majesty's Government certain base rights and was, once again, I stress, agreed by your predecessors. Not only to protect our citizens here but to act as a force of stability in the region as a whole against ... rising tensions. Another reason why we were hoping for your inclusion in the Baghdad Pact.

Nasser (*pause. Serious*)   When I became president, I vowed that my people would once again be free from the rule of Empire. And, at last, this is happening. I really do not see the need for an imperial Western power to / construct a treaty of alliance –

Eden   Imperial Western power?

Nasser   – between our Arab neighbours. This is something we should be doing for ourselves. We will not be joining your pact, Mr Eden.

Eden   Well you ... I must confess –

Nasser But enjoy the rest of your stay as guests in my country. As guests, you understand.

Eden Well you, you ... yes, I ... just –

Cairo and **Nasser** *disappear. A burst of tango as* **Eden** *collapses over to Washington.* **Dulles** *embraces him in a dance hold to steady him, and to lead him to his seat.*

Dulles Course, now there's NATO. There's the United Nations.

Eden Yes, of ... uh ...

Dulles Other people's affairs, well ... it's not only our responsibility now, but also our *right* to intervene when and where we see fit. And truth be told ... well, truth be told, we've opened our eyes since the War. And what we see is a lot to be done. And to that end, Mr Eden, my country ... well, like I say. Europe, we're nearly done with. Now we're looking ...

Dr Hume's *hand appears out from the darkness to tap* **Eden** *on the shoulder.*

Dulles (*smiling*) ... further afield.

Washington and **Dulles** *and the scene disappear. The tango ends.* **Dr Hume** *appears.*

Dr Hume Foreign Secretary. I ... I'm afraid the results have come back from your test and it's, uh ... not all good. We've found gallstones in your bile duct, and ... well, we should need to operate immediately.

Eden Well I ... I ... I really am – I'm rather busy at the moment, you know, and –

Dr Hume Oh, don't worry. It was partly the Prime Minister's suggestion you take some time off. In fact, he's all for it.

Eden (*beat*) Really? That so?

Dr Hume And he's impressed upon me how, uh ... well, how damn important you are. Kept telling me about the time –

Churchill *appears, barking in their direction.*

Churchill I had my appendix cut out of me with a bread knife on the kitchen table. Bah! You'll be fine, man. I shall make sure this chap knows exactly how important you are.

Operating theatre. **Dr Hume** *in a small pool of light, wielding a scalpel, looking down at a body covered in a white sheet. The beat of a heart monitor.* **Dr Hume** *looks around nervously before lowering the knife and beginning to cut. Suddenly, a red patch of blood begins forming underneath the white blanket. The beat of the heart monitor increases.* **Dr Hume** *begins to panic, his hands working away under the blanket, the level of blood swelling, as the heart monitor beats at a faster rate. Blackout.*

Dr Hume *with* **Eden***, who looks ill and very weak.*

Eden What ... do you mean?

Dr Hume The knife. It just, um ... slipped I'm afraid. And we ... accidentally ... severed your bile duct. (*Pause.*) Sorry.

Churchill *appears.* **Dr Hume** *disappears.*

Churchill Well, I was going to set a deadline for the transfer of power, Anthony. But I can't very well expect you to take over now. The doctors think it will kill you. And I cannot have that. You need to get fit, Anthony. Fit and well. Then we'll talk.

Silence. **Churchill** *disappears as* **Eden** *spins angrily into:*

Eden *and* **Clarissa***'s apartment, Carlton Gardens.* **Eden** *slams his hat onto the floor.*

Eden THAT INSUFFERABLE OLD FOOL!

He grabs his side in pain. **Clarissa** *goes to him, lowering him to a chair.*

Eden I'm fine!

Clarissa You are not fine, you need to rest. / Sit back.

Eden My life has been resting, and waiting, and sitting back, and *waiting*!

Clarissa That's not true.

Eden It was him! Put the fear of death into the surgeon. Be on drugs now for the rest of my ... Cholangitis of the liver, now! So there you are! Go in with one, come out with a-bloody-nother. The kiss of death, that's what he ... 'Heir Apparent'. Nothing 'apparent' about it. Positively indistinct! The life of the understudy! (*Sighs*.) We had a deal. And I swear he's taunting me with it! At the American dinner today, he's looking over the garden at Number 10 with the President and he says – knowing I can hear – that he's thinking of cutting down the poplars so he can see the Trooping of the Colour properly ... *next year*! So I end up storming over to him and yelling that they weren't his to cut down. And he just smiled. Lord knows what Eisenhower thought. And Cabinet's a mess, no one believes he knows what he's doing any more. Selwyn Lloyd's positive the only reason he's in the Foreign Office is because Winston thought he was *Geoffrey* Lloyd, and then couldn't be bothered with the paperwork to sort it out, and Walter Elliot missed out on the Cabinet because he was out of the house when Winston telephoned! Answer in three rings or you're out! That silly old man!

Clarissa Oh Anthony, you shouldn't let him get to you so.

Eden Reminds me of Eton when everyone in the years above were going off to war except me. The *first* war. (*Beat*.) And my housemaster there was called Churchill!

Clarissa Never.

Eden Would you believe it?! Probably part of the same bloody family! No offence. (*Pause*.) Said I had too soft a heart for war. Whilst all around me, friends left to fight.

Clarissa Well, you proved them wrong, darling. Men with soft hearts don't fight their way into the trenches and win a Military Cross, do they?

Eden For what it's worth. My sons fighting the same enemies years later. Only ... not being so fortunate.

Clarissa Oh, Anthony, stop.

Eden I just want the chance to ... make things better. And I could. I could! Given the chance I ... I could. Heal old wounds.

Eden's Empire 31

Clarissa Well, you need to get yourself better first. (*Softly, stroking his hair.*) And I'm afraid there are some wounds that politics can't heal.

Eden (*pause*) It was the waiting. Huh. (*Shakes his head.*) Again! Waiting … for news, after his plane went down. Nothing … nothing prepares you. (*Pause.*) Amongst, uh … Simon's things, they … in the wreckage, found a copy of … *Henry V.* (*Smiles.*) Kept up with his … just as I told him. And all the others, countless others who … never came … (*Bitterly.*) 'Once more unto the breach, dear friends, once more! Or close … (*Calmer.*) … close the wall up with our … English dead.' (*Tries to compose himself.*) They say the … the hardest thing a man has to do is … is bury his son. I think, though … *not* being able to bury him … is … is probably … far worse …

Clarissa *embraces him as he collapses into her. Lights fade.*

Churchill *appears in his quarters, sitting at his desk. His head leans to one side, as though asleep. For a time, all that can be heard is his heavy, rhythmic breathing, which sounds painful and wheezing. Half his face is slightly paralysed from a stroke. Footsteps from the darkness.* **Harold Macmillan** *enters.* **Churchill** *looks up.*

Churchill Mr Macmillan.

Macmillan Good evening, Prime Minister.

Churchill H-how are things in Housing, Harold, with all your success?

Macmillan We're building on it all the time.

They both chuckle politely. Pause.

Winston. We'd like to talk about your succession.

Churchill W … we?

Butler *enters.*

Butler Yes, Prime Minister. Wondered if you had any thoughts.

Macmillan   You did say you wouldn't fight another election. And we're going to need someone else in as soon as possible. Leave them enough time to build a campaign.

Churchill   Yes, well, it's … all very well to say … to say we'd like, we need. But it is a … a matter of choosing the best time.

Butler   What we need is an anniversary or something. An 'apt' time for a change. 'This many years' in power, or 'so many' as leader, that kind of thing.

Churchill   But the climate, gentlemen. The, the conditions.

Swinton *enters.*

Swinton   How about your eightieth birthday, Prime Minister? That might be an apt time.

Churchill   My … ? (*Pause.*) Yes, perhaps you're … (*Unsure.*) Yes.

Woolton *enters.* **Churchill** *is now practically encircled.*

Woolton   And then there's the matter of your successor.

Churchill   Well you … you know who my successor is to be. Anthony.

Swinton (*pause*)   Yes …

Churchill   Can you think of anyone better?

Woolton   Well – (*Indicating.*) Rab of course. And Harold.

Swinton   Personally I think anybody would be better. His health, for a start. And he can never seem to make up his mind, which doesn't bode well. And his temperament!

Butler   Let's not forget this is the man once considered to become the first ever Secretary General of the UN. He's a proven diplomat and an accomplished politician. And he's been in line for the throne for over a decade.

Woolton   Well, exactly. There's no point in arguing now. What's done is done.

Churchill Harold?

Macmillan I trust in your opinion, Prime Minister.

Churchill Well. You'll have to have him.

Macmillan (*pause*) When?

Butler, **Swinton**, **Woolton** and **Macmillan** *disappear.*

Eden *enters to stand in front of* **Churchill**. *Silence, punctured by* **Churchill**'s *wheezing, as they stare at each other.*

Churchill He ... is almost done with me, Anthony. I have been possessed ... my entire life ... by the history I was making. Time now ... to raise the white flag. A *stroke* ... of good fortune for you. 'Unto whomsoever much is given ... of him ... much shall be required.' Remember. Indecision is a most fatal vice. Better act wrongly but quickly ... than lose the chance of acting at all. I have not chosen you, Anthony. History has chosen you. You will find out ... soon enough ... why ...

Elgar's 'Nimrod' creeps in as the lights around **Churchill** *slowly die.*

Eden *steps onto a podium. Hung there is a poster emblazoned with the 1955 Tory Party election slogan, 'Working for Peace', as the hubbub of crowds and horns grows to become deafening.*

Eden My government will be one of efficiency and fair play. My Britain will be one of strong industry and manufacture, a happy employer and a happy workforce. I have fought all my life for Britain abroad. Now, at a momentous moment in the history of not only our country but our world, when there is not a single war in progress recorded anywhere on the surface of the earth, I am ready to fight for her at home!

The cheers and 'Jerusalem' explode. **Clarissa** *joins the waving* **Eden** *on the podium as a shower of ticker tape engulfs them, lit up by the flash of camera bulbs.*

Downing Street. Prime Minister's chambers. Desk, British flag, portrait of the Queen. **Eden** *alone.* **Bishop** *enters and shakes his hand.*

Bishop Prime Minister.

Eden Yes. Yes, I believe I am. Pleasure, Mr Bishop.

Bishop It is an honour to serve as your Private Secretary.

Eden Thank you, Fred.

Bishop Mr Harold Macmillan.

Macmillan *appears.*

Eden Harold. How does the Foreign Office grab you?

Macmillan (*pause*) Very nicely. Prime Minister.

Eden I've kept it nice and warm for you, eh?

Macmillan Thank you.

Macmillan *disappears.* **Lloyd** *appears.*

Bishop Mr Selwyn Lloyd.

Eden Selwyn. Fancy a go at Defence?

Lloyd Why the devil not? Thank you, Anthony.

Lloyd *disappears.* **Anthony Nutting** *appears.*

Bishop Mr Anthony Nutting. Junior Minister at the Foreign Office.

Eden Of course. Nice to keep you on board, Mr Nutting.

Nutting The pleasure is all mine, Prime Minister. You've been a great role model to me.

Eden Well. Your work in Egypt over the Base Agreement was commendable. Keep it up.

Nutting I shan't let you down.

Eden If I've learnt anything, Mr Nutting, it is to conduct foreign affairs with the utmost integrity, gentlemanly conduct and never, never, make it personal.

Nutting *disappears.* **Clarissa** *appears.*

Bishop Lady Clarissa Eden. Your wife.

Bishop *exits.*

Clarissa *takes off some gardener's gloves she's wearing.*

Clarissa (*beaming*) 'Prime Minister'.

Eden Ma'am.

A beat. **Clarissa** *skips excitedly over and kisses him on the cheek as they hug tight.*

Eden (*laughing*) How do you like your new home, darling?

Clarissa Suits me fine, thank you. Just fine. Though the garden has been practically reclaimed by nature. Lot of dirty work to be done.

Eden For both of us.

Clarissa I hear Winston is on the mend and feeling better now.

Eden (*beat, fearfully*) Well, I'm here now, we've moved in all our things.

Clarissa (*laughing*) Oh darling, I meant nothing by it. Silly thing. (*Looking at the portrait of the Queen.*) She has asked you to serve her, Anthony. Just don't forget. She is not the only woman in your life ... who needs you.

Prime Minister's chambers. **Eden** *is pacing, reading his notes.* **Bishop** *is listening.*

Eden ... 'Strikes overcome through' ... (*Scribbles.*) 'as a result of this government's partnership with industry.' (*Writes.*) 'Succeed in building three hundred thousand houses, a sustainable ... a sustainable growth our', uh ... (*Scribbles, then sighs.*) Gad, why do I find speaking to the House so fiendishly terrifying?

Bishop You always do fine, Prime Minister. You know, Winston used to take six hours practising his speeches.

Eden Hmm.

Bishop It will be Gaitskell who is terrified today. It's his first time at the Labour helm. You should just play the 'new opposition leader appealing to the middle ground just to make his party electable again' card. That ought to do it.

Eden Ye-es. (*With a newspaper.*) You know, it's being touted that I am weak at the despatch box, Fred. Have you seen this? 'To emphasise a point he will clash one fist to smash the open palm of the other, but the smash is seldom heard!' I mean really!

Bishop You shouldn't pay so much attention to the press, Prime Minister. The country rates you / as highly popular.

Eden Seldom heard! I ask you. (*Smacks his hand with the other.*) You can hear that, can't you? Trying to make me the laughing stock of Whitehall. And what is the talk in the smoking room? Any consensus so far?

Bishop You needn't worry, Prime Minister.

Eden (*pause*) How do you think Harold is faring at the Foreign Office? Good choice?

Bishop I believe fine, Prime Minister.

Eden Hmm. I'll telegram Menzies. Get word from the other side of the world, yes?

Bishop I could notify the Foreign Office on your behalf?

Eden No, that's all right. I'll do it. I should see how the preparations for the Commonwealth Conference are going anyway.

Bishop May I make a suggestion, Prime Minister?

Eden Yes, go on.

Bishop I think you can rely on your officials to keep their eyes on overseas. All that's being handled by someone else now.

Eden (*pause*) Yes, of ... no, of course. Just a, uh ... few little aches for my old job, you know. But you're right. After facing out to the rest of the world for so long, time to turn around and face in a little more, eh?

Bishop Quite right. Let someone else fret about that silly little Commonwealth.

Eden I beg your pardon?

Bishop Just a little joke, Prime Minister.

Eden Well, don't. They are our family, Bishop. And one must always respect one's family. They make Britain more than the sum of its parts. We are their parents. Not so long ago, our influence spread across a third of the world. But alas, like all children ... they're growing up. And leaving home. (*Facing the Queen's portrait.*) They don't need us any more, Fred. One day we shall be left this island alone. (*Pause.*) Do you know I familiarised myself with all our possessions by heart, Fred?

Bishop Really?

Eden Oh yes. My duty, you know. And something to do on all those flights everywhere.

Bishop How many is that, sir?

Eden Eight in the Commonwealth. Then forty other territories, protectorates and such.

Bishop And you know them all by heart?

Eden (*pause. Smiles*) You don't believe me.

Bishop Of course, Prime –

Eden Canada, Australia, New Zealand, South Africa, India, Pakistan, Ceylon, United Kingdom.

Bishop Very good, Prime –

Eden Then we have, well ... Gibraltar, Malta, Singapore. Hong Kong. Uh ... Zanzibar. The Seychelles. Jamaica. Maybe you should be writing these down.

Bishop I, I'm sorry?

Eden I'm saying maybe you should be writing these down. So we don't say the same ones twice. (*Pause.*) Come along.

Bishop (*pause. He takes a pad and pencil from his pocket*)   Sir.

Eden   Canada, Australia, New Zealand …

Westminster. Press room.

Caricaturist (*sketching on a pad*)   So. How do you think the old boy's doing, then?

Reporter (*writing. Sipping coffee*)   All right. Storming the polls, ain't he?

Caricaturist   Oh yeah. But then they always do the first year, don't they?

Reporter   Mm. Good campaign though, I thought.

Caricaturist   Did yer?

Reporter   Yes, I did. Fought like a gentleman.

Caricaturist   Oh yeah. Then he always was one of those, wasn't he?

Reporter   One of those?

Caricaturist   One of them. Born into it and all that. Eton.

Reporter   Oh yeah. Money.

Caricaturist   Buy yourself into it, can't you?

Reporter   Hmm.

Caricaturist   Pay for it. I could have been a gentleman if my old man had paid for me to be one.

Reporter   You are a gentleman, Fred.

Caricaturist   Ah. Thank you, Bill. So are you.

Downing Street. Prime Minister's chambers.

Eden   … Tanganyika. Uh, Swaziland. Bermuda. How many's that?

Bishop   That's thirty-eight.

Eden (*pause*) Hong Kong?

Bishop You've had that one, I'm afraid.

Eden Don't be pedantic, Bishop. (*Pause.*) Kenya! Kenya!

Bishop (*writing*) Kenya.

Eden Good old Kenya. (*Pause.*) How many's that?

Bishop You need one more, Prime Minister.

Eden Are you sure? (*Pause.*) Damn it man, one more.

Bishop If it's any consolation, that's pretty impressive off the top of your head, sir.

Eden No, no it's not. I know them all. (*Takes the pad.*)

Bishop Well, I'm afraid your audience with the Queen will be starting shortly, Prime Minister. We'll need to be getting you to the palace.

Eden Fine, fine. (*Gathering some files and making to leave.*) But this isn't over.

Bishop Perhaps Her Majesty could help.

Eden (*barking as he exits*) I don't need any help!

Downing Street. Bedroom. **Eden** *in bed has a telephone on his lap, the receiver rested on his cheek and shoulder, notes on his lap.* **Clarissa** *lies next to him, reading.*

Eden (*on the phone*) Ah, Harold. Yes. Now. (*Pause.*) Sorry? (*Pause.*) Yes, I'm aware of that, Harold. I just have a few amendments to your Iranian telegram. (*Pause.*) No, it's fine, I just … (*Pause.*) This part where you say – are you writing this down? (*Pause.*) Well you *should* keep a pencil by your bed, I do. (*Pause.*) Oh, listen, go and get one, I'll call you back. (*Pause.*) No, don't put me onto … Hello Dorothy. (*Pause.*) Yes, I do apologise. (*Sighs. Pause.*) Yes, w-would you like to speak to Clarissa?

Clarissa *shoots him a look, shaking her head.*

Eden Look, can – I'll call back in a minute. Tha – ye – bye.

(*Replacing the receiver.*) God, that man. He thinks every bloody telegram he writes is as sacred as the Bible.

Clarissa   You wouldn't have stood for Uncle Winston rewriting yours. You need to be careful, Anthony. You don't want a reputation as one who –

Eden   What?

Clarissa   Fusses.

Eden   It is a Prime Minister's duty to fuss. The bigger picture is made up of the minutiae.

Clarissa   Learn to trust your officials, Anthony. It's better for them and it's certainly better for you. And you're getting a cold.

Eden   Just a runny nose.

Clarissa   That's the first sign.

Eden   Not if all you've got is a runny nose, then it's the last sign.

Clarissa   You need to wrap up more. If Dr Evans saw you he'd have a fit. You should wear your homburg.

Eden   I do wear my homburg.

Clarissa   It's cold. You'll catch your death.

Eden   Well, what? Do you want me to wear it now, should I put it on now?

Clarissa (*pause. Smiles*)   Yes.

Eden (*pause. Smiles back, wryly*)   All right.

He hops out of bed and exits the light.

Clarissa   What did he give you?

Eden (*off*)   Nothing. More Benzedrine. Help with my circulation.

He returns and gets back into bed, wearing his homburg. He poses mockingly, and **Clarissa** *laughs.*

Clarissa What a handsome English gent you are!

Eden Why, thank you. (*Going back to his notes.*) Anyway. Things will calm down now the Russian visit is over.

Clarissa Until the next one. When is King Feisal coming to stay?

Eden *laughs.*

Clarissa What? What's so funny?

Eden Nothing. You ... It's a state visit from the King of Iraq. You phrase it as though it were your mother coming over for the Bank Holiday.

Clarissa Well, it's all the same, my mother or the King of Iraq. Still need to change the sheets, don't we? (*Pause.*) Well, we should get away after that. Somewhere warm. And quiet. (*She curls up to him.*) Just you and me. No one else for miles and miles. Relaxing. On the beach. In our bathing outfits. And no telephone!

Eden Well, I'll need a telephone, darling.

Clarissa Not on the beach. (*Beat.*) I thought my outfit for the Russians was ghastly on reflection. Get one of your cronies to check what Her Majesty is wearing for this one. Make sure we don't clash.

Eden I hardly think that's likely, darling.

Clarissa Why not?

Eden Just that ... Nothing. (*Chuckles.*) I don't think she goes to the same shops.

Clarissa What does that mean? She wears better clothes than me?

Eden She wears different clothes from you. (*Dialling another number on the phone.*)

Clarissa You think I'm going to embarrass you?

Eden I think it's incredible I can negotiate international treaties with foreign dictators, yet I'm diplomatically impotent when it comes to a conversation with my wife.

Clarissa I fancy Jamaica.

Eden Send me a postcard. (*On the phone.*) Ah. Mrs Butler? (*Pause.*) Hello. Prime Minister here. Is your husband available? (*Pause.*) Well, be a dear. Give him a nudge.

Downing Street. **Eden** *with* **Bishop**. **Lloyd** *appears.*

Eden Selwyn, old boy. Having a reshuffle. What do you say to the Foreign Office?

Lloyd (*nods*) Prime Minister.

Lloyd *disappears.* **Macmillan** *appears.*

Eden Harold. You're going to the Treasury. Congratulations. Chancellor of the Exchequer.

Macmillan (*pause*) Thank you, Prime Minister.

Macmillan *disappears.* **Eden** *claps his hands together in a 'job well done' fashion.*

Eden There.

Bishop Prime Minister? Making Harold Chancellor. Such a ... well, prominent man so close to the prize, as it were? (*Pause.*) Forgive my presumptions, Prime Minister.

Eden Thank you, Fred. Suggestion noted.

Westminster. Press room. **Caricaturist** *is pulling 'toothy' faces as he sketches.*

Caricaturist Quite 'toothy', Sir Anthony. Ain't he?

Reporter See he's shuffling people around already. Butler. Lloyd. Macmillan.

Caricaturist Hmm. All sounds very sensible to me, though, Bill.

Reporter Do you think? (*Pause.*) So, lot more work for Mac, then. Less time to, uh … check up on his wife, if you know what I mean.

Caricaturist I think there are plenty of gentlemen who know that, Bill. (*Laughs.*)

Reporter Word is, Mac has heard that too. Course, he'll never leave her.

Caricaturist Would you? (*Laughs.*) Why don't you, uh … you know. (*Gestures to the notepad.*) Slip something in. Quite a coup, wouldn't you say? That story?

Reporter There are certain things one shouldn't 'report', Fred. A gentlemen's private life has no bearing on his integrity as a politician. And I rue the day when serious journalism becomes nothing more than grotesque gossip for the hoi polloi.

Caricaturist Hmm. (*Glancing at his notepad.*) I'm thinking of giving Mac a forked tongue.

Downing Street. Prime Minister's chambers. **Eden** *is peeking through the window,* **Lloyd** *watching behind him.*

Eden Ye gods, would you look at that man. It's as though he thinks being Chancellor makes him Elvis Presley. Loitering on the steps so they can get a better shot of him. I've made the wrong choice, haven't I?

Lloyd You can't blame Harold, Anthony. We all do it.

Eden I don't do it! Always waving, playing to the crowds. A small salute is enough for me. But him. Desperate to get a cheer. Course Winston was the worst. All he'd have to do was give the victory fingers and he'd have women fainting into the road. Though at least Winston had earned it.

Bishop *enters, followed by* **Macmillan**. **Eden** *continues at the window, unaware.*

Eden What's this chap done? Flouncing around like he owns the place.

Macmillan Who is this, Prime Minister?

Eden (*turning. Beat*) Prince Philip. (*Pause.*) Can't stand the man.

Macmillan Ah.

Eden (*pause*) Don't tell him, will you?

Macmillan Safe with me, Prime Minister.

Lloyd (*pause, then hastily*) Right, we'll leave you to it, gentlemen.

Lloyd *and* **Bishop** *make a hasty exit. Silence.*

Eden Your budget has been emphatically received, Harold. Despite a cut of one hundred million in expenditure, the press seem to like you.

Macmillan Yes, I don't know why, really. But I've never had it so good. (*Beat.*) Hmm …

Eden Hmm – yes. Well, all in all we haven't been producing enough. We're consuming too much of domestic production ourselves, leaving not enough to export.

Macmillan I've ordered the banks to reduce advances to customers. Local authorities are to cut back on spending …

Eden But despite world trade expanding at a healthy rate, Harold, Britain is scarcely managing to balance its payments. (*Facing the Queen's portrait.*) We're the fathers of industry, Harold. Architects of modern manufacture and commerce. Now everyone has caught up and is leaving us behind. How is a small island to cope? (*Mopping his brow.*)

Macmillan As it stands, our biggest expenditure is still defence.

Eden Well, withdrawal from Egypt is all but complete.
Though we must keep on funding the atomic weapon research at Aldermaston. Cannot afford to be left behind there.

Macmillan And speaking of Egypt. Our finances are in place to fund the new Aswan Dam in the Nile. As are French and German. Any news from America?

Eden Mm. Dulles is giving the impression their enthusiasm is waning, given that Nasser keeps flip-flopping over the terms of the loan. God, he's getting to be bloody pain, that man. Lloyd rather suspects he was involved in Glubb's dismissal from Jordan as well.

Macmillan If the Americans withdraw their funding, the World Bank will do the same.

Eden Which will mean the end of the whole thing. Well. We'll keep an eye on it.

Downing Street. Prime Minister's chambers. **Eden**, **Bishop**, **Macmillan** *and* **Lord Mountbatten** *sit having tea.* **Mountbatten** *is dressed in naval officer's uniform.*

Eden Bit of good news, Lord Mountbatten. The Jordanians are joining the Baghdad pact.

Mountbatten Well, that is good. Keep one foot in that door, eh?

Macmillan Yes, we rather thought it might be a good idea to send them a present.

Eden Ah. Yes. Now. Mr Lloyd and I were chatting about this. Any thoughts?

Macmillan Perhaps a fighter aircraft. A sort of welcome gift.

Mountbatten Excellent idea.

Eden Very well. Bishop, could you make a note? We'll inform the Ministry of Defence.

Macmillan Although the Israelis may get unsettled if we're seen to be arming Jordan.

Eden Yes, perhaps. I'll telegraph Dulles in the States. Get him to move on the offer of a few military bits and pieces for the Israelis. That should keep them happy.

Mountbatten Well of course, if we're doing that, may as well make sure Iraq receives its tanks and equipment around the same time.

Macmillan   Ah, then what about the Lebanese?

Eden   The Lebanese?

Mountbatten   Yes, they'll need something if we're giving out to Israel.

Macmillan   And maybe the Sudanese.

Eden   Oh, for heaven's ... fine, we'll just hand over HMS *Belfast* !

Bishop (*writing*)   HMS –

Eden / Macmillan / Mountbatten (*together*)   No!

Eden   I think that should be enough for now, gentlemen.

Mountbatten (*pause*)   Hear the Americans pulled out of the Egyptian Dam deal.

Eden   Yes, which means we've pulled our support as well, I'm afraid. Though the danger is the Russians may get in there with funding now.

Mountbatten   Well, if you ask me it serves them right. Nasser blasting us on Radio Cairo. Ungrateful Arabs. If ... ha! ... if they don't give a dam, why should *we* give a dam! (*Laughs.*) Hope the Nile floods every day this year. (*Pause.*) Do you ever miss Durham, Prime Minister? Beautiful place. Wonderful cathedral, of course.

Eden   Oh yes. Stunning. I think one must always pine for one's first home occasionally.

Mountbatten   You know, I've always thought of Britain's geography like the anatomy of a woman. The top part is pretty enough, but can give you an awful lot of grief. When really, all the main action is from the Midlands down.

Eden (*pause. Mortified*)   Yes, that's ... I've never thought of it in, uh ...

Macmillan   Midlands down. Right.

Mountbatten Though I always enjoy a good feel around the Pennines, what? (*Nudges* **Macmillan** *and laughs.*) Well now, I won't keep you, Prime Minister. Have to head off and pay a little visit to our base in the Falklands. Check everything's shipshape.

Eden Yes, well. Thank you for stopping – Falklands! That's it! Falk –

He laughs, smiling smugly at **Bishop** *as he takes out the pad of paper and writes.*

Eden Ha! Forty. There. Got them. (*Noticing his bemused company.*) Excuse me. (*Exits.*)

Macmillan How is the mood in our forces, Dickie?

Mountbatten Oh fine, Harold. Fine. Truth be told, as we shut up shop in more and more places, there's getting less and less for them to do!

Downing Street. **Eden** *is standing alone by a radio. The sound of an Arabic speaker exclaiming with passion. Suddenly, and slowly,* **Nasser** *appears some distance from him.* **Eden** *looks up, a mixture of fear and anger.* **Nasser** *smiles, then disappears.*

Prime Minister's chambers. Night. **Eden** *alone, as before. He looks panicked, mopping his brow and breathing heavily.* **Bishop** *bursts in, closely followed by* **Lloyd**.

Lloyd Prime Minister. I've just heard.

Eden Mr Lloyd. Mr Bishop. Sorry ... uh, so sorry to drag you in so late.

Lloyd Heavens, what ... what on earth is that madman up to?

Macmillan *enters.*

Lloyd Harold, Nasser has –

Macmillan I know. The Egyptians have announced they're seizing control of the Suez Canal. (*Pause.*) I suppose we should have seen this on the cards.

Lloyd Well, I didn't, and I'm Foreign Secretary! It's, it's ... I mean, what is it?

Macmillan It's intolerable.

Lloyd You're right, in ... intolerable! God, that man!

Eden It's the seizing of international assets.

Lloyd Seizing? It is tantamount to theft.

Macmillan It is theft. (*Producing a note.*) Five million pounds withdrawn today from the Suez Canal Company account. From the Bank of Cairo.

Lloyd (*taking the note*) That's our money!

Macmillan So they're pickpockets as well. I can only assume it's a response to the United States and their withdrawal of aid towards their dam.

Lloyd Well, that's not our fault!

Macmillan We're all one. The West. It's an affront against us all.

Eden And as such ... as such, we respond, all of us, as one. The free world.

Macmillan Prime Minister.

Eden (*beat*) Dispatch telegrams to Paris and Washington immediately. I'll draft them.

Bishop Prime Minister.

Bishop *exits.* **Macmillan**, **Lloyd** *and* **Eden** *look at each other. Pause.*

Eden What ... what does he think he's doing? This is just a, a, a blatant violation of international law, and a huge public slap in our face that we cannot tolerate. I will not ... and the timing is incredible! We have King Feisal sleeping rooms away! It's been done to embarrass us. (*Pause.*) I MEAN, REALLY! Snatch and grab what isn't his. He, he's trying to humiliate us, damn it! (*He faces the Queen's portrait.*) How. Dare. He.

Macmillan   We must call the Cabinet to a meeting first thing tomorrow morning.

Eden   Then I must speak to the House.

Lloyd   I shall call the Chiefs of Staff to, um … God, to meet tomorrow as well.

Eden   Right.

Lloyd   I mean, no one is suggesting … You know, a response from our forces. It may not –

Macmillan   Although … quite. But. We must try and use this to our advantage.

Lloyd   Ad – ? What possible advantage can be – could be reaped from this?

Macmillan   Nasser is a ruthless dictator who has been troubling us for years. He's damaging our interests in the Middle East and threatening stability in the whole area. This is … well … an incentive to get the job finally done.

Eden (*pause*)   Overthrow his regime …

Macmillan   Whilst we're there …

Eden   You're right.

Lloyd   Prime Minister?

Eden   We've wanted him out for years.

Lloyd   But. If I, I could … you mustn't – we must wait to see what the situation is first.

Macmillan   The economic and trade situation is very dire indeed if Nasser obstructs our passage. He'll almost certainly use the revenue to fund the dam himself. More as an exercise in propaganda than because he actually cares for his people. Let alone what it would mean to our supply of oil!

Lloyd Yes, but you're ... I'm not disputing taking action on the Canal, against the breaking of UN regulations, but you're talking about deposing a / government.

Eden No, but it's more than that! We've been here before, gentlemen. I've ... I've been here before. When a dictator shows himself to have designs outside his nation and the world stands back until it's too late. Well. We stop this one dead before he gets going.

Macmillan Agreed. We lose this one, we lose them all.

Eden That man wants sole power in the Arab world, getting us out altogether. Leaving him free to suppress Jordan, Israel, the Sudan, whoever else he chooses.

Macmillan Not to mention what signal this sends out to the world if a vicious dictator is seen to take what doesn't belong to him and then just get away with it.

Eden Then we don't let him get away with it.

Lights down.

Act Two

Westminster. House of Commons. Loud commotion, which **Eden** *has to battle through.*

Eden No ... no notice was given, no formal statement made. In truth, nothing that amounts to any kind of fair play. This is aggression. From an aggressive dictator. Of an aggressive regime. That has repercussions not just for our nation, but all nations, when the mutually agreed rules between countries are publicly disobeyed. Her Majesty's ... Her Majesty's Government are acting swiftly in consulting the other governments of the world to assess this very serious situation, on a very international scale. May the House be assured that we will keep them informed!

War Rooms. **Mountbatten, Macmillan** *and* **Lloyd** *around a map on a table.* **Eden** *enters after* **Mountbatten** *has begun his analysis.*

Mountbatten Egypt. Its neighbours, Sudan and Libya. North-east we have Israel, Jordan, and here Saudi Arabia. Northern entrance to the Canal from the Med here. Southern exit to the Red Sea here. Port Said there. Alexandria here. Currently Port Said is the preferred choice of attack. Alexandria would be messier, with far more casualties.

Eden What are the Chiefs' suggestions on the kind of invasion force?

Mountbatten First assessments show that the most effective attack, certainly in terms of preparation time, would be paratroopers dropping here, at the northern entrance.

A phone rings. **Macmillan** *answers.*

Macmillan Macmillan.

Mountbatten Though it is incredibly perilous, as we know from our drops over Germany.

Eden No. This is not to be a campaign that results in significant loss of life. On any side.

Macmillan Thank you. (*Replaces the receiver.*)

Eden We would lose all support.

Macmillan That was the Minister for Fuel and Power. Our current oil reserves would last us six weeks, no more. Assuming the Egyptians place restrictions on our passage.

Lloyd Good God, man!

Macmillan Mr Jones and his staff are looking into the possibilities of sailing oil from the Persian Gulf around the Cape of Good Hope.

Lloyd Oh crikey, they'd better set off now, then!

Eden (*to* **Mountbatten**) What are the other initial suggestions?

Mountbatten Well, there's the possibility of unilateral action from naval and marine forces. Send the Maltese fleet to Cyprus, pick up ten, twelve thousand marine commandos, sail them to Port Said. Could be there within four days, a touch more.

Lloyd Though the problem then is maintaining control over the Canal once we are there.

Mountbatten I agree. Troops on the ground, probably backed up by the RAF. (*Sighs.*) Truth be told ... well, Britain does not really have the capacity for such an emergency.

Macmillan We have the largest navy, one of the most feared armies and the most admired air force in the world. I'm pretty sure we do have the capacity.

Mountbatten Yes, but this one is tricky. It warrants too small a campaign for a large-scale response. It's potentially very awkward. I mean the exact objectives are unclear.

Eden The Cabinet objective is to place the Canal under a new international commission.

Mountbatten Those are diplomatic objectives. What are our military objectives?

Macmillan To seize the Canal by force if we have to.

Mountbatten Well, with respect, I've never had to develop a strategy on such a basis.

Eden Which is why we are pursuing all other possible alternatives. Political pressure backed up by the threat of military action. Only the threat.

Mountbatten What's the situation regarding allied support?

Eden From the French, definitely. They own shares in the company, and Nasser is involved in Algeria. This would be a war of revenge for them. And quite frankly, they're tired of being humiliated. This is a war they might actually win.

Mountbatten And the Americans?

Eden Eisenhower's reply to our telegram wasn't as outraged as I'd hoped. And there is the November election. Military support is unlikely, so we'll have to bank on moral.

The phone rings. **Lloyd** *answers.*

Lloyd Lloyd.

Mountbatten And, Mr Macmillan, not that I need to see a statement or anything, but ...

Macmillan Financial measures have been put in place. As for your budget, well, I'll need to sift around the piggy bank in more detail, but needless to say –

Lloyd Thank you. (*Replaces receiver.*) Gentlemen. Our Cairo Embassy has been in touch.

Eden Yes?

Lloyd Our note of protest has been returned.

Eden Returned? Any note?

Lloyd Only ... 'Return to sender'.

Eden (*pause*) That devil.

Lloyd (*heading out*) And I'm afraid Nasser has been making speeches again. One moment. (*Exits.*)

Eden   Well, that's it then. (*To* **Mountbatten**.) He's clearly not going to co-operate.

Lloyd *returns, holding a large file.*

Eden   That can't be all of it.

Lloyd   It's at least shorter than the last two-hour one. (*Reads.*) Shout. Scream. Uh, wave of fist. It is within his nation's right to nationalise what already belongs to them. Uh, and that the ... imperial powers ... have no case to claim any ownership themselves.

Eden   Imperial powers? (*Taking the transcript.*)

As the War Rooms darken, **Nasser** *appears in front of a microphone.*

Nasser   This, oh citizens, is the battle in which we are now involved. It is a battle against imperialism! In the past, they used to keep us waiting in the British High Commission! Now, they pay their dues to us! Arab nationalism has been set alight from the Atlantic to the Persian Gulf! Arab nationalism feels its existence and its strength!

Nasser *disappears as the War Rooms return.* **Eden** *overlapping slightly with* **Nasser**.

Eden (*reading*)   'This is not called the Suez Canal, it is called the Arabs' Canal' ... 'The forces of Islam ... ' (*Glancing up, somewhat fearful.*) 'are to clean the land ... '

Macmillan (*pause. Turning to* **Mountbatten**)   A timetable of military operations as soon as possible, Lord Mountbatten.

Foreign Office. **Nutting** *enters to give* **Lloyd** *a report.*

Nutting   Our lawyers' findings.

Lloyd   Thank you, Nutting.

Nutting   It isn't promising, Foreign Secretary.

Lloyd   What do you mean?

Eden's Empire   55

Nutting   Based on the Joint Intelligence Committee report, Selywn, and ... and United Nations regulations, there is little to support a case for military action just yet.

Lloyd   What? Nasser has stolen international assets.

Nutting   He has nationalised a canal that runs through his land.

Lloyd   That isn't the point!

Nutting   I know, Selwyn. But no restrictions have been placed on our ships, even though they now pay their dues to Britain and not Egypt. He continues to employ all foreign nationals and the Egyptians, despite all fears, have proved capable of looking after the Canal themselves. Also, there has been ... well, no real act of military aggression. If we launch a pre-emptive strike against a nation that hasn't fired one bullet, attacked one British citizen, Britain would be the aggressors. We who were the warmongers.

Lloyd *turns into the Prime Minister's chambers.* **Eden,** **Macmillan** *and* **Bishop**

Macmillan   I really don't see the problem, I'm afraid!

Lloyd   You don't see the problem / in this?! (*Waves the report.*)

Macmillan   We are responding to / an act of aggression.

Lloyd   The problem is we need an irrefutable legal case to show the world we are acting legitimately. Britain cannot just go to war whenever she feels like it! As it stands, I think, legally speaking, our position is very weak indeed.

Macmillan   Then we don't speak legally, we speak politically! Anthony?

Eden   We need to guard ourselves, yes, Selwyn.

Lloyd   Thank you.

Eden   But seeing as our standpoint legally is not the strongest it could be, I agree with Harold that we shouldn't ... bring it up too often.

Macmillan   They're the ones who have acted illegally, Selwyn.

Lloyd   The Foreign Office cannot find substantial enough justification for war.

Macmillan   Then get them to try harder, damn it!

Lloyd   You want me to falsify intelligence!

Macmillan   We don't need to falsify intelligence! The world knows this is a vicious dictator. Their people will be grateful we overthrow him. As will the entire Middle East.

Lloyd   Why do you keep harping on about overthrowing him? One is one thing and one entirely another! I'm working on the basis of retrieving a canal. Through the right channels. Through the UN. Prime Minister, the Suez Canal Company is legally speaking a registered Egyptian Company operating under Egyptian law. He's compensating the shareholders. From a business point of view, he's … well, he's simply buying us out.

Eden   He's forcing us out.

Lloyd   It's his country.

Eden   It's our canal! We built it, we bought it, we own it.

Lloyd   I know, and I agree, both of you, Harold, you know I'm batting for the same team. But if we're accusing him of violating UN regulations, we can't respond by doing the same thing. Using these violations as an excuse to bring down a government we don't happen to like. This report bothers me. It bothers me, Prime Minister.

Eden (*pause*)   We will refer the matter to the UN Security Council.

Macmillan   Prime Minister, with all due respect, that would be / a waste of time.

Eden   Selwyn is right, Harold. We need to show the world we have every intention and every hope of sorting this out peacefully and diplomatically. And if that fails we then have no choice but to resort to the use of force. We need to push through a resolution.

Macmillan   They won't sanction any military action.

Lloyd If we don't refer such matters to the UN then what is the point of this organisation? Why did we build it not even fifteen years ago? It means nothing.

Macmillan Let us not forget this dictator has been flouting UN resolutions for years now, and the UN has done nothing. Which is precisely why we're going in to sort him out. Otherwise the UN really will mean nothing. That's the line we should take, Selwyn. That's what we should be focusing on, not the legality of a war, but the necessity for it. For international security against a mad dictator and his appalling regime! Winston would have razed Cairo to the ground by now, Anthony!

Eden I understand, Harold.

Macmillan And I am afraid I will have to resign if action is not taken. I cannot be a part of any administration that claims it will roar like a lion but hide like a mouse!

Eden Harold –

Macmillan And the Russians will only use their veto at the UN. They'll stop any resolution to take action against Egypt. You know they will, Anthony! So what is the point?!

Eden MR MACMILLAN!

Macmillan (*pause*) Prime Minister.

Eden The point is to show the world that we tried. It clears our conscience. Which is also why I think we should accept America's request for a conference of the main maritime powers. As soon as possible. Mr Lloyd?

Lloyd I'll get my staff onto it.

Eden That will be all for now, gentlemen.

Macmillan *and* **Lloyd** *exit.* **Eden** *writes a note and hands it to* **Bishop**.

Eden Fred, could you ... my prescription for Evans. I want to up the dosage of Benzedrine, and uh ... need more Sparine, and the, the purple ones. I can't remember their name.

Bishop Prime Minister. (*Exits.*)

Downing Street. **Bishop** *and* **Clarissa**.

Clarissa What do you mean?

Bishop I am sorry, Lady Eden, but there's nothing all day. He can't fit you in.

Clarissa He can't *what* ?

Bishop Uh ...

Clarissa Fit. Me. In?

Bishop He has appointments. People have to book rather in advance at the moment.

Clarissa (*beat*) Well, I'd better book an appointment, then.

Bishop (*pause*) Beg pardon?

Clarissa I would like to book an appointment with my husband, please.

Bishop (*beat*) All right. (*Opens a diary.*)

Clarissa Tomorrow morning?

Bishop Sorry.

Clarissa Afternoon? Evening?

Bishop Nothing really all day, I'm afraid.

Clarissa Night?

Bishop I'm sorry?

Clarissa Night.

Bishop Well ... you'll be ... 'seeing' him ... anyway. Won't you?

Clarissa You would think so, wouldn't you?

Bishop (*writing*) What business?

Clarissa *glowers at him.*

Bishop (*beat. Snapping the book closed*)   Right. There. You're in.

Downing Street. Prime Minister's chambers. **Eden** *and* **Macmillan**.

Eden   I received another telegram from Eisenhower. He's very worried we're too far ahead in our military plans. Thinks we've decided to go in guns blazing regardless of whether there's a diplomatic road to peace. He mentions you by name.

Macmillan   I'm touched.

Eden   Murphy relayed to him your talks. Sounds like you frightened the trousers off him.

Macmillan (*smiling*)   Really?

Eden   You're pleased?

Macmillan   The Americans will play along more readily if they think we're about to blow up the Middle East.

Eden   A rather dangerous game, Harold. Maybe play down the warlord rhetoric for now?

Macmillan   Very well. (*Beat.*) Prime Minister, I've reservations about the Port Said plan.

Eden   You ... do?

Macmillan   I think it limits our outcome to regaining the Canal.

Eden   Which is our primary objective, Harold.

Macmillan   Publicly, yes. Though ultimately isn't it to overthrow Nasser?

Eden   You have a better one?

Macmillan   I think we should invade through Alexandria. That way we enter the Canal Zone from behind, get a foothold, and advance through the rest of Egypt.

Eden (*pause*)   Well. Run it past Mountbatten, if you'd like.

Though, try to, uh … try to keep any paper trail to a limit, would you?

Macmillan Prime Minister. (*Beat.*) And Prime Minister? Might it be time to involve Israel?

Eden We've been in constant contact, of course. But perhaps it's not time to start enlisting other armed forces just yet, Harold. We need to show we're giving the conference and the UN a chance.

Macmillan It's only that they are on the border, and what with all the militia attacks from Egypt, they have been desperate to overthrow Nasser for some time now. (*Pause.*) Just a thought, Prime Minister.

Downing Street. Prime Minister's chambers. **Eden** *and* **Nutting**.

Eden Well, obviously the Foreign Office doesn't give a damn about British prestige, Mr Nutting, otherwise you wouldn't be doing all you could to hamper this campaign. If you got your way, Nasser will be the end of us! I mean, you, you've met him.

Nutting Yes, Prime Minister, and I found him quite charming. A little brash / perhaps.

Eden (*laugh*) Ch … charming? Ha!

Nutting A full-scale invasion will only give Nasser more support amongst his Arab neighbours. I fail to see how that would neutralise him.

Eden (*pause*) Neutralise him? Neu-tra-lise him? I want him gone. Do you understand? I. Want. Him. *Gone*.

Nutting (*pause. He nods, sadly*) Prime Minister.

Downing Street. Bedroom. **Clarissa** *in bed,* **Eden** *getting ready to join.*

Clarissa You're late.

Eden Hmm?

Clarissa For my appointment. I booked you in. And you look awful.

Eden   Thank you, darling.

Clarissa   And four a.m. is no time to be coming to bed. You'll be getting up in three hours.

Eden   Two. (*Taking his cycle of pills with a glass of water.*)

Clarissa   You should see Evans about getting off them. Apparently these amphetamines don't give you more energy, just use up what you have in bursts.

Eden   I need them at the moment, all right. The fevers and ... pains have ...

He clambers into bed and continues his cycle of pills.

Darling, you worked with this Anthony Nutting chap during the war, didn't you?

Clarissa   Yes, we decoded ciphers together in the Foreign Office.

Eden   What did you make of him?

Clarissa   I thought he was rather sweet. Why?

Eden   Hmm. Just ... (*Sighs.*)

Clarissa   Anthony, the news said you lost your temper in the House today. Try to stay calm. It isn't professional. They're trying to provoke you, and you're letting them win.

Eden *turns off the light and the room descends into darkness.*

Westminster. Press room. **Reporter** *is note-taking,* **Caricaturist** *is sketching.*

Reporter   See Egypt's rejected the conference demands. And the UN aren't playing ball.

Caricaturist   So it would seem. (*Sucking in air through his teeth.*) Looks like old Tony is taking the country to war, then. Whether they like it or not.

Reporter   Judging from our poll this morning, they like it not. Don't think a canal is worth a war. Think Egypt must do something else first. Something worse.

Caricaturist Reckon it'll harm our standing in the Middle East, Bill. Make those Arabs hate us even more.

Reporter Do they hate us, Fred?

Caricaturist They distrust us.

Reporter (*sucking in air*) Some tough decisions to be made at the top then, eh?

Caricaturist Yup. Where do you stand?

Reporter Where do I stand?

Caricaturist Yes.

Reporter I'd prefer to wait until the decision is proven right or wrong, Fred. Then I'll choose to stand in the appropriate place and say I have been standing there all along.

Caricaturist Sounds like a good idea, Bill. Mind if I join you?

Reporter Not at all, Fred. There'll be plenty of room for everyone.

Downing Street. Prime Minister's chambers. **Eden** *is on the phone, writing notes. Newspapers cover his desk.*

Eden Yes, well … (*Pause.*) But the four yellow ones at night are, are the, um … the equivalent of two red ones, right? (*Pause.*) Sometimes I find it better to take three yellows before bed and then maybe a red one if I wake in the night. (*Pause.*) What green – I don't have any green ones. (*Pause.*) Well, can I get some green ones?

He writes some notes. **Bishop** *enters.*

Eden OK. Yes. Bye. (*He writes, mumbling to himself.*) Red, green, blue, all the colours of the bloody rainbow. Right! Bishop.

Bishop Lord Mountbatten and Mr Lloyd are here with the operation details, sir.

Eden Have you seen these, Fred? (*Holding up the newspapers.*) Treacherous, the lot of them. Buckling under the pressure. Giving in to hysteria. Denouncing me one by one!

Bishop   That's not entirely the case, Prime Minister. Most bar a couple still support –

Eden   This one! Claims an increasing number of ministers are resigning! It's – how can any respectable government operate under such scrutiny? And betrayal!

Bishop   Right, well, we should get your press secretary to rush out a release stating these ministers aren't resigning over Suez.

Eden   I can't.

Bishop   Why not?

Eden   Because my press secretary has just resigned over Suez.

He swallows some tablets as **Lloyd**, **Macmillan** *and* **Mountbatten** *enter with plans.*

Mountbatten   Prime Minister.

Eden   Gentlemen. Let's get going on this, shall we?

Lloyd   I hear the French are getting impatient.

Macmillan   We're all getting impatient, Selwyn.

Eden   We mustn't dawdle. The people and the, the, the press have noticed we are arming ourselves but are seeing no action.

Mountbatten   How are they noticing?

Macmillan   Our navy has been on standby for a fortnight. And when you see tanks on the road painted a sandy colour you don't need to be Einstein to put two and two together.

Mountbatten   Christ! The secret service can't even fart any more without the press getting wind of it. (*Beat.*) So to speak.

Lloyd   Is everyone ready?

Mountbatten   Prime Minister, here is the joint plan of action as agreed by our Chiefs of Staff and the French officials. Alexandria will now be the landing point …

Eden *looks at* **Macmillan**, *who doesn't flinch.*

Mountbatten ... the operation will consist of eighty thousand men, including one French regiment. Phase One will be the RAF bombing of Egyptian bases. Once the Egyptian air force has been annihilated, our troops hit the ground from the Med to take Alexandria.

Eden The resistance in Alexandria was to be greater than in Port Said, I thought.

Lloyd It will be easier to occupy the northern regions after Nasser is overthrown.

Eden I wanted all options that prevented maximum casualties to be pursued. Is the speed of the Alexandria option really worth the extra loss?

Mountbatten This is the joint recommendation from the French and ourselves. Our main problem then is our exit strategy.

Eden What's the problem?

Mountbatten We don't really have one. If we're successful in regaining the Canal and toppling Nasser, we would have to make the always awkward transition from invasion force to occupying force until a new administration can be placed in power.

Lloyd Our prime concern would be to maintain good relationships with the locals. A Western army occupying an Arab country would do us few favours in the Middle East, let alone at home if we are there too long.

Eden Well. Detailed plans for an exit strategy pending, I agree to sign these off. (*Taking the proposals.*) What is the code-name?

Lloyd Ah. Now. I'm afraid 'Operation Hamilcar' can no longer work. Telegram from the French this morning. Apparently Hamilcar is, uh ... well it's spelt differently in French.

Mountbatten Differently?

Lloyd It's spelt with an 'A', not an 'H', sir.

Macmillan (*sighs*) Lord, all ...

Lloyd They want a different name. Make them feel more involved.

Eden And what do they suggest?

Lloyd Musketeer.

There is an eye-rolling from everyone.

Eden Very French. Fine. (*Begins to write.*) Do they spell Musketeer the same way we do?

Lloyd Uh, I assume so. Bishop?

Bishop Yes they do, Prime Minister.

Eden (*starts to write. Pause*) M-u-s?

Bishop / M-u-s-k ...

Macmillan (*overlapping*) M-u-s-k-e-t.

Eden E-t ...

Macmillan / Double 'e'.

Mountbatten E-e ...

Eden Double E, e-e. That's four 'e's.

Macmillan No, just –

Mountbatten Just two 'e's.

Eden Well can only one person speak, please?

They all start to spell it for him before **Macmillan** *breaks through as the loudest.*

Macmillan M-u-s-k-e-t-e-e-r.

Eden E-e-r. For heaven's sake, there ... (*Thrusts the document in* **Mountbatten**'s *hand.*) Right. Let's get this thing moving, shall we?

Television studio. **Eden** *sits in front of a camera, holding some notes. He shuffles in his seat, staring straight ahead. A stronger light shines on him, and he begins.*

Eden Naturally no one wants a war. But sometimes the decision is not made by us. It is made for us. By those who disobey the rules. Those who threaten the security of their own people, and of the world. Yes, we could give him the benefit of the doubt. Just like we gave Mussolini the benefit of the doubt. Just like we gave Hitler the benefit of the doubt. But forgive me if I am no longer willing to take the word of such reckless, untrustworthy men and their regimes. And God forbid any nation that does.

Westminster. Press room.

Reporter Taking his case direct into people's homes, Fred. That's a new one.

Caricaturist Mm. Thought he came across rather well, Bill. For what good it'll do him.

Downing Street. Prime Minister's chambers. **Bishop** *with* **Eden**, *who slams down a pile of papers, knocking items off his desk.*

Eden This is turning into a farce. A bloody farce! Can you believe it?

Bishop It is unfortunate, Prime Minister.

Eden Unfortunate?! It's like they're against me! First they want to change it to Alexandria. And now, now they're saying they've 'gone off' that and are back onto Port Said again. So. More time is needed. More time. Our armed forces will be in a state of readiness for the next seven years!

Macmillan *enters, holding up a document that he drops on the desk.*

Macmillan Prime Minister. 'Musketeer Revise'.

Eden Fred, could you ... leave us, please.

Bishop *leaves.*

Eden The Americans are worried about Russian intervention. Apparently they know of two Russian submarines that have taken on board Egyptian crews.

Macmillan Naturally they're going to be … tetchy, Prime Minister. But when the campaign is completed successfully and Nasser overthrown, the Russians won't have an ally in Egypt. And the Americans will be thanking us.

Eden Well, they needn't worry, anyway. Our generals take so long to get a war going, the Canal will have dried up before they finish! The French must be furious.

Macmillan From what I hear, they're beginning to look elsewhere.

Eden (*sighs*) The Israelis.

Macmillan They're tired of waiting.

Eden Well, do you know what … (*Trails.*)

Macmillan *fixes them a drink. He now talks in a very calm, dry and measured tone.*

Macmillan I have been made aware, Prime Minister, that the French legal team are looking at the 1954 treaty on our troop withdrawals from the Canal. It states, signed by the Egyptians, that British troops can return in an emergency.

Eden (*pause*) So I recall. But we've checked that. This doesn't constitute –

Macmillan I know. It doesn't. But something else might.

Eden (*pause*) I don't – what do you – ?

Macmillan Oh I don't know. We're just talking. (*Pause.*) But so are the French and Israelis. They were just wondering what would happen if, say … the Israelis sent a ship down the canal.

Eden The Israelis are sending a ship down the Canal?!

Macmillan No, they're not. We're just talking. (*Pause.*) But what if they did?

Eden The Egyptians would attack the ship, of course.

Macmillan Yes, they would. There'd be a fight. There could be ... a war.

Eden Harold ...

Macmillan We're just talking, remember. Just talking.

Eden We are?

Macmillan Yes. We are.

Eden (*pause*) If that happened, we would be under international obligation to –

Macmillan – to intervene, and restore order –

Eden – by occupying the Canal Zone –

Macmillan – and placing it back under international control. Asking both sides to retreat a set distance away from the Canal. Say, ten miles. Including the Egyptians.

Eden The Egyptians would never agree to that.

Macmillan No, Anthony, you're right. They wouldn't. Which means ... regrettably, but legitimately ... we would have to use force against Nasser and his regime. Regrettably. But. Legitimately. Prime Minister.

Eden (*pause*) I, I've ... fought against this kind ... Fought for peace my / entire –

Macmillan You still are. We all are. You know what appeasement of dictators means, Anthony. You more than anyone.

Eden *looks at the portrait of the Queen.*

Eden I remember the ... the time I was at Stalin's war rooms in Moscow. During the War. We were standing in front of this huge map of the world. The size of a house. Discussing various tactics and strategies. Stalin looked up at the map. At Britain. Looked at me, and said, with a hint of awe and wonder in his voice ... 'How can so much depend on one tiny little island?' And we both just stood there. Quietly. Looking ... (*Long pause.*) Send someone to Paris.

Macmillan Prime Minister.

Eden Discreetly.

Macmillan *smiles and toasts his glass.*

Macmillan I've never been anything but, Prime Minister.

Downing Street. Back room. Dimly lit. **Eden** *and* **Lloyd**.

Eden (*holding a sheet of paper*) There's written evidence!

Lloyd There's –

Eden Who gave you this?

Lloyd It was drawn up at the Quai d'Orsay in Paris.

Eden I cannot believe they have been so reckless! Why does it need to be written down?

Lloyd Something needs to be signed, Prime Minister.

Eden If this got out. If this got out do you realise ... (*Begins to cough.*) ... do you have any idea ... (*Trails off into a coughing fit.*)

Lloyd There are only two, Anthony.

Eden (*regains himself*) Burn this one.

Lloyd What?

Eden Burn it!

Lloyd *takes it.*

Eden And the other one?

Lloyd In a safe in the Quai d'Orsay. Signed by all of us, the French and Israelis.

Eden Send people over there. I want it destroyed.

Lloyd You ... want it what?

Eden I WANT IT DESTROYED!

Lloyd W-what kind of people? Secret service?

Eden No! Not – this isn't espionage, for heaven's sake! Just anyone. Two chaps on your staff. Just get them over there and get that copy. I mean it. Now.

Lloyd Prime Minister.

Eden *disappears.* **Lloyd** *steps forward, and sets the document alight.*

Eden *reappears, sitting in the Prime Minister's chambers, head in his hands, looking devastated.* **Macmillan** *standing over him. Silence.*

Macmillan They did wait several hours in the foyer, Anthony. Before the French came out to say they would keep a copy intact. For their records. Although it's an irrelevance now. A third copy was made of the agreement for the Israelis in Tel Aviv.

Pause. **Eden** *doesn't move.*

Macmillan No one will see it, Anthony.

Eden In thirty years ...

Macmillan By then it won't make any difference.

Eden My place in history ...

Macmillan There are more important things.

Eden A canal?!

Macmillan BRITAIN! *Long pause.*

Eden (*looks up, determined*) I know. (*Beat.*) It's just a shame, that's all. Just a shame.

Macmillan We need to prepare. The Israelis are going in. The movement of troops to the Jordan–Israeli border is under way as a diversion. Make people think Israel have ambitions for Jordan not Egypt. (*Beat.*) Remember what Winston always said.

Eden (*sighs*) What did Winston always say, Harold?

Macmillan History is written by the winners. It will be written by us.

Nutting *bursts in, followed by* **Lloyd** *and* **Bishop**.

Bishop   Mr Nutting!

Lloyd   Anthony, stop!

Eden   What's happened?

Nutting   Prime Minister, please, I beg you. End this sordid conspiracy now, I beg you.

Macmillan   Mr Nutting! What is the / meaning of this?

Nutting   This is not only highly illegal but highly immoral and your motives are so transparent / the whole world will know your intentions!

Macmillan   Selwyn! Can you not keep your staff under control? This is obscene!

Eden   It's all right, Harold, it's … it's OK. (*Pause.*) Nutting, I do understand –

Nutting   Please. I beg, I beg you. It's not too late to seek a legitimate, peaceful route. This action is in breach of the UN Charter and of the Base Agreement which you and I constructed and signed not two years ago!

Eden   Egypt broke that contract when they seized the Canal. They started this, man!

Nutting   So this is how Britain conducts her affairs now? Tit for tat?

Macmillan   Nutting! Don't forget whom you are talking to. Bishop?

Bishop   Prime Minister?

Eden   How dare you question my integrity!

Nutting   Integrity?! (*Referring to* **Lloyd**.) I've had to watch my minister over the past week taking secret night flights to France. Shredding documents, burning files.

Eden   We have nothing to hide!

Nutting Then why did you insist Bishop stop taking notes at the meeting with the French!

Eden How dare you! Do you know what, what I've, I've – how hard I have worked, how I have – my whole life dedicated to peace and, and …

Nutting I know of your impeccable record, Mr Eden, / that's why this shocks me so.

Eden Question my motives! I bloody well resigned from government over the appeasement of Hitler and, and the others! The lives, Nutting, the lives! That, that, that could have been saved! Well I won't / make the same mistake again!

Nutting Why have you got it into your head that Nasser is Hitler, Prime Minister?!

Eden Why are you so keen to protect him? Can't you see / what he's doing?!

Nutting You told me never to make it personal! Never. Why, why can't we follow through the good work Selwyn is doing at the UN?

Macmillan Because it isn't working!

Nutting And you're willing to sacrifice British soldiers on not trying!!

Macmillan Get out, man! Bishop!

Bishop Prime Minister?

Nutting I am afraid I will have to tender my resignation, Prime Minister.

Lloyd Nutting, Israel is attacking Egypt tonight.

Nutting Oh yes. Their 'surprise' attack. And then the French arrive tomorrow under the pretence of drawing up an ultimatum to the Israelis and Egyptians to cease fighting. An ultimatum I have been asked to draw up *now*. To save time tomorrow. Well, I won't. I won't. It is with a heavy heart, Prime Minister, that I must resign my post. I cannot serve an administration that chooses war as its first resort, not its last. The shame! I mean … look at … Can any of you even look me straight in the eye. Any of you?

Nutting *looks around at his company, all of whom shift their gaze, except* **Macmillan**, *whom he comes to last.* **Eden** *starts shifting things nervously on his desk.*

Eden Well, you … I would have thought you'd have been more concerned with, with the threat Israel poses to, to Jordan, wanting to protect them.

Nutting Oh yes, that's right. Though of course the Israeli threat to Jordan was something we made up to distract the international community. Wasn't it? Prime Minister?

Silence. **Eden** *looks down, shuffling papers with no purpose.*

Nutting Already you're struggling to remember what is real and what is your fictional world of lies and deceit. (*Pause.*) You know what you look like to me, Prime Minister?

Macmillan That's enough. Selwyn?

Lloyd Come on, Nutting. Let's go. This is / no way to conduct –

Nutting You look like a man who has seen his own terrifying downfall in front of him. I can see it in your eyes. The cavernous hole … getting bigger and deeper, spreading outwards, to swallow you up …

Eden, *eyes locked, begins to tremble.*

Eden G-go …

Nutting I tried, I did try!

Bishop Mr Nutting, I must ask you to leave.

Nutting But you won't even save yourself!

Macmillan May I remind you you're talking to / the Prime Minister!

Eden PLEASE STOP! GET HIM OUT!

Lloyd Mr Nutting, please. / Prime Minister, I'm so sorry.

Eden GET HIM OUT OF HERE!

Bishop *and* **Macmillan** *bundle him out.* **Lloyd** *follows.* **Eden** *collapses in his chair.*

Downing Street. Corridors. **Macmillan** *and* **Nutting***, who holds a letter.*

Nutting My resignation letter to the Commons. I have not included the details. For Anthony, you understand. Though I have a good mind to drop a copy off at the American Embassy. Alert Eisenhower of your plan. Stop this before it's too late.

Macmillan No. You won't.

He takes the letter, and rips it in two.

For the good of the government, Mr Nutting. There's a good chap.

Macmillan *disappears.*

Clarissa *appears.*

Clarissa I don't suppose there's any chance you'll change your mind. For an old friend. For two.

Nutting I'm so sorry, Clarissa. It breaks my heart. But I can't betray it.

Clarissa (*getting upset*) He's going the wrong way, isn't he?

Nutting *pauses. Nods his head slowly.*

Clarissa I know it. I know it, I can ...

Nutting Perhaps you could say something. They're all ... we're of a, a different generation. You and I. We see the future when all they see is the past.

Clarissa Please don't judge him so ... I see things you don't. There are things he ... like ... Don't tell him I spoke of this, but when he worked on the Anglo-Iranian oil deal as Foreign Secretary. Did you know he sold his shares in the company? To avoid a 'conflict of interest'. Despite it practically bankrupting him. He thought there were more important things than personal gain. I know you can't see that in him now but –

Nutting I can see that, now. That's why it … (*Pause. Sighs.*) That's *why*.

Clarissa You know, at the end of every day it feels as though he washes back to me like a tide. And every day it feels … like he washes out a little bit further. Each and every time. Until it feels like one day he won't come back at all.

Nutting I can't imagine how all this could ever be worth it. For you. How can it possibly be worth it?

Clarissa Because he's my husband. And when this is gone … I'm all he'll have. (*Pause. She laughs, tragically.*) He's already worried. About how he'll be remembered.

Nutting Oh, Clarissa. I don't think you … quite understand.

Clarissa Don't say that.

Nutting He's going –

Clarissa Don't ever say that to me!

Nutting Forgive me. (*Pause.*) If it's any consolation … and I hope it is … I fear his premiership will be such an anomaly he will barely be remembered at all. (*Pause.*) I'm so sorry.

He disappears.

Downing Street. Prime Minister's chambers. **Eden** *enters looking exhausted. He closes the door behind him, and rests against it with his back. He is surprised to see the room is empty. He slams his briefcase onto the desk and storms back to the door.*

Eden Hello?! Anyone there?!

He hops to the window and peeks out suspiciously. **Bishop** *enters.* **Eden** *spins.*

Eden Where the devil were you?

Bishop Prime Minister?

Eden Everyone jumping ship now the going has got rough? Where were you?

Bishop I'm not sure I understand, Prime Minister. I was ... I was here.

Eden You should have seen it, Fred. In the House. I announced our forces had set sail. There were nearly riots. They were actually ... booing me. I thought I was going to have to, to leave for my own ... (*Pause.*) Monckton's resigned from Defence, now. You heard that? It's all got so –

Macmillan *and* **Lloyd** *enter.*

Lloyd Well, that was a sight.

Eden Where have you been?

Macmillan Anthony. (*Handing him a report.*) Transcript from the press conference in America. It's worse than we thought.

Eden (*taking it*) Oh God ...

Macmillan Basically they've dissociated themselves from the whole situation. Eisenhower also ... uh, implied ... that they would never support a policy that is tantamount to ... (*Sighs.*) an imperialist power trying to hold together its empire.

Eden (*pause*) What?

Lloyd Correspondence in from others, I'm afraid, as well. New Zealand, India, Canada, all um ... all denouncing our course of action and demanding we turn our vessels back.

Macmillan And my conversation with Murphy in the States. They ... well, rather resent the idea of us starting a war on the assumption they would join in. 'Like the last one'.

Beat. **Eden** *slams the document down.*

Eden Like the last one?! This has got nothing to do with our empire! Or imperialism! Or ... It is to do with right and to do with wrong! Not wanting to stick our flag everywhere!

The phone rings. **Bishop** *answers.*

Bishop Bishop.

Eden But, but that doesn't mean we'll just … sit back and allow it to be trampled on!

Bishop (*offering the phone to* **Lloyd**) Mr Lloyd. The Foreign Office.

Macmillan Last time I checked we were still a superpower that made its own decisions.

Eden I have, I have Cabinet members resigning, a country divided, a parliament nearly in revolt. Our Commonwealth against us! And the press! Who still backs us in the press now, Bishop? What are they saying now?

Bishop Um, I'm afraid there is some increasing anti-Tory sentiment over the handling of the crisis. Even in the *Telegraph*.

There is a gasp from all. **Lloyd** *puts the phone down.*

Lloyd Right. That was the American Embassy. I think they smell a rat.

Macmillan Why, what have they said?

Lloyd The part of our ultimatum demanding both parties withdraw ten miles from the Canal. They say it reads like we drew it up long before Israel invaded Egypt.

Macmillan They're bluffing, how could they possibly know we did that?

Lloyd They … they just wondered, since our motive for sending in troops is to protect Egypt from Israel, and given that Egypt have managed to hold them at bay miles from the Canal, why we're moving Israel, the aggressors, *forward* sixty-five miles, and the victims we're defending … *back* one hundred and thirty-five.

Dumbfounded silence. Everyone turns to **Macmillan**.

Macmillan Whoopsie.

Eden *sighs and rubs his head in disbelief. The phone rings again.* **Lloyd** *answers.*

Eden We keep going. The fleet will be there any time now. Then we can sort this out.

Macmillan We just need to remain calm and strong, Anthony.

Lloyd OK. Right. Thank you. (*Replacing the receiver.*) Um …

Eden What now?

Lloyd Second query from the Americans. They wanted to know, if we're going in only to 'keep the peace', why flyers dropped from British planes have been retrieved, encouraging the people to … overthrow … Nasser.

Lloyd *winces. Everyone turns again to* **Macmillan**.

Macmillan Whoo –

Eden Whoopsie. Yes. Right. Can everyone leave me for a while.

Macmillan Anthony –

Eden I need to sort some things out on my own, Harold.

Lloyd Perhaps a stirring speech in the Commons, Anthony. Bolster their patriotism. Think of Winston, think of all he would have –

Eden WINSTON CHURCHILL IS NOT THE PRIME MINISTER! I AM!

Silence.

Eden Who is?

Lloyd You are.

Bishop You are, sir.

Eden Harold?

Macmillan You are. Prime Minister.

Eden Go. Now.

Westminster. Houses of Commons. Loud commotion. **Eden** *looks exhausted.*

Eden There ... there has been no collusion with Israel. We had ... no ... there was no foreknowledge of their attack. None. There was ... *none.*

The commotion dies. **Eden** *is alone, looking incredibly sad. He takes some tablets.*

Downing Street. Noise of horns and a demonstration outside begins to grow. **Eden** *paces nervously.* **Macmillan** *stands calm and still.*

Eden What's taking them so long?! How long ago did the fleet set sail?

Macmillan They are on their way from Malta, Prime Minister. I realise it's frustrating, but it is a long way.

Eden I know how far it is from Malta, Harold! Why wasn't this planned?

Macmillan There is no deep-water port in Cyprus. The nearest / was Malta.

Eden We should have deployed the fleet sooner. They were waiting –

Macmillan Do you not think the world would have got rather suspicious if the peacekeepers had set sail *before* the war?

Long pause. **Eden** *looks indignant.*

Macmillan The RAF is persisting in the bombing until the fleet arrive.

Eden They're fast running out of targets.

Macmillan With all due respect, Anthony, it was the emphasis you placed on sparing innocents that prompted the first phase of carpet-bombing / on military targets.

Eden Whereas you would have just sent in the troops and performed a massacre!

Macmillan I would have done what had to / be done, Prime Minister.

Eden Excuse me for not wanting slaughter and torture and death.

Macmillan Are you suggesting that –

Eden I have lost a son in war, Harold. I do know what it is to fight and to, to sacrifice.

Macmillan Anthony, I wasn't / suggesting for a moment –

Eden Please remember that! I have fought. And I have seen what horrors –

Macmillan Oh, and what was the Somme, Anthony?

Eden (*pause*) Harold –

Macmillan A shattered pelvis and months trapped in a hospital bed hasn't made me unsympathetic to the suffering of soldiers. And I resent the implication.

Eden (*pause*) I ... (*Sighs.*)

Macmillan I know ... when Simon ... How hard –

Eden The Cabinet will be reconvening. Though how we're supposed to think properly when we have that racket going on outside? Biggest peacetime rally ever, Harold. Something else for the history books!

Bishop *enters.*

Bishop Prime Minister –

Eden Not now, Fred, the Cabinet are returning to –

Bishop My apologies, Prime Minister. But this urgent telegram from the Foreign Office. It appears ... it appears the UN has called for a ceasefire between Israel and Egypt.

Macmillan ... I beg your pardon?

Bishop And Egypt have agreed.

Eden Oh heavens, no ... (*Taking the note in dismay.*)

Bishop The UN want to send their own peacekeeping corps in to occupy the area.

Eden Before we've even got there ... (*Pause.*) Leave us.

Bishop *leaves.*

Macmillan Damn. We must inform the Cabinet at once.

Eden We can't abort.

Macmillan Prime Minister?

Eden Well can we?

Macmillan If there is a ceasefire between Israel and Egypt then what do we say as our reason for going in?

Eden I don't know, but, but ... if the UN are occupying the area, we lose all hope of seizing back the Canal, let alone toppling Nasser.

Macmillan We need to think very carefully about what we are saying, Anthony. This is uncharted territory.

Eden Yes, well, so is Egypt, but we're going in there! How close are they?

Macmillan Couple of days.

Eden Too close not to be pulled back?

Macmillan Not in the eyes of the world. You are –

Eden – never too close to war that you can't pull back. Yes, I thought so. (*Pause.*) We should stay on our course. And we'll have to ... to veto the UN resolution to send in a peacekeeping force.

Macmillan That would confirm everyone's suspicion we were in on this from the start.

Eden What choice do we have? You, you ... realise what it would mean? For me. If we pull back now. You realise what I would ... have to do ... (*Trembling and opening his pills.*)

Macmillan   Anthony?

Clarissa *enters.*

Clarissa   Harold, would you excuse us?

Macmillan   Lady Eden, we have to return to –

Clarissa (*gesturing to the pills*)   Is that dinner today?

Eden (*pause*)   Harold. I'll … be there in a, a moment.

Macmillan   Prime Minister, we –

Eden   Just one bloody moment, Harold.

Pause. **Macmillan** *exits.*

Clarissa (*her hand out*)   Give them to me.

Eden   I need them. They're keeping me alive …

Clarissa   You need to rest. You need to throw them away. We need to get away!

Eden   How can I do that?!

Clarissa   YOU'RE KILLING YOURSELF! (*Pause.*) If it's a choice between losing you or losing that bloody canal …

Eden   It would be more than just … (*Pause.*) I'm … sorry. I'm truly … if this doesn't … work out. I'm sorry for the things you're going to find out that I've done.

Clarissa   You could never do wrong by me. (*Pause. Softly.*) Let's just go.

Eden   What?

Clarissa   Let's just run away. Whilst no one's looking. We could climb up the vines on the back wall. Up onto the poplars. And over. Two fugitives. No one would ever know.

Eden *smiles faintly, though he begins to look as frightened as a child.*

Clarissa (*moving to embrace him, whispering in his ear*)   Leave all this behind. Dressed all in black. Run onto the Mall. Flag down a bicycle. I could distract them, and you push them off. I'll sit on the back and you could ride us through Trafalgar Square, all the way to the Embankment. We'll hire a boat. Sail down the Thames, take us all the way to the coast. Find a ferry that will take us to France. Then get a car, all the way down to the south coast. And live out our days, together, in the sun …

Eden *smiles weakly, leaning against* **Clarissa**, *as they rock, back and forth, slowly …*

Clarissa Remember when we used to dance …

In the distance, muted, a shell goes off. Then another. Louder. There is machine-gun fire. And tanks. And planes swooping over. Lights fade on **Clarissa** *and* **Eden**.

Westminster. Press room.

Reporter Would you have it?! Nasser's gone and sunk his own ships, blocking the Canal!

Caricaturist Sneaky, Egyptians. Always said it. Sneaky. (*Beat.*) Bloody good idea, though.

Reporter Oh yeah. Smashing. (*Pause.*) Makes you wonder. How it's all going to end.

Downing Street. Prime Minister's chambers. **Eden** *and* **Bishop**.

Eden Always, always rely on, on the opposition party to change with the tide. One minute they're this, the next they're that! And what are these whispers about Mountbatten? Hmm, Fred? What's he been saying?

Bishop Uh, he … that he was never completely convinced by the operation.

Eden Well, this is the first I've heard of it!!

Bishop Apparently he talked his opinion through with a few Cabinet members.

Eden Oh well that's fine then. As long as my Chief of Staff mentioned his opposition to the war he was running to *some ministers*, that's absolutely bloody fine. Any news?!

Bishop   None since this morning, Prime Minister. Our troops are still holding on to Port Said, though there has been more bloodshed and resistance than expected. And ... messages are still coming in from a rather ... disgruntled international community.

Eden *raises his hands in frustration.* **Macmillan** *and* **Lloyd** *burst in. Pause.*

Macmillan   Imagine what is the worst thing that could happen to us?

Eden (*pause*)   The last time I heard that, the King was dead. (*Sighs, and laughs as though he no longer cares.*) What? What's the next 'worst' thing that could happen?

Macmillan   The Russians have announced their alliance with Egypt against us.

Blood drains from the frozen **Eden**'s *face. He smiles and shakes his head.*

Eden   Well I guess. That. Makes. Sense. (*Long pause.*) How, um ... how confirmed?

Macmillan   Unconfirmed from Moscow. No formal declaration of war. But they are moving troops, Anthony ...

Eden   Weapons?

Lloyd   Uh, I could ... I could get the Foreign Office to ...

Eden   Atomic weapons?

Lloyd   Probably ...

There is a deathly silence. **Eden** *covers his mouth with his shaking hand.*

Lloyd (*attempting a joking tone*)   Although ... if it's any consolation, not as many as us.

Eden (*whispering*)   Oh God. We've ... (*Laughs, tragically.*) I've started World War Three.

Macmillan We may have to consider moving you out of London, Anthony. Just in case.

Eden (*whispering*) Oh God ...

Macmillan And, um ... as expected, the Americans are ... well ... they're furious. Anthony. War with Russia is exactly what they feared would happen.

Lloyd I contacted Dulles immediately. Asked them not to say anything / in public.

Macmillan They are demanding we withdraw our forces immediately or else.

Eden (*looking up in horror*) Well, since ... since when do they ... we, we ... (*Looks to the others for show of confidence.*) We have a job to do. Right?

Lloyd We asked for a guarantee that they would not, um ... that they would not fire upon any British ships entering the Persian Gulf. They said ... (*Deep breath, trying to steady his nerves.*) They said they couldn't necessarily give us that guarantee.

Eden They ... they'd shoot at *us*. The Ameri ... the Ameri ... (*Begins a coughing fit that he slowly gets under control.*) Why ... why did it take us so long? I thought ... our navy ...

Macmillan It's just one of those things, Prime Minister.

Eden *slams his fist down onto the desk several times in succession. The others take a step back.* **Eden** *stops and holds his hand to his mouth to stop any more coughs. As he speaks, he begins to shake, and it gets worse as he goes on.*

Eden How did ... we used ... we used to be ... used to have – and now ... what? We're ... wrists slapped and being told ... what? To, to ... it's, it's our canal. If we ... if we ... if we ... a canal ... If we can't even ... even ... A CANAL! (*Quieter.*) Canada. Australia ...

Bishop Prime Minister?

Eden Falklands, Australia, Hong Kong, Singapore, Kenya. Yes, Kenya, must ... mustn't ...

Bishop Anthony?

Eden (*steadying himself. Pause*) Go.

Lloyd Anthony, please.

Eden Leave me. Please. I just need ... go ...

The others exit. **Eden** *takes a deep breath and tries to take a few steps forward. He starts to shiver violently, and bends over double.*

The map of the world grows brighter as Downing Street disappears. **Eden** *looks up, as the tango theme begins and* **Dulles** *appears.* **Eden** *makes to get into the dancing position, but* **Dulles** *spins on his heel, and holds* **Nasser**, *who appears behind him.*

Eden *watches aghast as they dance.* **Schuman** *appears and, ignoring* **Eden**, *cuts in on* **Dulles** *and* **Nasser** *as they interchange in the dance.* **Eden**, *hyperventilating, goes to grab* **Nasser** *by the neck, as* **Schuman**, **Dulles** *and* **Nasser** *disappear. Downing Street returns.* **Eden** *collapses back against his desk, exhausted and afraid.*

Macmillan *appears. Standing in front of a closed door. A* **Minister** *comes out.*

Minister You can go in. Don't say anything to upset or worry him. He is still very weak.

The **Minister** *exits.* **Macmillan** *walks through the door. A light shines from one side, out of our view. He turns to face it, and smiles.*

Macmillan Hello Winston. (*Pause.*) Got a minute?

Downing Street. Prime Minister's chambers. **Eden** *enters with* **Clarissa**'s *help. He rests on the edge of the desk, as* **Bishop** *follows with* **Lloyd** *and* **Macmillan**.

Bishop Glad to see you're feeling better, Prime Minister.

Lloyd Absolutely. Damn glad, Prime Minister.

Macmillan Very glad, Anthony.

Eden (*almost inaudibly*) What … ? (*Clears his throat.*) What news?

Lloyd The, uh … the tangible gains we made before the ceasefire are looking untenable with the resistance plus the Russian threats. The United Nations welcome our willingness to the discussion of a United Nations force.

Macmillan The Chiefs of Staff have drawn up three possible courses of action. One: to renew military action and occupy the whole canal. Two: maintain our position until a UN force is ready to take over. Or three … a complete withdrawal.

Lloyd But the Americans will not allow a UN force to assume control until the Anglo-French contingent has withdrawn and … well, buggered off home, Prime Minister.

Macmillan And I'm afraid the United States refuse to, uh … prop up our sterling until we're out completely, Prime Minister.

Eden *wraps himself up warmer. There is complete silence.*

Eden Withdraw …

Lloyd (*unable to hear*) I'm … sorry?

Eden (*louder*) Withdraw …

Lloyd Yes, Prime Minister.

They all exit. **Eden** *stands weakly, and totters around, without purpose. He looks at the Queen's portrait. The figure of* **Churchill** *slowly appears behind him.* **Eden** *turns to face him. Both look weak and feeble relics. Elgar's 'Nimrod' creeps softly in.*

Eden Who could ever follow you?

Churchill 'For what shall it profit a man if he shall gain the whole world … and lose his soul?'

Eden I … f-failed …

Churchill This was just our time, Anthony. Just our time.

Eden You were the saviour of Britain. And I ... I am her undertaker.

Churchill (*shakes his head*) Undertakers are not responsible for the deceased, Anthony. They merely see them safely down.

Eden ... After me?

Churchill Macmillan ...

Eden (*pause*) I sh-should have been ... stronger ...

Churchill You can deny, and ignore, the diminishing strength of something, and convince yourself, despite its age, it is as strong as those younger and healthier than he. But the time will always come ... when you must decide ... to sit this one out ...

He moves to **Eden**, *and pulls him into him, as the music swells and lights fade.*

Churchill My Anthony ...

Eden *and* **Clarissa**'s *garden.* **Eden** *is sitting in a chair, covered in blankets, eyes closed and breathing heavily.* **Clarissa** *enters, followed by* **Bishop**.

Clarissa Anthony? (*Pause.*) Anthony, look who's here.

Eden (*slowly opening his eyes, weakly*) F-fred?

Bishop Anthony. No, please don't get up.

Eden (*smiling*) Fred. What a wonderful surprise. What are you doing here?

Bishop Well I was passing and couldn't very well not pop in to see my old boss, could I?

Eden Fred, it's wonderful to see you. How are things? How's ... Harold?

Clarissa Anthony.

Eden I'm only asking.

Bishop So-so. He's run into a few problems with his 'Never had it so good' claim.

Eden Oh dear, too bad. (*Beat. Smiles.*) You must ... Clarissa, we must show Fred our cow in the field. Fine heifer. We entered her into the local fair. And look, have you seen our bluebells?

Bishop Yes, they're lovely. (*Beat. Laughs.*)

Eden What?

Bishop I'm in the Garden of Eden.

Clarissa Let me fetch you a glass of lemonade, Fred. (*Exits.*)

Bishop Lovely. Thank you.

Eden It's wonderful. You know. Fred. Gardening. Just wonderful ... Plant a seed, watch it grow. Tend to it. Care for it. Simple, and ... and honest. (*Long pause.*) To wait so long, Fred ... only to become the shortest serving Prime Minister of this century. And the shortest bar just three in nearly one hundred and fifty years.

Bishop You're *not* the shortest?

Eden Alas. Rosebery and Canning, last century. And Bonar Law in '22, in for just two hundred and nine days. Died of throat cancer.

Bishop Oh. That's a relief then. (*Pause.*) As one last task, I could always compile an official report? (*In knowing jest.*) See how badly you really do compare?

Eden I'm all right, actually, Fred.

Butler Very good, Prime Min ... Anthony.

Pause. They smile. **Clarissa** *enters with a glass of lemonade.*

Eden Win ... Winston's funeral, Fred ... the whole nation. Mourning. Did you see? All the cranes in London, bowing their head ... as his coffin sailed across the Thames. The whole city, the whole country ... leaning with them ... onto their knees.

Eden *closes his eyes, and rests his head back.* **Bishop** *places his hand on his.*

Clarissa Fred, dear. Would you mind running into the kitchen? His tablets are on the side.

Bishop Uh, yes. Yes, of ... of course.

He exits. **Clarissa** *gets to her knees, by* **Eden**. *He looks at her.*

Eden I know they will never bow for me. They loved him so much ...

Clarissa Come on. Stand up. It's getting cold.

She helps him to his feet. Pause.

Eden After him, they had no more left to give. That love ...

Clarissa It isn't real, Anthony. This ... this is real. And it's all that matters in the world ...

The waltz theme creeps in. The map of the world beneath them twinkles again. **Eden** *and* **Clarissa** *embrace, and begin slowly to turn and move across the world together.*

Alaska

DC Moore

*To Luckster and Hufford
for making me a (slightly) better person*

Alaska was first performed at the Royal Court Jerwood Theatre Upstairs, London on 24 May 2007, with the following cast:

Adam	Sebastian Armesto
Emma	Christine Bottomley
Russell	Harry Hepple
Chris	Thomas Morrison
Frank	Rafe Spall
Mamta	Fiona Wade
Director	Maria Aberg
Designer	Fred Meller
Lighting	David Holmes
Sound	Carolyn Downing

Characters

Frank, *twenty-four*
Adam, *eighteen*
Russell, *eighteen*
Emma, *twenty-three*
Mamta, *nineteen*
Chris, *seventeen*

Part One

Scene One

December. **Frank**'s *bedroom in halls of residence at university.* **Frank** *is in bed.*

We hear some drunken commotion from outside in the hallway. Then **Adam**, *shushing aggressively and saying 'Shut up' repeatedly under his breath.*

Knocking at the door.

Silence.

More knocking, before the door opens and **Adam** *peers round. He is drunk.*

Adam (*half-whisper*) Frank? Frank? (*Louder.*) *Frank.*

Frank (*still half asleep*) What?

Adam I know it's late but can we get some … cannabis?

Frank (*still half asleep*) What you doing?

Adam Got the money. Be dead quick, mate.

Pause. **Frank** *turns a lamp on.*

Frank Do you know how late it is?

Adam, *who is smoking, comes into the room.* **Frank** *sits up on his bed.*

Adam We got pizza in the kitchen, mate, if you want some.

No response.

So, is an eighth gonna be alright?

Frank *shrugs an offhand 'Yes'.*

Adam Cool. How much is that gonna be exactly?

Frank Forty.

Adam Pounds?

Frank *nods and takes a swig from a two-litre bottle of water by his bed.*

Adam Simon's sister can get us that much for like … twenty quid. That's all we've got.

Frank Supply, mate. Demand, mate.

Adam Right.

Frank Though actually. Maybe. Maybe I could go into your room, steal a moment or two with your lady. Make up the shortfall. Called Anna, in't she? I see her down the library …

Adam Is it skunk or weed?

Frank Yeah, see her all the time, the library.

Adam Is it … skunk / or?

Frank Beavering away. It's solid. Helps me study.

Adam Really? Always makes me a bit …

Frank You're never with her. Are ya?

Adam Can barely read, let alone some. Textbook.

Frank Cos I wouldn't let her out of my sight. Peach like that.

Silence.

Alright. How 'bout, how 'bout you give me an essay?

Adam (*not understanding*) Right.

Frank Just to read. No one ever shows nothing. To me. You do history. I seen ya. I like history. So. An essay and twenty quid and we're done.

Adam Um. OK.

Adam's *cigarette has run out. He looks around, before casually putting it out in the water bottle.* **Frank** *smiles with disgust.* **Adam** *smiles back, exits.*

A pause before **Frank** *takes the water bottle and inspects it. Puts* *the top back on it. Shakes it. Looks at it, holds it up, watching the fag end floating round.*

Adam *returns with an essay, offers it to* **Frank**.

Frank *takes the essay and starts reading.* **Adam** *passes him the money.* **Frank** *pockets it, continues to read.* **Adam** *watches* **Frank***, perplexed, waiting for some sign of cannabis.*

Adam Can we just … ? Can I just … ?

Frank Can you just … ?

Adam Get the … the drugs. Everyone's in the kitchen. Waiting.

Frank But I ain't finished.

Adam Well, can you not read it like … later?

Frank That wasn't the agreement, mate. I'm not a bank.

Frank *goes back to reading.*

Adam But …

Annoyed but accepting that he will have to wait, **Adam** *relaxes. Takes in the room, sees an open Bible, which he picks up, reads.*

Silence.

Frank (*having read three paragraphs or so, genuinely impressed*) This. Seems. Very. Very good.

Adam Yeah?

Frank Your prose. It's very. Clear. Precise. I mean, this a fucking good intro. Can I keep it? Finish it?

Adam If you want.

Frank Great.

He smiles at **Adam***, briefly forgetting why* **Adam** *is in his room.*

Adam Are you gonna … ?

Frank Oh. Yeah. Course. Sorry, mate. Forget me head.

Frank *gets out a small wooden box from under his bed.*

Frank You wanna be an academic then, or … ? Look like you got the, the smarts for it.

As they talk **Frank** *opens the box, takes out a little hunting knife and cannabis resin.*

Adam No. Wanna do something different. You know. Like, media stuff. (*Referencing Bible.*) Do you *really* believe in all this? I know you're very …

Frank How d'ya mean, 'different'?

He begins cutting the eighth.

Adam Yeah, my dad's. Erm. Professor.

Frank Of … ?

Adam History.

Frank Right. That's gotta be. Useful.

Adam Yeah, he's always emailing me, helping me out, you know?

Frank Helping out?

Adam (*referencing Bible*) So do you believe in miracles / and – ?

Frank Helping out with what?

Adam (*gestures towards the essay in* **Frank***'s hands*) On the. With the essays.

Frank *twigs.*

Frank That's a fucking. That's. (*Gesturing to the essay.*) So let's get this straight, you didn't even … ?

Adam What? It's first year. Doesn't count. And … and Dad didn't write *all of it*. He just gets … got. Excited. Thought of the title and then. Wrote. Some of it. You know what dads are like.

Frank Not really.

Adam How d'ya mean?

Frank Lost mine. Falklands.

Adam Shit.

Frank Yeah.

Adam How did he … how did he … ?

Frank What?

Adam Die. Was it in … combat?

Frank What? What you talking about? Course it was.

Adam (*puts the Bible down*) Must be very hard to … to have to, deal with that.

Frank Yeah. But I do, you know? I do. I deal with it. Every day. Whereas, what you ever dealt with, yeah? I mean, coming in here. You're just a … a kid. A fucking … Adam. Adam, mate. Do you know how many times you've knocked on that door?

Adam *shrugs.*

Frank Twice. Other time. You wanted some Rizlas.

Adam Right?

Frank Twice. In four months.

Adam Yeah, well, I'm not being funny but when you came out with us in Freshers' Week you told Priya she was going to Hell. You know? What is that?

Frank That's not exactly what I said, mate. Don't be –

Adam And all that shit about sewing people up inside pigs. D'ya not get that maybe that's a bit rude?

Frank *stands, still holding the knife from cutting gear.*

Frank What about you cheating me out of a degree I paid good money for by copying off your posh cunt dad?

No response.

I didn't work and save for three years to go clubbing with Pakis.

Adam Right. Right, can I just get the gear?

No response.

OK. Will you just give me the money?

Frank Sorry. We don't do cashback.

Adam *visibly begins to sober.*

Adam Just cos you're poor doesn't mean you're hard.

Frank Just cos you're a cunt doesn't make you a cunt.

Adam Right. Is that the sound of the streets?

Frank Why don't you and your haircut fuck off out my room?

Knocking at the door, which is now slightly ajar.

Russell (*off*) Adam? Adam? Adam, mate?

Adam Yeah?

Enter **Russell**. *He is white but blacked up, dressed to look like Mr T.*

Russell You alright, mate? How ya doing? Dave just lit one of his farts in the kitchen. Massive flame. Yeah? Like – (*Makes impressive explosion sound and gesture.*) You got the gear, mate?

Adam It's all good, mate.

Russell Wicked, mate. You alright, mate?

Frank …

Russell *Yeah*. Thanks for the gear, mate. Sorry if we woke you up. (*As Mr T.*) 'I pity the fool who wakes Frank up! I ain't gonna get on no plane! Damn fool!' (*No response.*) You having a good night, mate?

Frank Just got worse, to be honest.

Russell (*not registering*) I licked sambuca off this girl's belly.

Alaska 103

Then, I fingered her in the bar. Was awesome. Got a picture of her boobs, like, on my phone.

He laughs.

Silence.

Cool. Just gonna go and, er. Have a. A dump. Thanks for the er … the ganja, Frank. You're a good man, yeah? You're alright. (*To* **Adam**.) See ya back in the kitchen in a bit, mate, yeah?

Adam *nods.*

Russell *exits, bellowing 'I pity the fool! Damn fool!' as he goes down the hallway before slipping into a Bo' Selecta Michael Jackson impression.*

Pause.

Frank What does he study?

Adam Politics.

Pause. **Adam** *moves towards the gear,* **Frank** *puts himself in the way.* **Adam** *reaches anyway.* **Frank** *threatens with his knife and pushes him with his other arm.* **Adam** *swiftly and expertly takes* **Frank**'s *knife-carrying arm and twists it behind his back while pushing him to the ground.* **Frank** *struggles but the pain is too much.*

Adam Tell you what. While we're getting all. Manly. You talk shit like that about Anna again and I will fucking hurt you.

Frank Do your worst, you …

Adam *gives a quick and painful twist of* **Frank**'s *arm and leans in towards him.*

Frank *grunts with pain.*

Adam Look, why don't you just crawl back to your little estate?

Frank (*through gritted teeth, determined*) There's this black geezer. She's very friendly with. *Anna*. In the library.

Adam *delivers a violent twist which is close to breaking* **Frank**'s *arm.*

Frank   Arh! I'm sorry. I'm sorry! Just stop, mate. You're gonna. FUCK.

Content that **Frank** *is beaten,* **Adam** *releases the pressure on his arm.* **Adam** *stands up, picks up the gear and goes to exit.*

Adam (*remembering, turning back*)   Actually. Do you have any Rizlas?

Frank *is still face down on the floor, breathing deeply.*

Frank   Top drawer.

Adam *goes to the drawer, takes a packet of Rizlas.*

Adam   Awesome.

He exits.

Silence.

We hear cheers from the kitchen as **Adam** *returns, drugs in hand.*

Blackout.

Scene Two

February of the following year. A Tuesday afternoon. The staffroom of a multiplex cinema. **Emma**, *who is wearing her cinema uniform, is eating an apple and reading a newspaper. In the background,* The Simpsons *is on a TV/video combination, which is fitted high in a corner of the room.*

Enter **Mamta**.

As she has her back to her, **Emma** *hasn't noticed* **Mamta**, *who is unsure of how best to get* **Emma**'s *attention.*

Silence.

Emma *stands up to fetch something from her coat. She gets a fright as she sees* **Mamta**.

Emma *Jesus wept*. Where'd you sneak up from?

Mamta Um. / Martin said –

Emma (*not listening*) Sorry, take it ya realise this is the staffroom? As much as this does look like Screen Five, I'm not actually, believe it or not, Sigourney fucking Weaver.

Mamta Yeah, I just –

Emma So do you mind going back out through the double doors, and turning left, yeah? Better hurry, cos you only got about another minute or two of previews left before it starts. Well, go on. Toddle on then.

Silence.

Are you deaf or summat? Do. You. Mind. Going. / Back out –

Mamta I *work* here.

Emma What?

Mamta I'm starting tomorrow. Had an interview last week and they told me to come in today to get my uniform.

Emma Oh. Right. (*Realising.*) Shit. *Shit*. You're. You must be. Saw your name on the rota, thought it were new. You're … (*Struggling to remember her name*.) … Mumra?

Mamta Not quite. Erm. Mamta.

Emma Sorry?

Mamta Mamta.

Emma Mamtra?

Mamta Mam-*ta*.

Emma Mam-tar?

Mamta Mamta.

Emma (*nods*) Right. Right. Could you just, could you just say it one more time and a little bit slower for me? Is that alright? Sorry, you don't mind, do ya?

Mamta No. It's fine. It's. Right. It's. Mam. Ta. Mamta.

Pause.

Emma Mamta?

Mamta That's the one.

Emma Lovely. (*Pause.*) What kinda name is that?

Mamta It's mine.

Emma Oh. Anyway. I'm. Emma. (*Making a joke, as if having to explain how it is pronounced.*) Em-ma.

Mamta *nods and tries a smile.*

Emma It's a pretty exotic name. Emma. Everyone at school was dead jealous. (*Pause.*) Sorry for being a bit … *off* with ya, when you came in. We just get a load of gyppos coming back here, scabbing about, looking for shit to nick. Though obviously you're not one.

Mamta Gyppos?

Emma Yeah. Do you not see 'em at the bottom of the car park? Twice a year they rock up. Regular as fuck. We lost three tellies and a kettle last year. And a life-size cut-out of Will Smith. (*Pause.*) Where they putting ya?

Mamta Box office.

Emma Oh, you'll be right then. You mainly have to deal with 'em – gyppos – when you're on kiosk. They always come in scouting for toffee popcorn.

Mamta Right.

Emma I work on bar. Upstairs.

Mamta Could I just get my uniform? I kinda have to be somewhere.

Emma Oh, yeah. Course. What colour?

Mamta Sorry?

Emma You got three options. Yellow. Blue. Red. For your top. Which do you want?

Mamta Erm. (*Gesturing to* **Emma***'s blue worktop.*) Blue?

Emma (*moving towards the door as she speaks*) Ooh, good choice, madam. Right, now wait here and I'll just go and get one for ya. I'll do me best to grab a new one, cos sometimes they do try and fob you off with some old second-hand musky bastard and it'll have a load of stains on it, which look like and – thinking about some of the people who work here – probably actually are. Semen. So, wish me luck you don't get a spunky one.

Emma *exits.*

Mamta (*after her*) Erm. Good luck.

Emma (*off*) Cheers. Take a seat and I'll be back in a minute.

Mamta *takes in the staffroom but doesn't sit down. Blackout.*

Scene Three

The same day as Scene Two. Early evening. Outside the delivery doors of the cinema, overlooking a car park, which serves a large retail park.

Note: the delivery doors are also a fire exit. This means that, whenever anyone goes for a smoke, a brick must be wedged into the door to stop the smokers getting locked out. So these doors are ajar for nearly every scene.

Frank*, wearing the uniform of the cinema, is smoking and drinking a can of Diet Coke. Lost in thought.*

Enter **Chris***, also wearing the cinema uniform.*

Frank *acknowledges* **Chris** *and* **Chris** *smiles back.*

Frank Can I help you?

Chris ... ?

Frank Am I needed, back inside?

Chris No, I just, I just came out cos I thought you might want some company on your break.

Frank Right. Well, I'm alright, so ... *Pause.*

Frank *takes a drag of his cigarette.*

Chris Like it out here.

Pause.

Frank Why's that?

Chris The view.

Frank The view?

Chris *gestures to the space in front of them.*

Frank Would that be of the car park or all the caravans at the end of it?

Chris No, of the sky. You get a big view of it out here, wide, cos there's no houses in the way. (*Referring to the sky above him.*) Can't see this much sky most places.

Frank And that's good?

Chris Course it is. But it's best in autumn.

Frank Well, hopefully I won't be round that long.

Chris Why, do you not like it here? Are you being bullied?

Frank No. No, I just. Well, it's a bit. It's a bit shit, isn't it?

Chris No. It's *brilliant*. You get to go see films for free.

There's loads of free food. Everyone's really nice. And you get paid. And. You like Emma, I've seen you smiling with her, you *really* like her. And ...

Frank Alright, alright, you've convinced me. It's fucking brilliant, Chris, alright?

Chris *smiles.*

Pause.

Frank Want a fag then?

Chris Erm. OK.

Chris *takes a cigarette and* **Frank** *lights it for him. It's clear that* **Chris** *is not normally a smoker.*

Frank *is now looking up admiringly at the sky.*

Frank 'And God made two great lights: the greater light to rule the day, and the lesser light to rule the night.'

Chris Is that religious?

Frank Yeah. Genesis.

Chris Like, from the Bible?

Frank Chapter One. Verse Sixteen.

Chris Sounds good.

Frank Yeah. (*Pause.*) 'And God made two great lights: the greater light to rule the day, and the lesser light to rule the night.'

Chris And it rhymes.

Frank *nods a little.*

Frank It's great to memorise, you know? I was at uni for a bit, learnt whole chunks of it

Pause. **Chris** *takes a drag, coughs a little.*

Frank *smiles, catches* **Chris***'s eye.*

Chris What?

Frank You.

Chris Why?

Frank You're funny.

Chris Why?

Frank You do that dopey little cough every time you have a drag.

Chris Do I?

He looks at **Frank** *before taking a determined drag. He holds his breath, trying not to cough. Fails with an outward breath.*

Chris I don't think I did it before you said about it.

Frank It's alright. You just gotta breathe it in a bit deeper. And slower as it comes out. How long you been smoking for?

Chris I only coughed just then. I don't normally –

Frank How many a, a day?

Chris About. One.

Frank Cos I been here a month now and I ain't seen you have one before.

Chris I just like it.

Frank Well, breathe it proper. Deep. If you're gonna do it, enjoy it, yeah? (*He demonstrates.*) Out.

Chris *copies him. Coughs again.*

Frank *smiles and, noticing that* **Chris** *is a bit despondent, takes a softer approach.*

Frank Try it again.

Chris No.

Frank Please, go on. Just. Relax.

Chris You're being horrible.

Frank No, I'm not. I'm helping. (*Waiting till he has concrete eye contact with* **Chris**.) Just – in, two, three. Hold it, enjoy it. Out, two, three. Like it's air. But better. Come on.

Chris *takes a drag and with concentrated effort breathes out the smoke, managing to stifle his cough reflex.*

Frank There we go. (*Toasts him with the can of Coke.*) To Chris.

Chris (*smiling*) Idiot.

Frank *plays offended and playfully cuffs* **Chris** *on his arm.*

Frank Well, this idiot's just been offered kiosk supervisor.

Chris That's brilliant.

Frank Martin just had a word. Extra quid-fifty an hour. And you get the shirt-and-tie number.

Chris I'd like that. I'd love that. Hate baseball caps. Gets all sweaty when you're doing the hotdogs.

Frank Told 'em I'd think it over.

Chris You'd be a good boss.

Frank That's not the ... it's just that I'm better than ...

Chris Yeah, you are, but you could, you could get me so I don't ever have to do floor again. Don't like ushering. Drunk people saying, 'I don't care whose seat it is!' and calling me a 'wankstain'. But if you were the boss I could work with you on kiosk all the time and just make popcorn and ...

Frank Sorry, mate, but I'm, I'm too old to get excited about supervising people, cleaning ... drink dispensers. Making nachos. I'm twenty-four, you know? Time is just. Fucking off. Leaving me with my dick up my arse.

Chris But you're so clever, you'll be OK, won't you? Bet you it will all work out in the end. Just like it does in the Bible.

Frank Maybe. I dunno. (*Sighing.*) *Fuck.*

Silence, during which he stubs out his cigarette.

Look, I better get off. (*Starting to go.*) See ya in a bit, yeah?

Chris Could … ? Do you … ?

Frank What?

Chris Do you like … ?

Frank What? (*Pause.*) What?

Chris Would you like to go bowling?

Frank I'm back on three minutes.

Chris No. I mean on Sunday.

Frank Well, I've got Sunday off.

Chris I know. So have I.

Frank Oh. Right.

Chris You don't have to.

Frank No. Yeah. Cool. OK.

Chris Really?

Frank Yeah.

Chris Thank you.

Frank Don't be silly.

Chris OK.

Frank You want my number then, or … ?

Chris Got it off the rosters.

Frank Right. Well. It's a date.

Chris *smiles.*

Frank Well, not a … but. Yeah. I better be er … Yeah, see ya.

Frank *exits.*

Chris *takes in the view, smiles.*

Blackout.

Alaska 113

Scene Four

The staffroom. The day after Scene Three. Wednesday evening. The TV is off.

Frank *is sitting reading a book.*

Enter **Mamta**, *who goes to her coat to check her phone.*

Mamta   Hiya.

She smiles. **Frank** *continues reading.*

Mamta   You alright?

Frank *gives her a quick look.*

Mamta   Just seeing if I've got any messages.

Frank *goes back to reading.*

Mamta   Can't believe some of the customers today. First day here and I'm like: urgh. They make me wanna be sick. Though, I'm not anorexic or anything. Just allergic to the General Public, I think. I don't really put on weight. I'm an ectomorph apparently, just burn it off. (*Pause.*) I'm. Mamta. I just started. It's my first day. Today. Hello.

Frank   Right.

Mamta   And you're ... Frank?

Frank   Apparently.

Mamta   Martin said, he was saying you went to uni, in Nottingham. I've got / family in ...

Frank   I left. Dropped out.

Mamta   Well, I've got family. Own a restaurant in Nottingham, in the city centre. It's called the Palace. D'ya know it?

Frank   No.

Mamta   Oh, well, it's good. Really good. Won awards and stuff. If you ever go back, let us know and I'll put in a good word for you. Discount or whatever.

Frank, *still reading, shrugs vaguely.*

Mamta *receives a text.*

Mamta Ooh, here we go. (*Reads the text.*) It's a joke. What drugs do ducks take?

Frank *looks at her briefly.*

Mamta Quack.

She smiles at **Frank**, *pleadingly.*

Mamta No takers? Yeah, that is a bit rubbish. It's not from my mates or anything. They're *slightly* funnier than that. I get sent these random texts. From this weird number. Like jokes and chart positions. D'you get them?

Frank No.

Mamta Well. Probably. Different network or like, something … tedious.

She smiles, flatly. Puts her phone back in her coat.

So, do you … do you know any, any good jokes?

Frank Yeah.

Mamta I'm all ears.

Frank You ever see a black kid on a bus?

Mamta What? Sorry, what d'ya say? Cos my hearing's a bit. I'm deaf in one ear. So I can't actually be all ears. Shouldn't really use that phrase, should I? Fell off a swing when I was three, landed really badly. So now I'm a bit …

She rolls up her tongue in her bottom lip, does a 'spastic' face and groan, as well as the requisite shaky, twisted-out hand movements. Then relaxes back to normal, smiling with a mixture of silly pride and embarrassment. A pause. She does the 'spastic' face/groan/ hands again, just to fill the silence. Again, she finds herself quite funny/embarrassing.

(*Normal voice.*) Sorry. (*Reverting to the 'spastic' voice/posture.*)

Alaska   115

Sorry. Deaf in this ear. (*Another 'spastic' groan before going back to her normal voice.*) Sorry, I shouldn't really do that, should I? Bit wrong. Completely wrong, really. Something I do with my friends. The voice and the. But not usually with people I've just, I've just met. So, what was your joke? Something about a kid on a bus?

Frank *has found himself smirking at* **Mamta**'s *shtick.*

Frank   Alright. Alright. Here's one for ya. How many feminists does it take to change a light bulb?

Mamta   Erm. Dunno.

Frank   Two. One to do it. One to suck my cock.

Mamta *smiles.*

Mamta   I like that. That's good. Erm. OK. Why do women wear make-up and perfume?

Frank   No idea.

Mamta   Cos they're ugly and they smell.

Frank *nods his approval.*

Frank   Not bad. Alright. Try this one. What's the difference between Patrick Kielty and a vagina that can't read?

Mamta *considers.*

Mamta   Oh shit. I know this, I've heard this. God, what was it? Oh, this is gonna kill me. Erm. Hang on. No, hang on. It's coming.

She twists her face up, trying to remember the punchline. **Frank** *smiles in anticipation.*

Mamta   Has it got anything to do with the fact that he's Irish?

Frank *shakes his head.* **Mamta**   Oh. Shame. *Blackout.*

Scene Five

A club: 'Lava & Ignite'. The day after Scene Four. Late Thursday evening.

Frank *and* **Emma** *at the bar, people-watching, looking over a dance floor.*

Emma God. This place. Makes me feel like my hymen's grown back. Got your sights set?

Frank What?

Emma Got your eye on any ladies?

Frank Not really.

Emma You must of got loads at uni. All those hormones. Bet you couldn't move for ... (*conjuring the imagery, failing*) ... minge. Get much?

Frank Can't say I did, to be honest.

Emma How come?

Frank Well, they were all a bit *young* and. Posh. Good-looking, yeah, but in that horrible plastic way, you know? All fucking bangles and stupid hair.

Emma So you don't regret it then? Leaving?

Frank No. I just, I just wanted so much for it to be. Better. You know? I mean, there were so many books there. Whole library. Whole world to learn about. But all these *kids* with their cliquey little gangs, they'd rather. They'd rather get pissed up on cheap vodka and dance like a twat to Abba in some overpriced warehouse.

Emma What's wrong with Abba?

Frank What?

Emma Good band, Abba. Great tunes. Can't argue with great tunes.

Frank Well, I'm not because, because that's not really my point, is it? My point is –

Emma And I like cheap vodka. Gets you pissed dead quick.

Frank *Emma.*

Emma Yeah, calm down, alright? I'm just pulling your chain, Jesus. (*Pause.*) I was gonna go. Uni. Got the A levels for it. Did all the open days, interviews, got a place n' that

Frank Oh, right. Doin' … ?

Emma Law.

Frank Shit.

Emma Yeah, can you not sound quite so surprised?

Frank Sorry, I just didn't know you …

Emma Just cos I talk a bit rough don't mean I'm not an intellectual fucking powerhouse, alright? Anyway, I didn't go in the end, did I?

Frank Why not?

Emma Well. Mainly, primarily, it was because I couldn't really be arsed.

Frank *laughs.* **Emma** *joins in.*

Emma Ooh. Hang on. You just got a look. Green strappy top. Eleven o'clock.

Frank *works out the clock and spots Green Top on the dance floor.*

Emma She proper clocked you then.

Frank (*noticing her, but not interested*) Did she?

Emma You should get in there. Looks keen.

Frank (*dismissive*) Got funny eyes.

Emma (*matter-of-fact*) Good bum though.

They watch her dance.

Imagine hanging out the back of that. Be alright.

Frank Well, you couldn't do it facing her.

Emma Ooh, here we go. You see him? Black guy with the, with the silver earring. He's circling. Giving it the old. Tenner says he goes for her within two drinks. If you don't.

She gives him a knowing look, telling him off for not going and doing something about it.

Go on. Open goal there. Before he gets it.

Frank Na, I'm alright, thanks. What about you? Spotted anyone?

Emma Don't think any of these boys are ready to see me naked. Shock'd kill 'em.

Frank Well, I didn't have no complaints.

Emma Frank.

Frank What? I didn't. All seemed very much in working order.

*He smiles at **Emma**, who smiles back, a little embarrassed, before checking her phone for messages.*

Frank Fancy some shots then or … ?

Emma Nah. Gonna head off. Tell you what though, you should go over there and just straight out ask for her number. Mean it. Bet he won't. He'll just go for the grope. Being all … black.

Frank Emma. Emma. If I said that, if I said that, you'd have a fucking *eppy*.

Emma Shut up, I'm only mucking about. Don't mean it.

Frank The shit I get …

Emma (*stern*) *Frank*. Let's not, yeah?

Silence.

Alaska 119

You seen that new girl? Just started? (*Pause.*) You gonna leave her be?

Frank What?

Emma I said, are you gonna leave her alone? Cos I swear if you say anything to her, I'll … Just don't, yeah?

Frank OK. (*Pause.*) You want me … get us a, a taxi then? If you wanna go 'n that?

Emma No need.

Frank No?

Emma I'm fine.

Frank How come?

Emma Make my own way. Got a lift.

Frank Right.

Emma *smiles, not entirely convincingly, checks her messages again. Pause.*

Frank Got the anniversary coming up. Next month.

Emma Of ?

Frank You know. Dad. Passing on.

Emma God. Didn't realise. Sorry, mate.

Frank Well, you know. Fuck it. It's alright. It's not like I knew him or anything, is it?

Emma Still.

Frank Yeah. Anniversary's always a bit. Weird more than anything. (*Pause.*) Sure you don't want just some shots or … ? Just like, one for the road?

Emma Yeah. Best not.

Frank Come on. Not drinking on my own.

Emma *starts to write a text message but is simultaneously looking over her phone at Green Top.*

Emma Well, you don't have to. Look. She's talking about you with her mate. Sussing out if you're with me or not. Go on, go over now whilst she's still looking at ya. I can distract … him. I'm a great Wing Man.

She sends message, puts her phone away.

Frank Fuck that.

Emma Oh well, ta very much. Alright, fuck it, one more drink. What you having?

Frank Guinness and black.

Emma I told ya, I'm not ordering that. Two words: gay and, er … (*Pretending not to be able to find the word, then, as if suddenly enlightened.*) Oh yeah, gay.

Frank Alright, I'll have a Carlsberg. Fascist.

Emma Ooh, look. There we go. (*Facing Green Top's direction.*) *Told ya.* Our black friend wins. You lose. Look at his hands. Gone right up. And she's let him. (*Pause.*) Dirty cow.

They watch them kiss.

Blackout.

Scene Six

A week later. Thursday afternoon. A storeroom in the cinema. **Mamta** *is on the floor, rummaging through a cardboard box.*

Frank *is behind her with a pen and clipboard.*

Mamta Fifteen. Seventeen. Eighteen. (*Pause.*) Eighteen Minstrels. Plus four, five. Five Fruit Pastilles.

Frank Bang on. (*Notes it down.*) What about the Maltesers? Do them, we're pretty much done.

Mamta Just a sec.

She pulls another box nearer. Starts going through it.

Fuck sake.

Frank What?

Mamta They've all. Split. But they don't look too bad. You hungry?

Frank (*after looking round to make sure no one is about*) Yeah, fuck it, do the honours.

Mamta *reaches in. Pulls out a handful of loose Maltesers. Shares them with* **Frank**.

Frank Cheers.

Mamta 'S alright. (*Back to the stocktake. With her mouth full.*) Three, five. God. Are yours … ? A bit … stale?

Frank (*also with his mouth full*) No, they're alright. How many full packs are there?

Mamta Erm. Nine.

Frank (*noting it down*) Fucking hell. Actually … they're … fucking …

Mamta *grabs a nearby small empty cardboard box and spits her mouthful of Maltesers into it.*

Mamta Ugh. Here you go.

She offers him the box. He takes it and spits out the Maltesers.

You alright?

Frank Not sure I should say this out loud but. We have had a bit of a rat problem.

Mamta Really?

Frank *nods.*

Mamta Is that what that tangy taste is?

Frank *nods.*

Frank Why I tend to eat from sealed packs.

Mamta God. I might, I might actually be sick.

Frank No you won't.

Mamta *can't control herself and is sick into the box containing Maltesers.*

Frank Or. Maybe, you will.

Mamta Ugh. / Ugh.

Frank You alright? Want some water or summat?

Mamta *nods.*

Frank *goes.*

Mamta *gags and dry-vomits. Tries to force more sick out but can't. Tries to control her breathing, pulls her hair out of her face. Exhales deeply.*

Frank *returns with a glass of water for her. She takes it.*

Frank It's cold.

Mamta *takes a sip.*

Mamta (*referring to the Maltesers*) Think we might have to write those off.

Frank I reckon.

Mamta And you're also lucky cos I happen to look very sexy when I'm vomiting.

Frank I can see that. Really brings out your eyes. Like. Literally. You want more water?

Mamta No, I'm good. Thank you, though.

Frank And you've got some, on you. On your ... *He gestures to her top.*

Mamta Oh, that's, that's nasty. That's. That's never gonna come out.

She licks her thumb and starts to rub it off, which she continues to do through the next section of speech.

Oh God. You know. If we were in a fifties film and you were Jimmy Stewart and I was Katharine Hepburn, you'd have pointed it out, then wiped it clean with your hanky. Though cos it's the fifties it wouldn't be sick. It would be cake or. Something. And then our eyes'd meet after. And we'd. Kiss.

Pause.

Frank How about I just get you another top?

Mamta OK.

Frank *goes.*

Mamta *tries to seal down the lid of the box* (*the one she's been sick in*), *but the flaps keep coming back up.*

Mamta Fucking. Stop it.

Pause. **Frank** *returns with a top.*

Frank Here you go. Got a big one, just to be safe. I'm not saying you're fat or anything.

Throws the top to her. **Frank** *then turns round, with his back to her.*

Mamta Thanks.

Frank I'll make sure no one's coming.

Mamta …

She changes her top as she talks to him

Martin. Martin was, talking about me maybe taking a supervisor role on.

Frank Already?

Mamta What? Do you think it'd be too soon?

Frank No, it's just. Watch him. Martin. He's a bit of a. Lech. Bit of a 'C' word.

Mamta 'C' word?

Frank Cunt.

Mamta Oh. He seemed alright. Quite. Sweet.

She puts her old top in the box she's been sick in.

Frank Yeah, he does at first.

Mamta So do ya think I should take it?

Frank Do what you like.

Mamta Be good for my CV. Before uni. So. And it's better pay. Makes sense. I think I fancy you.

Pause.

Frank What?

Mamta I know you're not meant to say that outright to someone. And Emma was saying she doesn't think that you like me or anything, and she's clearly right by the fact that you're not saying anything. So it doesn't matter that I said it, does it? We can just forget it and talk about something else.

Pause. **Frank** *turns to face her.*

Frank To be honest. I'll be honest. You're not really. My type.

Mamta Was it the being sick thing? Because I barely ever throw up. Unless I eat crab.

Frank (*smiling a little*) No. We'll just. We'll just leave it at that. Alright? You're not. My type.

Mamta I like that you don't say everything that you're thinking. It's nice, that. Some people just keep talking and talking about everything and anything, don't they? But you don't. I like that.

Frank Yeah.

Mamta Loads.

Mamta *takes one of* **Frank**'s *hands. Pause.*

Alaska 125

Frank What you doing?

Mamta Holding your hand.

Frank Why?

Mamta Do you not like it? (*Pause.*) You don't like it?

Frank What d'you reckon?

Mamta I don't know.

Frank Well, I do. I don't need you. (*Pulling his hand back.*) Touching me.

Mamta What?

Frank You heard. You ain't that deaf.

Mamta What did I do ... wrong? What?

Frank And. And. You. You. Been here, been here five, five fucking minutes, think you can be my boss now?

Mamta *No*. It got offered me. I was just asking your opinion. I mean. You turned it down. Martin said. So they need *someone* to –

Frank Been here, what, two weeks?

Mamta It's not exactly a difficult job, is it?

Frank *shakes his head.*

Frank Almost had me for a bit.

Mamta Had you?

Frank Thinking you're. Alright. Different. But. Look at ya.

Mamta You said it was OK.

Frank Well, *it's not*.

Mamta Why not?

Frank God, you fucking reek of sick. You know that? Your mouth. Dirty. Look at it. Don't ya? *Reek*.

Mamta Jesus. Why are you being such a ... ? Knob now?

Frank Sorry, boss, is that not allowed? Speak my fucking mind? Bother you that much, yeah? Hearing the fucking truth.

Mamta *shakes her head.*

Mamta I don't. I don't understand what you're … doing. If you just, tell me. I'll listen. Promise. Whatever it is.

She looks at him, desperate to find an answer.

OK. Fine.

She exits.

Frank (*after her but under his breath*) Yeah, go on. Piss off, you fucking …

He can't say the word.

Blackout.

Part Two

Scene One

April. A small room upstairs in the cinema. **Emma** *and* **Mamta** *are sitting at one side of the room. They are filling out forms.* **Frank** *is sitting at the other side of the room. He has a small bottle of water.*

Emma *and* **Frank** *both wear the normal cinema uniform.* **Mamta** *is wearing a shirt, as she is now kiosk supervisor.*

Mamta (*to* **Frank**)   Would you like to talk through what happened?

No response.

Emma   Just say what happened. Just get it over.

No response.

Frank.

No response.

Frank.

Mamta   It might be better if you started this.

Frank *takes a sip of water.*

Emma   Frank.

Mamta   No, let him. This will get written down. He's shooting his own foot off

Frank   Nicely put.

Emma   Frank.

Mamta   Do you want to just talk through what happened? That might make it easier. And quicker.

Frank *scoffs instinctively and looks at* **Mamta,** *incredulous at her tone.*

Frank I find this pretty *extraordinary*, actually. When Pete was on bar, turned up *hammered* and set fire to the kitchen, he got a quiet word. How come I'm getting a *bollocking* / for – ?

Mamta Frank. I didn't deal with that. Martin did. I wasn't here then.

Frank What, did he tell you about it, over breakfast?

Emma *Frank.*

Mamta (*abrupt*) Why were you *smoking* in the *foyer*?

Frank *attempts to contain his rage, takes a big in-breath and takes another sip of water.*

Frank Alright. OK. Alright. Had a big night. Alright? Feeling a bit like, nauseous. Like, I'm gonna be sick. So. I'm on my way to the toilet. I see Chris and he's having a cheeky cigarette in the foyer. While I'm there. Ask him for a drag. That's all. Which will settle me, my stomach. As I'm having it, you walk past. That simple.

Mamta It's not quite that simple.

Frank Well, it's not complicated. I smoke, or I puke in the popcorn. You want me to do a flow chart? I. Had a fag. With Chris.

Mamta Yes. But. Chris had a coat on. Chris was on a break. Chris wasn't smoking in front of customers, wearing his uniform. About to go back and handle food, which he would then serve to those same customers. (*Pause.*) Have I got that wrong, at all?

Frank You know that shirt quite suits ya. Brings out your eyes.

Mamta Technically, this does deserve a written warning.

Frank Is that. Are you serious?

Emma Mamta, can we just … ?

Mamta What?

Emma I just don't think. This is a bit … you know?

Mamta I am actually going to leave this as a verbal warning. It'll only stay on his record for six months. I'm doing him a favour.

Frank If it's verbal, why are you writing things down?

Mamta Well, there needs to be some record.

Frank Of a verbal warning?

Mamta Yeah. So we know that whatever you do next, you know, merits a written warning. Cos of the cumulative. Effect.

Frank Can you not just, remember? Surely if it's written down and it's a warning ... ? Then, technically – fucking *literally* – it's a written warning.

Mamta If you've got nothing else to say ...

Frank I've got an absolute ... *legion* of things to say.

Mamta Well, that's partly why I haven't let this go.

Emma Let's just. Chill out, yeah?

Pause.

Frank (*half sings, under his breath*) Brown girl in the ring. Da, da da da da.

Mamta What?

Emma He doesn't mean ...

Mamta What are / you ... ?

Frank What? Boney M.

Emma *looks at* **Frank***, pleading.*

Mamta Have you got anything else – *relevant* – to add?

Frank Do you not like disco?

Emma Frank.

Frank D'ya prefer bhangra?

Emma Shut the fuck up.

Frank Cos, I don't wanna stereotype or nothing. Lot o' your lot into hip hop, in't they? Like a solidarity, like *empathy* with black, oppressed culture thing. You gotta respect that, yeah?

No? Sorry, am I, am I out of turn? Am I not being, am I not being PC enough? Cos if I'm not just tell me and I'll. Keep it. Shtum. Promise. Cross my fucking. Just get confused about what I can and can't say these days, you know? Gets difficult to know where the line is. (*Pause*.) But then maybe, maybe you're right, maybe I should be a bit more careful with my phrasing on this kind of issue. Cos a better man than me, once said: 'Every idle word that men shall speak, they shall give account thereof in the day of judgement.' Every idle word. Imagine that. Everything that you've ever said and you'd have to stand there and defend it. Now. As an idea. That's. It's. Mental. But also. Brilliant. Do you not think?

No response.

Well, duty calls, I got nachos to prepare.

He stands and exits.

Mamta How can you stay friends with … ? (*She gestures after* **Frank**.)

Emma He's just. Ignore him, yeah? He's just a bit … upset. It was. You should know like … you know I said his dad died. Well, yesterday was the … the anniversary. And he was, he was drinking last night. A lot. On his own. To help him … get over it, you know? He was a marine, I think, and he, he drowned on some operation or summat before, before Frank was born. So, it's made things pretty hard for him, yeah? His mum's still a wreck about it and every year she goes a bit …

Mamta Right. OK.

Awkward pause.

Emma Do you want me to, to write that all up?

Mamta If you don't mind.

Emma What do you want me to put?

Mamta Just. Say that he was … *cooperative.* Whatever. Keep it vague. Put it in my pigeonhole. And I'll, I'll give it to Martin tomorrow.

Emma Yeah.

Mamta Thanks, Em.

Emma Yeah.

She goes to leave, stops.

Just wanna say. Thanks. For not kicking off. I know he can be a shit. He's got no right. And. Just so you know. People call me Emma. Not Em.

She tries a smile and exits.

A pause before **Mamta** *notices some dirt on her sleeve, licks her thumb and tries to scratch it off.*

Blackout.

Scene Two

Later that day. **Frank** *and* **Chris**, *by the delivery doors. They are playing Dictators Top Trumps.*

Frank Right. Height.

Chris Musso … lini. Five foot eight.

Frank Idi Amin. Six foot four. Give it.

Chris *passes card to* **Frank**.

Frank OK. Erm. Countries invaded.

Chris Vlad the … Im-parlour.

Frank No, no, it's Vlad the Impaler.

Chris Who was that?

Frank Mad Russian bastard.

Chris (*nods*) Countries invaded. One.

Frank And here's another one. Stalin. Ten. Sorry, mate.

Chris *passes the card to* **Frank**.

Frank Length of reign.

Chris Fidel ... Cas ... tro. Forty-five years.

Frank *passes card to* **Chris**, *who reads it.*

Chris Who is that?

Frank Pinochet. Bloke from Chile. Army fella, bit of a shit. You want a cig?

He takes out packet of Marlboro Lights.

Chris No.

Frank *offers cigarette.*

Frank No?

Chris (*unsure*) OK, yes.

He doesn't take one.

Frank You don't have to.

Chris OK.

Frank It's your choice, mate.

Chris (*deciding*) I won't.

Frank OK. Good on ya.

Chris I have been practising but they make my throat dry.

Frank *accepts the explanation and puts the cigarette in his mouth, while casually searching his pockets for a lighter.*

Chris Facial hair.

Frank George W. Bush. None.

Chris Saddam Hussein. (*Smiles.*) Three.

Frank *passes card to* **Chris**. **Frank** *hasn't found a lighter.*

Chris I've got some matches if you want.

Frank You know what? Fuck 'em.

Puts the cigarette behind his ear.

Good little game, this. Where do you get 'em from?

Chris Internet. Length of reign.

Frank Ceaușescu. Twenty-four.

Chris *passes card to* **Frank**.

Chris Here.

Frank (*looking at the card*) Hello. Is that Pol Pot? Didn't know he looked like that. Nice little face.

He screws up his face and holds up the Pol Pot card next to his face, doing a little show for **Chris** *and putting on a 'Chinky' accent.*

Chinky-wink. Chinky chow-wow wing-wang wow-pow. Me love you long time, sucky-sucky? Five dollar. *Five dollar*. FIVE DOLLAR.

Chris *laughs*.

Frank Sucky-sucky?

Emma *enters.*

Frank (*not having seen* **Emma**) Sucky-sucky?

Emma You alright, boys? Having a good time?

Chris Yeah, we are.

Emma (*to* **Chris**, *referring to* **Frank**) How's the big man?

Frank (*to* **Emma**, *referring to* **Mamta**) She speaks to me again.

Emma You said that without moving your lips. / Amazing.

Frank Pete set fire to half of upstairs, always stealing. Fucking. Stinks.

Chris I like Pete.

Emma She's just trying to, to piss out her territory.

Chris Pete's funny.

Frank So why's she pissing on me?

Chris But he does smell. Which category? / Frank?

Emma Because you need to cut out all the ... disco ... bollocks. That's not good, mate. At all.

Chris What's disco bollocks?

Frank Body count.

Chris Is there a disco?

Frank I said, body count.

Chris Robert ... Magoo ... bee. A hundred thousand.

Frank *passes card to* **Chris**.

Emma I just wanted to. You know. Make sure we're alright.

Frank Yeah. Course we are. (*Pause.*) You. Um. Fancy getting a drink in tonight?

Emma Er. Yeah, OK.

Chris Height.

Frank We can. Just have a chat or ...

Emma Alright.

Chris What height?

Frank Be good, yeah.

Emma And you know what, fuck her, you know? She's just. She's a blatant, like, Little Hitler.

Chris   He was five foot eight. (*Gestures to the cards.*) Adolf Hitler. Not that little.

Emma   Right. Thank you, Chris. Well. Fun as this is, I'll be …

She motions that she is leaving.

Frank   Cool. Yeah.

Emma   See ya later.

Frank   We'll get a taxi. Yeah?

Emma   OK. I'll book it now. See you later, Chris.

*No response from **Chris**, who is looking at his cards. **Emma** exits.*

Chris   Height.

Frank   What?

Chris   What height?

Frank   Right. Kim Jong-Il. Approx. Five foot two.

Chris (*smiling*)   Have you made that up? Stupid, name.

Frank (*distracted, throwaway*)   Don't be a twat, course not.
*The insult hangs in the air and **Chris** buries himself in the cards. Silence.*

Frank   Well? What you got?

Chris   She's just being nice.

Frank   What?

Chris   She doesn't fancy you.

Frank   Are you drunk?

Chris   I heard her.

Frank   Do wanna play this or what?

Chris   What.

Pause.

Frank Wha' she say?

Chris She's got a man. And she really likes him. He's in the army, like your dad was. She told Mamta. I heard them. He's called Paul. But she calls him Big Paul.

Frank She chats all kindsa shit, yeah? You've got it wrong, yeah?

Chris I'm not a liar.

Pause.

Frank What else she say?

Chris She told Mamta that you had a thing. I heard them. A little one-off fling, Emma said. But it was only cos she was so drunk.

Frank You've completely. You're a little fucking … *and* it was more than once, so that's just … you're just wrong.

Chris She said … that.

Frank *gestures for him to say more.*

Chris She said that … she just felt sorry for you, just cos of what happened to your dad. She said it was a. (*Pause.*) Sympathy. Fuck.

Silence.

Frank Chris.

Chris *offers his card to* **Frank**, *who doesn't take it. Silence.*

Frank *places his cards neatly on the ground. Takes the cigarette from behind his ear. Presents it.*

Frank Eat it.

Chris What?

Frank You heard.

Chris Don't. That's horrible. No.

Frank All of it. Right down. Now.

A moment. **Frank** *pounces violently on* **Chris***. Pins him, struggling, to the floor. Forces open his mouth. Rams the cigarette in, despite* **Chris***'s spluttering and struggling. Forces* **Chris***'s mouth shut.*

Frank Swallow. Is that a problem? Is that a fucking problem? Your throat too dry?

Chris *nods frantically.*

Frank Well, that is a shame. WHAT. A. FUCKING. PITY.

Blackout.

Scene Three

The next morning. **Emma***'s room.* **Frank** *and* **Emma** *are sitting on her bed.* **Emma** *is in a dressing gown.* **Frank** *is just in his boxers.*

Frank Don't think I'm gonna go in today. My head's.

Emma Yeah?

Frank We can go into town. If you want. Get some lunch or …

Emma I'm not. Not all that hungry.

Frank Right. (*Pause.*) I like your room. Nice … layout. (*Pause.*) Was it OK, that we didn't use a … ? Like, is that gonna be OK?

Emma Doesn't … matter.

Frank Are you on the … ?

Emma Yeah.

Pause.

Frank Are you, erm … are you alright?

Emma Yeah. fine.

Frank You just seem a bit … (*Pause.*) I heard that you're … is it right that you're … seeing someone?

Pause. **Emma** *nods.*

Frank How long? How long for?

Emma 'Bout, two months.

Frank Is it ... serious then or ... ?

Emma (*shrugs*) I like him, yeah. And he's not ... better than you or anything. If you're thinking that. He's just. Decent, you know? I know it sounds shitty but ...

Frank Will I get to meet him?

Emma Frank.

Frank I know, I'm just ...

Emma *digs out a packet of cigarettes.*

Frank Thought you give up.

Emma *offers* **Frank** *one, he declines.* **Emma** *has a cigarette.*

Frank *watches her.*

Emma You know, I think, I think Chris might just have a bit of a crush on you.

No response.

Bet you twenty quid I'm right.

No response.

We can't do this again, yeah?

Frank I know.

Emma This is, like. I don't want this to happen every time we ...

Frank Yeah.

Emma You know? Because it could really mess things up for me if Paul finds out and ...

Frank Yeah, I know how it goes. It's fine.

Emma So we should probably stop going. For drinks and stuff.

Frank *nods.*

Pause.

Emma   Thanks. For …

Frank   What?

Emma   Being cool with that.

Pause.

Frank   You're right by the way. About Chris. He does have a, a crush on me. Well. Did have.

Emma   Did have? What happened?

Pause.

Frank   Nothing. I just. Set him straight.

Emma   Bless him.

Frank   Yeah.

Silence.

Emma   Think I might have a shower. Go to work.

Frank   …

Emma   So … could you go? So I can have one?

Pause. **Frank** *nods.*

Emma   Thank you.

Neither of them moves.

Blackout.

Scene Four

Later, the same day. Early evening. **Frank** *is sitting on the steps of a large church in the centre of town. Wearing the same clothes. Deep in thought.*

Enter **Mamta**. *She is wearing a long red coat, which has a floral design, and is holding various shopping bags. She puts these down as she approaches* **Frank**.

Mamta Thought it was you. Saw you from the high street. (*Pause.*) Look. I know you're probably just wanting me to go away already but I thought I should just come over and say hi. (*Pause.*) Hi. (*Pause.*) Is this your church? It's. Huge. Isn't it? Pillars and. Must be dead old. Never been inside. Always see it walking past. Sometimes have my lunch here on the steps but. Never gone in. What's it like? Inside? (*Pause.*) Are you not meant to be at work today?

Frank *looks up at her.*

Mamta Have you called in sick or … ? What ya doing?

Frank Thinking. What you doing?

Mamta Shopping. Then I'm meeting my brother for dinner. We're going for Thai. Are you gonna make a joke about that? Something about Thai brides or ladyboys or … ?

Frank Are you gonna tell anyone? Like Martin? That you saw me?

Mamta You look awful.

Frank (*sarcastic*) Thanks. Are you?

Mamta I'm sure they'll cope.

Frank (*surprised*) Right. (*Genuine.*) Thank you.

Mamta Look tired. Should try and get a bit more. Sleep. When you're. Upset. Look like you might need it. (*Pause.*) Alright. OK, I'll leave you to it.

She goes to go.

Frank Why am I … why am I upset?

Mamta Because. You look it.

Frank I look *shit*, I don't look *upset*.

Mamta Sorry, I was. Just trying to help.

Frank Help?

Mamta Yeah.

Frank Help what?

Mamta Your. Situation.

Frank *stares at her, searchingly.*

Mamta Cos of. Your dad. I don't know how I'd cope with that, I really don't. I mean the whole anniversary thing every year must be … awful.

Frank Shame about your coat. Nice design but. Red and brown. Clashes.

Mamta *Frank*. Who are you saying that for?

Frank What?

Mamta Yeah, well, I'm sorry, you can't play me like I'm fresh off the boat. I'm from St Albans.

Frank That doesn't change a thing.

Mamta What do you mean?

Frank Just that. Right. Your lot, back home, got the caste thing, yeah? Which is like. Light at the top. Then darker as you get further down. Well, that ain't too far, give or take, from my way of thinking. Just give it a bit of a Doppler shift and you're there. But …

Mamta But what?

Frank But it's bigger than that, yeah? Where I'm coming from.

Mamta Well, OK. I'm all ears.

Frank You sure? Yeah? *Yeah?* Alright. Alright. Moses right? Moses, yeah? Moses saved the Hebrews, yeah? Jews. Led 'em out. But. This is the trick. Hebrew was a misprint. The original – listen, *listen*, yeah? – the original, the original translation, was,

was 'hapiru'. H-A-P-I-R-U. Meaning. Light-skinned. Literally, that's all it means. 'Hapiru'. And they were the ones pulled out of Egypt. So the light, you see, the light were saved. And the dark, they drowned. Yeah? So, wind it back, wind it back, it's not a tribe, not Jews, it's people. White people. We were. We are. *Chosen*. So that's why the world is what it is.

Mamta   And what is it?

Frank   Right. You see a black kid on a bus, yeah? If he's on his own. Do an experiment for me. I mean it. Try this. Watch him, yeah? Young black kid, yeah? Watch him come up the stairs. First. First thing. Wass he do? He looks round. Quick. Straight away. Choosing where he's gonna sit. Yeah? Now, what's he looking for? I'll tell ya. Other black kids. *The threat*. He can't see me. I'm nothing. Like air, yeah? Like fucking. Tippex. Cos he's looking for them. He's looking for trouble.

Mamta   Have you rehearsed that?

Frank   No, but the little black kid has. Save him getting stabbed. Save him getting Damilola Taylor'd. Save him from. Trying to be safe in this country. That's what it takes.

Mamta   Two words. Jamie. Bulger.

Frank   Alright. Fuck that. Brixton. Riots.

Mamta   OK. Er. Police. Brutality.

Frank   Fuck off. History. Africa.

Mamta   You fuck off. Slave. Trade.

Frank   Feisty, in't ya? But I think you'll find there was a fairly prosperous, *historic* – fuck it, *prehistoric* – trade in that before we got there. We just redirected it. Made a bit o' dollar. And don't tell me, you see 'em in the paper, on telly, down in London, their self-created little ghettos, stabbing and shooting each other up, you *care*. *Fuck that*. You. Just glad it ain't you. Glad they keep it themselves. What's the phrase? Black on black.

Mamta   I do care. Don't –

Frank (*genuine*) Darling, I don't believe you. As long as they keep it to themselves, you really don't give a fuck. Honestly, you don't –

Mamta Frank, I'm not –

Frank Now, I mean, you might wank on about it for appearance sake like all the other cunts. Like, blame it on the government. Or, or the media. Police. Or … legacy of Empire. But let's fucking face it, where's the poor white kids shooting each other up over the next shipment of crack coming in? Where the fuck are they, yeah? Where's the white kids setting up a whole genre of music so they can rap on about what hateful fucking animals they are?

Mamta Frank, that's mental, you're …

Frank OK. OK. Alright. OK. History lesson, yeah? Back in the day, India, motherland, whenever they had a revolt. British Army, British Army would sew up any rioter inside a pig-skin and fire 'em out of a cannon. Over the crowd. To get the message across. To the locals. Teach 'em right from wrong. Now, now it weren't right, was it? Was it? It was wrong. Completely. And we've apologised for it, ain't we? But. Right. Think about it, it's no different that, no different, to what your lot are doing *now*. To their own. No different. We've civilised. Got law. Respect it. Obey it. But your lot. All over. India. Pakistan. Kashmir. Like the tenth fucking circle. Or, or, if I wanna pull out the heavyweights. Sudan. Congo. You go deepest, darkest. Fuck it, you look at any non-white country. It's immense. Makes us, our fuck-ups, look like a cherry picnic. Makes me look like a fucking saint. So, who had to pitch in Kosovo? Sierra Leone? Who pitched in? Was it Nigeria? Was it Egypt? India? Bangladesh? Was it fuck. It was us. My lot. *Me*. Cos really, you don't give a fuck about a million dark faces over there, do ya? You're the fucking racist. Suffering. Death. Screams of a continent. Cos I'm white, you care more about what I *say* than what all those billions of black and brown fuckers actually *do*. To each other. To themselves. Now. Why is that? Do you wanna know why?

Mamta *shakes her head in disbelief.*

Frank Two reasons. First off, you know deep down that I'm better than you. So you expect more. Demand more. Second off, you're past caring. Cos it's just black on black. Whole countries, but still, it's the same principle. Let's just leave 'em to it, let 'em wipe each other out. Like. You've got to this country, yeah? Posh area. White area. Nice school.

Mamta Frank …

Frank *White school.* So you've left it all behind, ain't ya? And that's why we got on first off. Because you've embraced me and what I think. (*Pause.*) Now I mean, I know you've got all these liberal good intentions and off-the-shelf morals and you're there, you're there looking down at me now, like I'm, some kind of … monster, but actually, honestly. Be honest with yourself. Just for one second. Because, let's face it, just like everybody else you don't care about anyone or anything that doesn't directly benefit you or people like you. Cos if you did, you wouldn't be here now. You'd be out there doing something to make things better for these people. So. When it comes down to it. Now we've talked it all through. It turns out, you think and feel exactly like I do. Exactly. It's just that I've got the heart and the balls to say it out loud.

Silence.

Mamta Are you done?

Frank *nods.*

Mamta You know. I hope. (*Referring to the the church.*) If your God is in there, I really hope He can hear you. All this.

Frank Me too.

Mamta I mean. Does talking like that, all that, speaking like this to me, does that give you a boner / or – ?

Frank No. Why, does it get you wet?

Mamta Charming. Really. I can see why Emma went for you. Or was it cos she was too drunk to stand up?

Alaska   145

Frank You're not funny, yeah?

Mamta I fucking am. What's black and eats bananas? Half of London. What do you call a dead Paki? A good start. Don't be thinking you can shock me, alright? Or push me around. Fucking ... lecture me. You know the funny thing is, you actually sound a bit like my dad. He was always saying stuff like that. Like, doesn't matter who I marry as long as they're not either black or Muslim and he'll rant on about everything that happened back in Uganda. So actually as well as being wrong, you're also being. Very. Deeply. Unoriginal. (*Pause.*) But I think, I think some people need to keep talking like you do. Cos if they stopped they'd realise that, God, I've got. Nothing. The only way I can function is by directing all this shit out at other people. Because if I stopped. If I stopped doing it for one second and looked at my life. And was truly honest with myself, I'd have to take the nearest knife and stab myself in the heart. (*Pause.*) And. And d'ya know what's really funny?

Frank What?

Mamta Having listened to you now, I do think Emma was genuinely mad for letting you and your tiny white cock anywhere near her.

Pausing briefly for effect, **Mamta** *picks up her shopping and exits.*

Frank *watches her go.*

Blackout.

Scene Five

We hear rainfall. Gradually at first but it soon becomes torrential. As the sound eventually fades, lights come up on –

Later that night. The garden of **Chris**'s *family home.* **Frank** *is standing out on the patio in the dark.* **Frank**'s *face is bloodied and bruised, particularly around his nose. There is also blood on his hands and his top. He is breathing heavily, noisily, and has* *clearly been crying. He is a mess, soaked through with rain.* **Chris** *is inside, wearing pyjamas, a dressing gown and slippers, having just turned the living-room light on. Both* **Frank** *and* **Chris** *are holding mobile phones to their ears.*

Having only just turned the light on, **Chris** *sees* **Frank** *for the first time, through the glass of the locked patio door.*

They look at each other.

Chris (*talking to the mobile rather than* **Frank**)   What are you doing in my garden?

No response.

It's late.

No response.

(*Looking directly at* **Frank**.) I was in bed.

Chris *lowers the mobile phone and places it in his dressing-gown pocket.* **Frank** *lowers his too, pockets it, as* **Chris** *unlocks the door with a key and comes out onto the patio, making sure he locks the door behind him.*

Chris   What do you want?

Frank   Can I ... could I just ... can I come in, yeah?

Chris (*shaking his head*)   Not allowed visitors.

Frank   Just ... just for a bit, yeah?

Chris   Mum and Dad are very strict.

Frank   Just ...

Chris   And you're not even very nice, so ...

Frank   Chris.

Chris   So just ... *Silence.*

What happened to your face?

Frank   So you won't ... ?

Alaska   147

Chris   Looks sore.

Frank Can we not ... can we not just ... talk? For a bit. Inside, yeah? It'll be fine, it will. I promise. I won't hurt you or ... I mean, I mean we could just go up to your room and ... and just ... talk. Play cards or ...

Chris *shakes his head.*

Frank   I just wanna. I just wanna clean up. Get warm. Dry. *Chris.*

Chris   Then go to your own house. Your own room.

Frank   Chris. I'm so cold, yeah? I'm ... I'm ... Fuck sake, I'll be ten minutes, five minutes. Tops. I just need to clean up. Look at me, for fuck sake. Look at me.

Chris   I am. But you can't. That's not ... It's not fair.

Frank   Chris.

Chris   And what even happened to your face?

Frank   ...

Chris   Why is there blood?

Frank   It's ... it's nothing, yeah? I'm just ... I fell over and, and ...

Chris   If it was nothing then you wouldn't be on my patio late at night crying.

Frank I'm ... Look, look, alright, it was Mamta, yeah? It was. Mamta. Mamta. She ... I ... I was ... I followed her, yeah?

Chris   I don't believe anything you say anyway, so ...

Frank   Look, I told you I ... I followed her and ...

Chris (*hushed, so as not to wake anyone*)   Frank, I don't care what you say, *you're not coming in my house so you can just ... go.*

Frank *looks at* **Chris** *and takes a second to slow down/control his breathing.*

Frank Right. (*Pause.*) She was with her, her brother. In town. They had dinner together, but … then, then he left. So, she was, she was on her own. And I … I follow her. (*Pause.*) I watch her go down off the high street and she … gets her bus. Then. Quickly like, I sneak on after. (*Pause.*) So, so she's upstairs and I'm down, downstairs, at the back. Tucked away, and I'm watching. Waiting. For like ten, twenty minutes. Eventually, we stop and she comes down. I watch her, watch her slow, like slow motion, coming down, wearing this coat, this red coat, down the stairs, through the doors, off. And she still ain't seen me. Fucking. Oblivious. So I go. Follow. Just slip through the doors. Driver says summat behind me but I don't hear him. Can't. Just. Focus. And I go. (*Pause.*) Then, suddenly I'm. Was very. Very. Quiet. Dark. I'm on the street and it's. Quiet. Empty. And I thought. And I thought. I watched her walking ahead of me, away from me, and I thought. Yeah. Yeah. (*Pause.*) So I got her. I just ran quick and I got her. Easy. Lift her up. Catch her. Lift her up off the street. And I, I put her down hard in this, this alley. And she's struggling and screaming but I, I shut her up, yeah? Quick. I hit her, yeah? Like reaction, like. Her face. Hit her. And she screams, like. So, so I hit her 'gain. But she jumps up. Jumps for me. Goes for me. And this punch, like she gets this one, like, this one lucky punch at me, yeah? Lunge, gets me here and I'm straight off, bleeding. So I'm shocked, yeah? Hurt. But the punch. Just made it worse, yeah? Made me worse, yeah? Then I. When she did that I just. Then I just. Lost it. Got her down with this kick in her stomach, then these punches coming over and over, quick, then this last one, like this kick when she's down. In her. Into her. I kick her and. I mean, her neck, it. It just. It just. Broke. Snap. And her eyes … her eyes were … gone.

Chris Gone?

Frank *nods.*

Frank Heard it. Her neck. And her eyes were …

Chris So you … ? You're saying that you … ?

Frank *nods.*

Frank And I hold her. Her body. I pick her up and I rest her on me. She ain't breathing and I can feel the weight of her on me, her body. And I take one of her arms and I hold it in my hand. Feel the weight of it. Look at it. Then I take it and I push it, I push it down on this railing behind her. And the spike, the railing, it comes up, through, like through the wrist. And she don't scream or … so she must be … and it's actually … easy. To do that. You wouldn't think. To push it down, through it. But it is. Easy. (*Pause.*) So I take her other arm. Do the same. Push it down on this railing. It comes up through it. See her blood. Bone. Metal. And I've done it now so she's, she's hanging there. Like. Cross. Like a. A cross. She's there. And then I … She's there, so I … I touch her. My hand in her jeans, feel her. She's still warm. Soft. Wet. (*Pause.*) And then I …

Silence.

Chris You're so … horrible.

Frank *nods.*

Chris Why do you … ? (*Pause.*) I don't understand why …

Pause. **Frank** *starts to back away.*

Chris Where are you going?

Frank *edges further away.*

Chris Where are you going, Frank?

Pause.

Frank Away.

Frank *exits.*

Chris (*after him*) Frank? (*Pause.*) Frank.

A moment.

Blackout.

150   Contemporary English Plays

Scene Six

Early evening, the next day. The lights fade up on the staffroom at the cinema. **Emma** *is eating and watching a* Sopranos *video.*

Enter **Mamta**, *coming in to get her coat and purse.*

Mamta   You alright?

Emma   Yeah, cool. Just. You know.

Mamta   I'm off to McDonald's, want anything?

Emma (*gestures to her salad, which is in a Tupperware container on her lap*)   Nah, I'm alright, thanks.

Mamta   You had a good day?

Emma   Magic.

Mamta   I've been completely 'argh'. Feet are killing me. This gyppo guy, this idiot. Tells me women shouldn't get to be managers. Cos I won't let his nine-year-old into an eighteen. They've always got a chip on their shoulder, apparently. Women.

Emma   Yeah. My uncle says that.

Mamta   Right. God. Is he a wanker?

Emma   No, he's my uncle. (*Pause.*) Have you seen Frank about?

Mamta   Yeah. I meant to tell you, actually.

Emma   What?

As **Mamta** *pauses,* **Emma** *mutes the TV. A brief silence.*

Mamta   Met him in town. This is. Yesterday. I tried to be nice. Make things alright. Went over to him. Really made the effort. But. He started being all. All in my face. And. We had a few … words. He was being an absolute *arse*. All this racist shit.

Emma   I'm sorry. He's such a. We had a … *relapse* after we went for a drink the other night, and I, I shouldn't have. I know that. So. Then I told him. That we couldn't like. See each other. Or … So he was probably still. Upset.

Alaska 151

Mamta Why are you making ... excuses for him?

Emma I'm not. I'm just saying. He just takes stuff out on people. And this time it was ... it was you, you know?

Mamta It's not just been this one time.

Emma I know. Fair point. But this whole thing with his dad's really fucked him up, you know? It makes him say stuff. Snap at people. He doesn't mean it. I can't believe that he can actually mean it. Saying all that. To you.

Mamta Well, it sounded pretty convincing. And. What I don't get. At all. Is how can you sleep with someone who comes out with stuff like that. The way he looks at me. Like I'm ...

Emma It just. He's ... / *nice*.

Mamta Like I'm to blame for ...

Emma I know it's hard to ... to justify. But. He can be so lovely. So ... soft. (*Pause*.) What did he say?

Mamta He was giving it the full white-power shit. So. I walked away. I wasn't gonna put up with that. Lower myself to listen to that. Then, bit later, he came over, out of nowhere, told me and my brother that I was up my own arse and that I need a good lay to sort me out.

Emma Right.

Mamta And he said he'd heard that Gandhi was good in bed and ...

Emma He's such a mong. I'm sorry.

Mamta So my brother. Wasn't gonna take that. Knocked him out. We were by the car park. Near the. Fire station. He'd followed me. From the high street. Weirdo.

Emma Did 'e hurt him?

Mamta Busted his face up a bit. Kicked him. It was funny, really, more than anything. Bit cartoony. All this blood. Didn't look real. I think he was actually crying. But. We left him to it. Went for dinner.

Emma   That's a bit ... fucking ...

Mamta   What?

Emma   *Harsh*. For saying Gandhi was ... randy.

Mamta   That's not what he meant.

Emma   Yeah, but that's what he said. No wonder he hasn't come back in.

Mamta   Well, he won't be. I've talked to Martin.

Emma (*shocked*)   *Have you?*

Mamta   Yeah.

Emma   You *punched* him, so you *sacked* him?

Mamta   That's not someone I want to work with.

Emma   Oh, and we couldn't have you being upset, could we?

Mamta   Are you still ... are you still siding with him?

Emma   No, but *for fuck sake*. I know you're a good girl. But. I'm struggling to ... (*Pause.*) Right. Frank talks a lot of *shit* but I never seen him *hit* anyone. Never seem him beat someone up in the street, leave 'em there to rot. Then laugh about it. Eating a fucking curry.

Mamta   It was Thai.

Emma   Whatever. You get Thai curry, don't ya?

Mamta   He'll be *fine*. It was just a few cuts, bit o' blood.

Emma   Mamta. Much as I feel for ya. For what he said. Which I'm sure was awful and spiteful and stupid. And it must be terrible to hear that. And I know I could never know what that's like. Hearing that. But. (*Pause.*) I'm not sure I can jump up and down with joy knowing my mate's had his face kicked in by your idiot brother. I don't think that's *fine*.

Mamta Mate?

Emma Yeah, mate.

Mamta Even now?

Emma Yeah.

Mamta That's pretty ... shit.

Emma Maybe it is. So what?

Mamta So what?

Emma Yeah. I mean, what gives you the right to be so fucking ... high and mighty? Have you looked in the mirror lately?

Mamta I haven't done anything.

Emma Oh, fuck that. Fuck. That. You watch and laugh as Frank gets beat up. You manage everyone here like they're fucking retards or summat.

Mamta Well, look. Everyone here acts like. Trash. So that's how I'm gonna treat 'em. Simple as that. That's how it works. People fuck around, I'm not gonna put up with it, some fake smile. I mean, how do you want me to treat everyone? Like they're all my best mate?

Emma *No.* Just. With a bit of *respect*, yeah? (*Pause.*) I'll tell you what, though. I'll tell ya summat for nothing. The more I listen to you, the more it all makes sense. Cos, you know, all my worst experiences in clubs, bars, have been. Asian guys. Yeah? Calling me a white ... whatever. Threatening ya. Grabbing up ya skirt. Pushing ya round. Treating ya like cheap meat.

Mamta OK. But I've seen the way you dress, Emma, when you're going out, and maybe there's a reason for that.

Emma Yeah, well, I think it's a different kinda reason, but I won't say it out loud, case ya get your brother in here, beat fuck out me.

Mamta Could be a good idea.

Emma Oh yeah?

Mamta Yeah. (*Pause.*) But for now. I'll tell you what. I'll tell *you* something. I'm going out to get some food. Then I'm gonna go for a bit of a walk. Bit of fresh air. So I'll be off for about half an hour. When I get back. I want you gone. Or if not, I'll get security to do it.

Emma You what?

Mamta You heard.

They look at each other.

Emma Well, I may as well save you the walk.

She stands, calmly collects her coat and bag. As she gets to the door, she turns and looks one last time at **Mamta**.

Emma And you know what else? I don't believe in God, yeah? Heaven. Hell. Or any of that stuff that Frank does. (*Pause.*) But I do hope, sincerely, that you *fucking burn*.

Silence.

She exits.

A pause before **Mamta** *takes a seat.*

Blackout.

Scene Seven

By the delivery doors, which are closed. A few hours after Scene Five. **Frank** *is sitting on the ground in a heap.*

Silence.

Enter **Chris**.

Chris Thought you'd be here.

Frank I'm not. I'm really not. I'm not anywhere, mate.

Chris I got this at the garage.

Chris *takes a can of Diet Coke from his coat pocket and offers it to* **Frank**. **Frank** *looks at* **Chris** *for a second before taking* *the can gratefully. As they talk,* **Frank** *opens the can and drinks from it.*

Frank I just didn't know where to go.

Chris Alright.

Frank I'm an adult.

Chris I called Mamta.

Frank And the place I run to is …

Chris To make sure that she was OK.

Frank I couldn't think of anywhere else.

Chris And she was. Apart from being annoyed I woke her up.

Frank Coming from town, first thing I saw. Light from the gyppos' campfire.

Chris But it's OK, I didn't tell her what you said about her. Just said I got the wrong number. (*Pause.*) You are a rubbish liar.

Frank *takes out a crumpled pack of cigarettes. Takes out a bent cigarette, which is snapped in the middle.* **Frank** *has to push it together with his fingers to be able to smoke it successfully. He does so, lights it, takes a drag.*

Frank Share it. Please.

He passes it.

Have to keep your fingers on it.

Chris *does so, smokes.* **Frank** *waits for a cough. It doesn't come.* **Frank** *smiles.*

Frank I'm sorry, mate. I am.

Chris *offers back the cigarette.*

Chris What for?

Frank *takes the cigarette.*

Frank Why did you … why did you come here?

Chris Don't know. Just did.

Pause.

Frank What's the, what's the worst thing you've ever done?

Chris We went camping in Scotland with my family once and I hid my sister's medicine and she went into a coma.

Frank Fuck. How long for?

Chris Eight weeks.

Frank Shit.

Chris What about you?

Frank Don't even know. *Pause.*

Chris I bought you some face-wipes.

Frank (*confused*) OK.

Chris *takes out the wipes.*

Chris For your face.

Frank What?

Chris So you don't get infected.

A pause. **Chris** *takes out a wipe. He moves towards* **Frank**, *who initially flinches as the wipe touches his face.* **Chris** *gently starts to clean* **Frank**'s *face, which he tilts back, and continues to do so as they speak.*

Frank Thank you.

Chris *nods.*

Pause.

Frank You should probably ask me where I'm going on me holidays.

Pause.

Chris Where are you going on your holidays?

Frank Suppose it'll have to be here. (*Pause.*) What about you?

Chris Alaska.

Frank What?

Chris Alaska. Like cold places. Snow. Mountains. And I like grizzly bears. Would like to see them. Catching salmon.

Frank Reckon I'd look good with one of them hats. With the. Flaps.

Chris Maybe.

Frank Hunt for bears.

Chris Yeah.

Silence apart from **Chris** *cleaning* **Frank**.

Chris Kill them.

Frank *nods gently.*

Chris *stops cleaning, looks at* **Frank**, *before awkwardly leaning in and kissing him. Taken by the moment,* **Frank** *kisses him back.* **Chris** *puts his hand on* **Frank**'s *shoulders and pulls himself away from him, looking tenderly at* **Frank**'s *face.* **Frank** *looks down, evading eye contact.*

Frank What do you even … like about me?

Chris Your stretch marks.

Frank What?

Chris You were changing once and I saw them while you were pulling your top down. Like little lightning flashes. My sister hates hers, but I like yours.

A smile edges onto **Frank**'s *face before he successfully swallows it with a frown.*

Frank I'm sorry, mate. But you shouldn't, look at me like that. That's not what I'm about.

Silence.

Chris I saw your house today. (*Pause.*) After my shift, cos you was on the rota and I was a bit worried cos you never have days off. Thought you might be in trouble or … so I got your address off the taxi list. (*Pause.*) Took me ages to get there. I was on my bike and there was loads of country lanes to get over. And when I got there. (*Pause.*) Never seen a house that big. Least not on my estate. Had stables. And a gazebo. Thought I must have got the wrong house by being thick as usual or something. But a man answered your door and I asked him who he was and where you were and he said that he was your dad and that you were at the cinema. I told him I thought he was dead, though, and he asked me if I was on drugs or something and said he would call the police if I didn't get the fuck away from his house. So I left. Went home and just had a pizza.

Frank Chris.

Chris And then you turn up and claim all that rubbish about Mamta. Why are you such a *liar*? About everything? I mean, why do you pretend like you're poor and you did that thing to Mamta when … ?

Frank That's such a stupid question. You don't know anything. About me or *anything*. Little story, yeah?

Chris What story? / I asked a question.

Frank Shut up. Shut up, *listen. Listen.* Gehenna, right, Gehenna was the original word for Hell. You understand? *Hell.* And Gehenna was an actual place, like a valley where they sacrificed children. So, at the time scripture was like, be good or you'll be damned to go to what now would be, er, Dunblane or … Lockerbie. Somewhere shit, somewhere associated with death and fucking … evil. Yeah?

Chris What … like Corby?

Frank But they were wrong. It isn't even that far away. It never is. It isn't a valley somewhere. It isn't just fucking Corby, twat. It isn't removed from us in like a distant plain or place. Wherever you live, wherever you are, they're stood around us, like fucking demons. They live with us. Eat with us. Shit with us. Fucking.

Everywhere. See 'em. You see 'em? And it's fucked to ignore that. Or think that I'm *lucky*. My house and my fucking ... furnishings has got nothing to do with *me* or *what I am* or *what the world is*, you fucking *girl*.

Chris Do you wanna swap houses then? Cos I'd love to live in your house.

Frank Yeah, well then, you're completely fucked and missing the point.

Chris Prob'ly. But I don't think I'm the only one. Who is fucked.

Silence.

Can I have the can back, please? To recycle.

Frank *looks at him. Picks up the can, throws it at the feet of* **Chris**.

Chris Thank you.

Frank You're welcome.

Chris I won't tell anyone you kissed me. They might think less of you. (*Pause.*) And I do think it's sad that you lie so much. I think it's prob'ly the saddest things in the whole world. (*Pause.*) Because I wanted so much to stay here. With you. On your lips. (*Pause.*) Like. For about a whole month I thought I was in love with you. (*Pause.*) I must be very, very stupid. More stupid than I even thought. (*Pause.*) But then at least I'm not as stupid as you.

He picks up the can of Diet Coke and puts it into his coat pocket.

Goodnight.

He exits.

Frank *watches him go. Silence.*

Frank *takes out his lighter. Flicks it on and watches the flame. Does this a few times before putting his hand above the flame, feeling the heat until it becomes too much. He does this a few* *times, gradually breaking into a broad grin as he starts to savour the pain/sensation of it.*

Blackout.

Shades

Alia Bano

Shades was first performed at the Royal Court Jerwood Theatre Upstairs, London, on 28 January 2009, with the following cast (in order of appearance):

Sabrina	Stephanie Street
Zain	Navin Chowdhry
Ali	Elyes Gabel
Mark	Matthew Needham
Reza	Amit Shah
Nazia	Chetna Pandya
Director	Nina Raine
Designer	Lucy Osborne
Lighting	Matt Drury
Sound	David McSeveney

Characters

Sabrina Khan, *Pathan*
Zain Miah, *Bengali*
Ali Mahmood, *Pakistani*
Mark Blaine, *white*
Reza Qureishi, *Pakistani*
Nazia Qureishi, *Pakistani*
Waitress (*can be doubled by the actress playing Nazia*)

Scene One

A table. A man and a woman, in a short-sleeved, quite low-cut top, are sitting opposite each other. They are in mid-conversation.

Sab Why did we come here?

Zain I'm helping you with your Bridget Jones status.

Sab They're just merging into one, IT, accountant, consultant – it's the bloody twilight zone.

Zain You could always marry me.

She laughs.

Sab They keep looking me up and down.

Zain You are dressed like the Whore of Babylon.

Sab (*looks down at her clothing*) I'm not!

Zain This is Muslim speed dating.

Sab You said I should come as I normally dress.

Zain I may have made a mistake about the clothing – overestimated the, um, ah … I hope you've been hiding that inquisitive mind to compensate.

Sab Shall we go home?

Zain You'll be doing the dishes for the month. I'm not ready to leave, this is better than I thought. The ladies are lapping me up. I haven't had so much fun in ages.

Sab Of course they are. You're liberal, you're an artist – basically white, but you're brown, perfect.

Zain I've already heard a few of them give out orgasmic murmurs.

Sab *laughs.*

Zain You know you can always marry me.

Sab Ask me again at thirty.

Zain When you're as good as dead to the Asian male – (*beat*) I'll have you.

Sab Let's go.

Zain Walk out midway?

Sab Why not?

Zain Controversial. But I'm gonna stay.

Sab Zee.

Zain I'm as happy as Larry.

Sab Come on, Zee. I'm leaving.

Zain But the guy coming up has been giving you the eye ever since we walked in.

Sab Really?

Zain He's quite cute.

Sab Is he?

Zain Uh-huh. This could be the one.

Sab *looks at him sceptically.*

Zain He could be!

Sab At least he'll be eye candy.

Bell rings.

Zain Just know you have my tick of approval. Let me know how it goes.

Kisses her on the cheek just as a man in a suit appears.

Ali *Salaam alakum.*

Sab *Walakum salaam.*

Ali An eager suitor?

Sab A friend.

Ali I'm Ali.

Sab Sabrina.

Ali Nice to meet you. So, what do you do?

Sab I'm an events organiser. You?

Ali I'm an accountant. An events organiser – must be exciting, your job.

Sab It can be tiring, but nice seeing the finished product.

Ali So, you're a party girl.

Sab Occupational hazard.

Ali Perhaps another occupation might more suitable.

Sab You don't approve of my job?

Ali I'm sure you're very good at it.

Sab I am.

Ali You must work late nights.

Sab Sometimes.

Ali Aren't you scared as a woman / to –

Sab I get a cab on the company just like all the guys do.

Ali Can I ask you a question?

Sab Sure.

Ali Are you seriously looking?

Sab Yeah.

Ali How do you think your partner would feel about you working late?

Sab He'd understand. I would, if he needed to.

Ali I guess he would.

Quite a long pause. **Sab** *feels uncomfortable under* **Ali***'s intense stare.*

Sab What do you do in your spare time?

Ali Read, mainly history. Play football, go to the gym, do some voluntary work. You?

Sab The same, not football really.

Ali Not really?

Sab Unless England is playing.

Ali 'Come on England!' Even I head into a pub at that time of year.

Sab The vibe's great! Shame it's not like that all year round.

Ali I wouldn't know. Pubs are just a work or football thing for me.

Sab Oh, right.

Pause.

Ali How religious are you?

Sab I never know how to answer that question. I mean, how do you measure religiousness?

Ali Do you pray?

Sab Sometimes.

Ali Do you drink?

Sab *looks round as if she wants to escape.*

Sab What is this, the Spanish Inquisition?

Ali I'm just interested.

Silence.

Have you ever been in a relationship?

Sab What?

Ali Have you ever been out with someone?

Sab I don't see how that's any of your business.

Ali I just can't believe someone with your looks and dress hasn't –

Sab Hasn't what?

Pause. **Ali** *tries to choose his words carefully.*

Ali – attracted the attention of the opposite sex.

Sab Right. (*Beat.*) What about you?

Ali What about me?

Sab Have you ever 'attracted the attention of the opposite sex'?

Ali I don't think I'm going to answer that question.

Sab Then neither am I.

Pause.

Ali I think you'd look great in an Asian suit. Do you wear them?

Sab That's a stupid question. Of course I do, sometimes.

Ali I'm glad you said that. (*Pause.*) So, Sabrina what's your favourite food?

Sab Why?

Bell rings.

Ali I would love to take you to dinner, anywhere you like. It was really intriguing meeting you.

Beat. He stares at her and takes out his card from his jacket pocket.

I know this is against the process, but take my card. Call me.

Ali *exits.* **Sab** *is left by herself. She looks at the card in her hand.*

Sab What the fuck.

Beat. A buzzer goes. Zain comes up.

Zain Come on. Give me your matches, we've got to hand them in, they're going to email us by the end of the day.

Sab *breathes a sigh of relief, looks at the match list in her hand and begins to rip it up.* **Zain** *pulls it from her hand before she can do much damage.*

Zain What are you doing? (*He looks at the match list.*) You haven't ticked anyone. Give me that pen.

He takes her pen and ticks all boxes.

Sab Zain, it's not your email they're getting.

Zain We need to know who got the most matches, remember. So what happened with Mr Cute?

Sab Nothing.

Zain Nothing?

Sab He was a moron.

Zain Ah, the condition of the Asian man! Thank God exceptions such as me exist. Shall we mingle?

Sab Not here.

Zain Come on then, Bridget, I'll grab a bottle from the newsagent's and then we can check who the real heartthrob is.

Blackout.

Scene Two

Back at the flat. **Sab** *is looking at the laptop,* **Zain** *is standing drinking with a glass of wine.*

Sab I can't believe it!

Zain Did I get more interest then you?

Sab (*looking at the laptop*)   Mr Cute!

Zain He ticked you!

Sab He was such a creep.

Zain He wasn't bad-looking and he ticked you!

Sab He was fucking intense.

Zain Fucking intense can be good, really good.

Sab He was the *haram* police.

Zain Shame. They come in all disguises. He so didn't look the type. Are you sure you're not just – [*being paranoid*]?

Sab (*ironically*)　　Great!

Zain What?

Sab He's emailed me.

Zain Already!

He pushes her aside, picks up the laptop and walks around the flat, reading the following in a sensual tone.

'Dear Sabrina, it was delightful meeting you, don't forget to call me.' (*He wolf-whistles.*) There's no number.

Sab He gave me his card.

Zain You never said! God, he's keen. Call him.

Sab (*patronising tone*)　　Yeah, right, Zee, I'm really going to call him.

Zain A one-night stand with a misogynist could be fun.

Sab *chucks pillow at him.* *He ducks.*

Zain You're such a prude. You should really let loose.

Sab What, just sleep with anyone?

Zain It's worked for me. Made me less grumpy.

Sab *chucks another pillow at him.* **Zain** *ducks, his attention to the laptop barely affected.*

Zain Ooh, that cute little girl in the *shalwar kameez* ticked me. I may not be marrying you after all.

Sab Great! Destined to solitude.

Zain What exactly do you want, Sab?

Sab You know what I want.

Zain What?

Sab Come on.

Zain Seriously.

Sab Just a normal guy.

Zain There's plenty out there.

Sab I just wish they were Muslim.

Zain Stick to wanting diamonds.

Sab I just want someone with a pulse and a brain. And that's hard to find round here.

Zain So log onto shaadi.com

Sab More like shag-me.com. I said pulse and brain. Can you imagine the guys that I'll meet there? Like the midget firefighter Fatimah met. Five foot four in his stockinged feet and obsessed with his sister-in-law – 'Oh, she's the perfect lady!' Anyway, I did try shaadi.com.

Zain You never told me! I didn't know it got that bad!

Sab Yeah, well, why would you tell anyone? I only did it for about five minutes. I was attracting the wrong types. I was attracting the really religious types, God knows why.

Zain Just face it: you want to marry a white guy.

Sab Marry a white guy when there's millions of Pakis about? My mother would just love that.

Zain Rage, rage against the machine.

Sab *looks at him.*

Zain OK, it's not easy, but make a stand.

Beat.

Sab Don't you ever wish – [*you could tell your parents*]?

Zain All the time, Sab.

Sab I'm just tired.

Zain You're getting old.

Sab Look who's talking!

Zain I'm a man – I have a longer shelf life.

Sab Do you think I'm past my sell-by date?

Zain Look, when you hit thirty, just stick on a scarf. Your marriage rating would go up –

Sab Exponentially.

Zain And you wouldn't have to bother with your GHD straighteners any more. Seriously – you haven't got much time left. The sell-by date is two or three years after uni. More if you do a Master's.

Sab You get a longer shelf life if you do a Master's? I might do one!

Zain You might need to – my sister's getting married.

Sab She's only twenty-one! Mubarak.

Zain You can be so traditional and blonde sometimes. Asian weddings are a pain, especially if you're single.

Sab Tell me about it.

Zain Who do you think will be in the firing line for the whole wedding? (*Beat.*) That's why you're coming.

Sab Nice try. But I'm not coming.

Zain It's a wedding, you love weddings.

Sab I'm not going as your dummy girlfriend.

Zain Who said anything about – ?

Sab I don't want your mum thinking I'm the reason why you won't marry the plethora of girls she's paraded in front of you.

Zain It's not like I haven't offered. I keep saying –

Sab Marry you. I just might.

Blackout.

Scene Three

Zain *is pacing up and down outside a building in central London.*

Zain Roll me a joint.

Mark You'll smell.

Zain She's bloody late.

Mark It's not unusual.

Zain Give me a cigarette.

Mark *lights cigarettes for himself and* **Zain**.

Mark Why don't we go in without her?

Zain I'm running the bloody thing tonight –

Mark She'll be fine to meet us there.

Zain I wanted her to check the roles I allocated. Let's go in. (*Smokes cigarette indecisively.*) We'll give her five minutes.

Both smoke their cigarettes.

This is the first bloody two-day festival we're organising. I just want it to be good.

Mark It will be. She cares about the cause just as much as you do.

Zain She promised she'd be on time.

Mark There's nothing we can do about that now. Let's go in.

Zain I'm going to put her with the scholar's son.

Mark Don't do that.

Zain I'm gonna make her regret it.

Mark She's only a few minutes late.

Zain It'll teach her a lesson.

Mark She'll kill you.

Zain No pain, no gain. A little bit of suffering might improve her timekeeping. Let's get this show on the road.

Zain and Mark move off. A few seconds later Sab runs on in a pair of jeans and a jacket. She walks in on Zain, giving his speech. The crowd is mixed. She finds Mark and stands next to him.

Zain The event will take place eight weeks from today, so we haven't got long. I've designated everyone in pairings to cater to our strengths. Remember, the more people that come, the more awareness we raise about the injustices occurring in the West Bank and the more money we raise for the orphanage. There'll be a fashion show, a photography exhibition and a gala dinner. Guys, every *job* is a self-portrait of the person who *does it*, so let's autograph this event with our excellence.

Round of applause.

Sab He's not pissed off, is he?

Mark I calmed him down.

Sab (*gives him a kiss on the cheek*) I knew there was a reason why I loved you. Do you know what I'm doing in regards to the event?

Mark The fashion show. Sab, don't go mad, but as you were late Zain's put you with this guy –

Reza Excuse me.

Mark Hi.

Reza I was sent here by the organiser, Zah, Zahid … ?

Mark Zain.

Reza I'm Reza Qureishi, and you're Sabrina Khan, right?

Sab Yeah.

Reza Great, I've been allocated to help you organise the fashion show.

Sab The fashion show?

Reza Yes.

Sab With me?

Reza Yes.

Sab Fabulous. Have you done this kind of thing before?

Reza I've helped with events, not really a fashion show.

Mark There's a first time for everything.

Sab (*to* **Mark**) There really is.

Reza I was a bit surprised to be assigned it, but Zain thought I'd be just what you needed.

Sab Right, did he? If you're uncomfortable with the role, we can always ask –

Reza I don't mind – it'll be a good challenge.

Sab Yeah, it will.

Reza Is this your first fashion – [*show too*]?

Sab (*shakes her head*) I'm an events organiser. I'm feeling a little thirsty, I might just –

Mark Let me get you that drink.

Sab Thanks.

Reza An events organiser. That's unusual for an Asian girl.

Sab Not really.

Reza It must be very creative.

Sab It is.

Reza I envy you. You're really lucky.

Sab (*surprised*) Really?

Reza To create something different every time. I miss that in my job.

Sab What do you do? No, no, let me guess. You're in a suit, you could be a consultant.

Reza In IT, perhaps?

Sab A little too arrogant for IT.

Reza I'm not arrogant.

Sab You're not *arrogant* arrogant, so you're not a solicitor. I'd say an accountant.

Reza Impressive.

Sab The choice of occupations is limited.

Reza *laughs.*

Sab So, you work for PWC?

Reza Deloitte. (*Beat.*) You didn't settle on accountant because you thought I was boring?

Sab Now you mention it –

They both laugh.

I'm sure all the Asian mums and dads are glad you're an accountant.

Reza You don't approve of my job?

Sab I'm sure you're very good at it.

Pause.

Reza Are you Pakistani?

Sab Yeah, why?

Reza I wasn't sure. You're quite fair, you could be Arab.

Sab We're from the North West Frontier.

Reza That explains it then.

Sab I gathered you were Pakistani.

Reza It seems I'm an open book.

Sab It seems you are.

Zain *walks in with* **Mark**.

Zain Ah, Sabrina.

Sab Ah, Zain!

Zain Great, you found each other. Sab's a real star to work with, but you'll have to watch out for her timekeeping.

Sab Zain!

Zain It's true.

Reza As long as we reach the end goal, I'm sure we can compromise on the timekeeping.

Mark I couldn't agree more – compromise is key.

Sab If only they thought like that in the Middle East, but I guess once you feel that you've been unjustifiably wronged, all you can think about is revenge.

Zain If both sides didn't keep breaking their promises they wouldn't be in this mess.

Reza It's terrible.

Zain It is.

Sab If the retaliation to the crimes was proportionate you could understand.

Mark I'm sure both parties think they're justified.

Sab I just don't know if there can be peace in those circumstances.

Reza Forgiveness is the better option.

Shades 181

Sab You're right, there are other methods like Gandhi, passive resistance, an organised campaign of non-cooperation.

Zain Non-cooperation?

Sab Imagine the person you regularly confide in, shop with, stops hanging about with you for a few months.

Zain A few months.

Sab You'd give in to their demands.

Reza I'm not sure that strategy would work in the Middle East. On a personal level, sure, when my sister gives her husband the cold shoulder, he can't stand it for more than a few days. He has to apologise and take her to dinner in a nice restaurant as well.

Mark Does that keep the peace?

Reza *Alhumdillah.*

Sab I'm not sure that'd work for me.

Beat.

Zain I guess the best always demand more.

Reza Don't tell my sister that. There'll be no – [*pleasing her*].

His phone beeps, and he quickly reads a text message.

I'm sorry, Sabrina, do you mind if we exchange numbers? My friend will be arriving in a bit, we're gonna go pray. It'll be the easiest way to get in contact.

Zain What, praying?

Reza No, phoning.

Mark He was joking.

She gives **Reza** *her phone. He types his number in and hands it back.*

Sab I'll call you now.

Reza's *phone rings once only.*

Sab Have you got it?

Reza *looks at his phone. While he is distracted* **Ali** *walks up behind him and taps him on the shoulder.*

Ali I thought I'd come and get you, otherwise we're gonna miss … prayer.

Reza I'll just be a minute. I'm just gonna save Sabrina's number. Everyone, this is Ali.

Ali *nods his head in acknowledgement and then extends his hand to* **Sab** *for a handshake.* **Sab** *reluctantly takes it.* **Reza** *is deep in his phone.*

Ali Nice to meet you. (*To* **Sab**.) I believe we've met before.

Sab Very briefly.

Zain Wasn't it for three minutes, to be exact?

Reza We better be going, but it was nice meeting you all. *Khudafiz.*

Ali *Khudafiz.* (*He looks at* **Sab**.)

The spotlight follows **Reza** *and* **Ali** *as they leave.* **Ali** *gives* **Reza** *a quizzical look.*

Reza Did they say you've met before?

Ali In passing.

Reza At least one of us will know what we're doing – she's an events organiser.

Ali So you'll be working with her for the next few weeks.

Reza Yeah.

Ali That's great, really great.

Blackout.

Shades 183

Scene Four

Reza's *house.* **Reza** *is sitting watching TV surrounded by a few magazines. He seems engrossed. He turns one of the magazines on its side and closely inspects it as if he can't believe what he's seeing. Footsteps arrive behind him. He quickly tries to hide the magazine. Enter* **Nazia**, *wearing a headscarf.*

Nazia I thought you might be thirsty. What are you up to?

Reza Nothing.

Nazia Are you reading a magazine?

Reza It's something for work.

Nazia Boring.

Reza Why is everyone saying that lately?

Nazia Are you reading *Vogue?*

Reza Where's Shoomie?

Nazia She's asleep.

Reza Shame.

Nazia More like *alhumdillah.* The terrible twos are a nightmare. She threw a tantrum in Tesco's.

Reza Why?

Nazia I wouldn't buy her yet another Barbie.

Reza Did she get her way, though?

Nazia Yeah.

Reza So she's already taking after you then.

Nazia Are you sure that's not *Vogue?* Let me have a look.

Reza It's just boring work – *[stuff]*.

Nazia Reza!

A pause he hands over Vogue

Reza It's for research, Bhaj.

Nazia Is that what they're calling it these days?

Reza It's for this charity event.

Nazia I thought your charity was raising money, not looking at naked women.

Reza I'm organising a fashion show.

Nazia You? (*She laughs.*)

Reza Yeah.

Nazia I thought you were going to do something sensible like design leaflets, PR.

Reza The guy who organised it seemed to have made this meticulous plan and I didn't want to disrupt things.

Nazia I hope you're not gonna – (*Taps the magazine.*)

Reza Of course not! I was just trying to get ideas so I actually know something and I'm not a hindrance.

Nazia Speaking of hindrances, I need a favour.

Reza What?

Nazia I was wondering if you would help wallpaper the house. Mum's offered, but –

Reza Mum's offered – (*He starts to laugh.*)

Nazia You saw what she did with the living room.

He laughs a little harder.

Reza Modern art – it's all the rage.

Nazia Reza.

Reza I'm really sorry, Bhaj, I can't. I've made plans to help out on this charity gig.

They turn round as the door opens and **Ali** *walks in.*

Nazia Ali, *salaam alakum*.

Ali Bhaji, *walakum salaam*.

Nazia How are you?

Ali Good, *alhumdillah*, busy with work.

Nazia So, you're not like Reza then – he has plenty of time on his hands.

Ali Really?

Nazia He's taken up reading –

Reza Bhaji!

Nazia He makes a good point, it's not really reading.

She chucks **Ali** *the copy of Vogue.*

Ali You're reading *Vogue*?

He flicks through the magazine and stares appreciatively at some of the shots.

Reza It's research for the fashion show.

Ali I wouldn't worry, Bhaji, the three most beautiful women I know are in this house.

Nazia *laughs.*

Nazia I'm surprised that silver tongue hasn't got you in trouble.

Ali I'm only commenting on the great beauty that Allah has created. A *sharif* boy like me only tells the truth. Don't worry, I'll make sure he isn't led astray.

Reza I can hear you, you know. I am in the room.

Nazia Yeah, look out for him, he is a bit trusting.

Ali Simple. Yeah.

Reza We can't all be as complex as you.

Nazia *Borhat mast hai.* I'm going to leave you to it. Do you want some tea, Ali?

Ali I'm cool, Bhaj.

Nazia *exits.*

Reza I can't believe what you get away with saying to my sister.

Ali Watch and learn.

Reza How's work?

Ali Big project, you know the score.

Reza Yeah.

Ali If all goes well, I'll be promoted. And get out of auditing at long last.

Reza Fantastic!

Ali So how's all with you?

Reza Work's fine, it's just this fashion show.

Ali We're still on for Friday evening, though?

Reza Of course.

Ali Great, all the guys are coming.

Reza Even Tariq?

Ali Yeah, even Tariq. Who's well under the thumb. Sometimes I don't know who the man is in that relationship. Poor sod – he thought he was safe marrying the village girl from back home … How wrong could he be? So, how's it going? (*Gesturing at the magazine.*)

Reza We're meeting this weekend to discuss themes. (*Tapping on* Vogue.) But this isn't really helping with sensible ones.

Ali It's about the Middle East – why not the dress of the Muslim world?

Reza Great idea.

Ali Do you think so?

Reza Yeah, I might mention it to her. Thanks, Ali.

Ali Cool.

Reza *gets out his laptop.*

Ali Rez, do you think it's too late to get involved?

Reza With what?

Ali The charity event.

Reza That'd be great.

Ali Yeah, and it'll all be in a good cause.

Blackout.

Scene Five

A coffee shop. **Reza** *and* **Sab** *at a table scattered with papers and photos.* **Reza** *is in a suit,* **Sab** *is in a knee-length skirt.* **Sab** *is making notes.*

Sab You think that should be the theme?

Reza Yeah, it just came to me. I thought it fitted with the cause.

Sab Really?

Reza (*hesitant*) Yeah, I mean –

Sab It's bad enough the media has defined all Palestinians as Muslims they're Christian, Druze, atheists ...

Reza Right. I didn't think.

Sab I just hate the way everyone tries to simplify things.

Reza I guess we better go back to the drawing board.

Sab It should be lively and fun.

Reza Yeah.

Sab Something for everyone, inclusive not exclusive.

Reza Sure.

Sab Something that says 'summer'.

Reza Right.

Sab Beachwear.

Reza Beachwear?

Sab Uh-huh, you know – kaftan, summery skirts, bikinis. (*Beat.*) What do you say?

Reza It's an idea.

Sab A good one.

Reza Don't you think … ?

Sab What?

Reza Some people might –

Sab 'Might'?

Reza – think that's more bare than wear. (*Beat.*) And if my parents are coming, I wouldn't be able to lift my head for the shame. I don't really want to be associated with –

Sab I was winding you up.

Reza Right.

Sab I was actually thinking we could do the ultimate in glamour and kitsch. Bring two worlds together.

Reza Kitsch?

Sab As in bad taste. (*Pause.*) You know, the plastic flowers mums decorate the living rooms with. Eastern kitsch meets Western ironic cool.

Reza (*laughs*) God, yeah.

Sab So, people can come in a whole range of styles.

Shades 189

Reza It's a good idea.

Sab We can have the standard three sections – daywear, evening wear and matrimonial. I was thinking that maybe we could get some –

Sound of text message arriving. **Reza** *gets his phone.*

Reza (*reads*) Ali. Can't make it.

Sab Shame.

Reza He says to apologise and hopes he will be able to help out soon. He's working on this big project.

Sab (*relieved*) You should really tell him not to stress himself out – we're fine without him.

Reza I've made a start on the leaflets and posters. It'd be best for our budget if we went for black and white.

Sab I'd rather we had colour. Different colours to attract the eye –

Reza The more colours you have, the more expensive it gets.

Sab How about we have a few shades? Black and white is so amateur.

Reza We're gonna have to cut the cost somewhere else.

Sab Let's do that. Models – know anyone we could recruit?

Zain *walks in.*

Zain Hiya guys. Taking my name in vain?

Sab 'Vain' being the operative word.

Reza *Salaam alakum.*

Zain *Walakum salaam.*

Sab What are you doing here?

Zain I thought I'd see how you were doing.

190   Contemporary English Plays

Sab   I was just asking Reza if he knew any models for the fashion show; we should get them early.

They share a look of amusement. **Reza** *notices.*

Zain   That's a good idea.

Sab   So?

Beat.

Reza   Actually, I might.

Zain   Really?

Sab   Great, who?

Reza   Some sisters from the Islamic centre would really be interested.

Sab   Sisters.

Reza   They'd love it, walking down the catwalk in the latest *jilbabs*.

Zain   *Jilbabs.*

He looks at **Sab** *as if to say, how could you let this happen.*

Reza   Yeah, I mean, surely we're going have a few in the show.

Sab   I don't think that really fits the theme.

Reza   We could have green, red, yellow – they'll get to flaunt their ankles. I thought we were going to cater for everyone.

Sab   I don't think –

Reza   It's financially viable. We'd make a killing. There'll be sisters in our audience and we can't let down all two of them, it would be – (*beginning to laugh*) a tragedy.

Sab   You're winding me up?

Reza (*laughs*)   Taste of your own medicine.

Zain   It was a joke.

Reza The tickets I can take care of. Just tell me what you want.

A **Waitress** *approaches.*

Waitress I'm sorry, but we're closing in fifteen minutes.

Reza/Sab Thanks.

Reza Maybe we should continue this tomorrow.

Sab I'm working.

Reza Thurs—

Sab I won't be free until Saturday.

Reza We need to decide the tickets, logo, colour. Shall we go somewhere else?

Sab I think Brick Lounge is open.

Reza I'd rather not go anywhere where's there's alcohol.

Zain (*touches his head as if he has remembered his migraine*) I know what you mean.

Sab We can go back to mine. It's only fifteen mins away.

Reza To yours?

Sab Yeah, you and Mark are going to the cinema, right?

Zain Yeah.

Reza We'd be alone.

Sab Yeah. We can get some work done. Without having to suffer Zain's music taste for once.

Reza I don't think it would be appropriate.

Sab What?

Reza I don't think it would be appropriate.

Sab Are you winding me up?

Reza *shakes his head.*

Sab OK.

Reza Perhaps we should discuss it over lunch one day this week.

Sab Sure.

Reza I'll email you to know what lunchtimes are best for me.

Sab OK.

Reza *Khudafiz.*

Sab Bye.

Zain See you.

Reza *exits.*

Zain I didn't know times were that desperate.

Sab What?

Zain You just propositioned a brother.

Sab I didn't.

Zain (*mimics* **Sab**) 'Why don't you come back to my place, we'll be alone.'

Sab To work.

Zain 'Would you like me to seduce you?' Do the words boy, girl and chaperone when not in public ring a bell?

Sab Oh God!

Zain Poor guy, you probably had him running out of here with a hard-on.

Sab Zain!

Zain You really should be more sensitive – he's probably had no sexual experience.

Sab Zain!

Zain What? I wasn't the one behaving like the local slapper.

Sab I'm gonna have to see him again with him thinking –

Zain Shut up, Sab. That's what I think the real problem is with these fundos.

Sab What?

Zain If they weren't so busy denying their sexual frustration, they'd lose all that aggression and forget about *shariah*.

Sab (*sarcastic*) Let's turn Planet Earth into one giant orgy.

Zain I'll have you know a man can go crazy from sexual deprivation. I came to make sure he hadn't declared *jihad* on you.

Sab (*laughs*) I hate you when you're hungover.

Blackout.

Scene Six

An array of clothes on hangers. **Sab** *takes off a few and puts them in front of her as if she is looking in a mirror trying them on. She picks up a long dress and begins to sway and then twirl around in it, humming a tune.* **Sab** *does not realise* **Reza** *has come back from praying. He coughs to let her know of his presence.* **Sab** *jumps and stops what she is doing.*

Sab That was quick.

Reza Five times every day, it gets like that.

Sab *goes back to looking through the clothes.*

Reza What were you doing?

Sab Looking through the clothes.

Reza Were you dancing?

Sab I was trying to imagine how the clothes would look down the catwalk. Nothing wrong with that.

Reza No, there isn't.

Sab I guess we better get on with picking what we actually want. Everything on that rail is a 'no', on this a 'yes'.

They work in silence. **Reza** *flicks through a few things and picks out a male T-shirt.*

Reza (*badly pronounced*)   L'état, c'est moi!

Sab 'I am the state.'

Reza What?

Sab '*L'état c'est moi*' – it means, 'I am the state.'

Reza You're really knowledgeable.

Sab I did French for A level.

Reza I was always really terrible at French.

Sab (*looking at the top*)   Definitely a 'yes'. And that – is definitely a 'no'.

She goes to put the top on the 'yes' rail. Meanwhile, **Reza** *notices a piece of paper. He picks it up, reads it.*

Reza You've written out the playlist.

Sab Yeah?

Reza I would have liked to have had a say.

Sab I didn't think it'd be your thing.

Reza Why?

Sab I didn't think you really listened to music.

Reza *begins to laugh.*

Sab What's so funny?

Reza You don't think I listen to music?

Sab No, I just thought with you being religious. You – [*didn't really listen to popular music*].

Reza Only listened to *nasheeds* and *qawwali*?

Shades 195

Beat.

Sab Most brothers don't listen to music, I just thought –

Reza I was a stereotype of a Muslim brother that you have in your head.

Sab I'm the last person to encourage stereotypes.

Reza The little digs, the constant worry I'd bring *shariah* to the stage. Not every brother wants to radicalise the world.

Beat.

Sab I'm sorry. I've been a bitch.

Reza You really do have a good command of French.

Sab *laughs.*

Reza I guess you have good reason to think that with Captain Hook and his gang running about.

Sab (*laughs*) You can be quite funny.

Reza I know.

Sab I guess I haven't had the best experience with Muslims.

Reza Why?

Sab They always seem to be telling you what you can't do and sending you to Hell for every little thing. Some Muslims have a superiority complex, and it doesn't matter if you're Muslim, you're not as good as them.

Reza We're not all like that.

Sab I know.

Reza I wish everyone else did.

Sab I guess I'm talking about my brother. (*Beat.*) Have you ever thought of shaving it off?

Reza After the first attacks, having it made me feel like somehow I colluded with them. That people would think I believed what they did. I felt let down because I felt I was being asked to choose between Britishness and being a Muslim, and it's never been separate for me. (*Beat.*) I'm the kind of person – and it's a very British characteristic – I'll always side with the underdog. The underdog at the moment is a Muslim, and in an ironic way, by standing up for Muslims, I think I'm being very British. Anyway. I did come close, but I realised it's just a beard, for me it doesn't mean any of those things, for me it means something else entirely.

Sab looks at Reza.

Sab It's weird, for me it was the other way round. My brother always used to go on and on about how I should dress more like an Asian girl. Wear a scarf on my head so people would know I was a decent girl. And I was like, I know girls who smoke, drink, sleep around, but no one thinks they have because they wear the *hijab*.

Reza *is about to speak, but* **Sab** *continues before he can say anything.*

Sab I know not all the girls are like that. It's really weird, but if my brother had told me to wear boob tubes and a miniskirt, I probably would have worn a headscarf and everything. I nearly wore it just to give my mum some peace from constantly stopping the battle between us.

Reza Why didn't you wear it?

Sab I think people should be judged for what they do, and then before I could, I got offered a place at uni and I left home. I'm not really a practising Muslim like you are.

Reza What –

Sab (*interrupting*) Like even at uni I felt more comfortable among the non-Muslims because they didn't think a skirt, or the sip of a drink, made me a bad person.

Reza You've drank?

Sab I know it's wrong but –

Shades 197

Reza What was it like?

Sab You want to know?

Reza I always wondered. When did you try it?

Sab First year of uni.

Reza What did you have?

Sab A lime Bacardi Breezer. And I had about six of them.

Reza You got drunk.

Sab Smashed. I just wanted to try it. The thing I absolutely hate about Islam is that everything is subject to interpretation. 'Consumption of alcohol is not permitted.' I'd like to know what the definition of 'alcohol' is. Like a few years ago we were told, don't wear perfume or deodorant with alcohol in it. That's just ridiculous. Now I'm hearing from my aunt, who is actually – I wouldn't say, 'by the book', more 'by the headline' –

Reza (*laughs*) 'By the headline', I like that –

Sab – say, 'You can't have drink in your medicines.' I said, 'Shame – whenever I needed that little something I'd just down the Benylin.'

Reza *laughs.*

Sab I guess I'm not really religious like you are.

Reza Why do you think that?

Sab I think you have to have a bit more of a pious nature.

Reza This is what I'm really interested by. A few minutes ago, you said I'm not really a practising Muslim.

Sab Yeah.

Reza And then you said I'm not really religious.

Sab Yeah.

Reza And now you're saying you have to be of a pious nature. I just want to know what makes someone a practising Muslim? And what's this 'pious nature'? How do you know that you don't have this pious nature?

Sab Look, all I'm saying is –

Reza No, I'm interested – someone who drinks, are they not really a practising Muslim? Because I know people who, let's say, dabble in drinking, but they also dabble a lot in praying.

Sab Then you're not repenting. You're going through a cycle that suits you, and your religion isn't supposed to suit you. A lifestyle is there to suit you, but not religion. If part of religion is sacrifice –

Reza So you're saying you have to sacrifice things to be a Muslim?

Beat.

Sab I don't know what I'm saying.

Reza (*jokey*) I think you're actually quite hard line.

Sab (*smiles*) I don't know the answer, and I don't care so long as I don't have to debate it. That's why I avoided the Islamic Society at university, because they will argue to death. Anyway. Being tipsy was nice, an escape to a wonderful place, but, trust me, you're not missing much.

Reza Sometimes, I wish I could escape everything.

Sab How?

Reza Go to the Amazon forest.

Sab The Amazon!

Reza It's always been a dream.

Sab It's really beautiful.

Reza You've been?

Sab Yeah. I'd always wanted to go since I was a teen and I went last year, Brazil. The whole thing was amazing.

Shades 199

Reza There's an exhibition on at the moment where you get to see all the early tools used in the Amazon.

Sab Where?

Reza At the Horniman Museum. Forest Hill.

Sab That's brilliant. I'll have to check it out.

Reza *laughs.*

Sab What?

Reza I don't know many girls who'd be that enthusiastic about seeing Amazonian tools. (*Beat.*) I'm thinking of going after one of the rehearsals, do you want to come? (*Beat.*) We can see if any of the other guys want to go?

Sab Sure, why not? It might be fun.

Blackout.

Scene Seven

Mark *and* **Sab** *sitting on the sofa.* **Sab** *is leaning against* **Mark***, her feet hanging over the sofa.* **Zain** *is sifting through a pile of CDs.*

Mark What's taking you so long?

Zain I can't find the CD! Sab, why do you never put them back where you find them?

Sab Because I'm not anal like you are.

Zain I'm not anal. Have you any idea how long it took me to put them all into alphabetical order!

Mark I told you we should have moved on to Fire.

Zain Yeah, and spent twenty quid on a cab home? We have to work on the charity event tomorrow, anyway. You guys would have just whinged about the music once you started coming down.

Sab Can we just dance?

Mark I think that CD's upstairs.

Zain I'll go get it.

He exits.

Sab It was a good night.

Mark And it's not ending yet. A few more dances to –

Sab Hits of the eighties and nineties.

Mark I really like that new Madonna song.

Sab You just fancy her because she looks like a blok

He begins to sing a Madonna lyric. **Sab** *joins in.*

Sab Hurry up, Zain!

Mark I don't know why he arranged to meet the food suppliers on a Sunday. It's meant to be the bloody day of rest.

Sab *groans.*

Sab I don't think I'll be able to cope.

Mark Maybe we should get some sleep. How's it going with son of a preacher man?

Sab His name's Reza.

Mark (*laughs*) I'd forgotten, especially with the nickname.

Sab He's not as bad as I thought.

Mark So no more digs at Zain.

Sab I can't promise no more ever.

Mark (*laughs*) That would really be a miracle.

Pause as they listen to music.

Sab Mark.

Mark Yeah?

Sab Nothing.

Mark What?

Sab Have you ever liked someone you never imagined liking?

Mark Yeah, why?

Sab Nothing. I was just wondering.

Mark *looks at* **Sab**. *He gets up.*

Mark Do you like someone? **Sab** *shakes her head.*

Mark You like someone. (*Beat.*) Oh my fucking Lord!

Sab What? **Mark** Admit it.

Sab What?

Mark You fancy him!

Sab Who?

Mark Son of a preacher man.

Sab No, I don't.

Mark I know you, Sab. Admit it.

Sab Maybe a little.

Mark I knew it, I knew it. Sabrina has a crush, Sabrina has a crush. ZAIN, ZAIN, Sabrina –

Sab *tries to stop* **Mark** *from calling out to* **Zain**.

Sab Don't –

Mark Why not? This is big – weird but big.

Sab I don't want him to know.

Mark You tell him everything.

Sab This is different.

Mark Why?

Sab It's not supposed to happen.

Mark You can't help who you fancy.

Sab I don't fancy him, it's just a little crush.

Mark Zain will be pleased.

Sab He'll think I've lost the plot. I think I've lost the plot.

Mark It's OK to fancy someone.

Sab But not him.

Mark You can't help who you fancy.

Sab You don't understand –

Mark Tell me what you like about him.

Sab He's funny, really respectful – always opening doors and checking if I got home OK; making sure I'm safe not because he likes me, because he'd do that for anyone.

Mark The problem is?

Sab If anything was ever to happen, things would have to change. He'd expect me to give up certain things.

Mark You always have to compromise in relationships. For the moment just enjoy liking someone.

Sab I'm gonna get over it.

Mark You've barely given him a chance. (*Beat.*) Zain would tell you the same thing I am. You should give this a go. Go on, tell him.

Sab I will when there's something to tell.

Mark (*sighs*)   In the meantime don't be so quick to shut down.

Zain *comes down the stairs.*

Zain Shut down? You're not planning to go to bed, are you?

Sab No, I'm wide awake.

Zain Good, because I found the CD. Let's dance.

Shades 203

Blackout.

Scene Eight

Models rehearsing in clothes. Music playing in the background as they rehearse their walk etc. **Sab** *is giving them instructions.* **Reza** *walks in.*

Reza You started without me.

Sab We literally started.

Reza You could have waited. I was stuck in traffic.

Sab This way everyone gets home quicker.

Reza Are you OK?

Sab Yeah.

Reza You just seem a little out of sorts.

Sab I guess I'm still tired from the week I've had.

Beat.

Reza You didn't come to the exhibition.

Sab Work's still hectic

She hesitates slightly.

Reza If you want me to do more here

Sab It's fine. I just want these rehearsals to be efficient so we can all get home early.

Reza Right.

They watch the models.

Sab Great, guys, but can we get on our cues faster? We don't wanna be here all night.

Reza I'll drive you home.

Sab What?

Reza I was gonna give Ali a lift. I'll drop you off on the way.

Sab I'll be fine. (*Beat.*) I don't want to put you out.

Reza It'll spare you the tube journey. If you really want your cortisol levels to soar, the Northern Line'll do it for you nicely.

Sab I'll think about it.

Reza Are you annoyed with me?

Sab Why would I be?

Reza I don't know. *Beat.*

Sab I'm gonna go backstage and check everything's OK. You can keep an eye here.

Sab *goes, leaving* **Reza** *confused.* **Ali** *walks in carrying a book.*

Ali *Salaams!* I see it's all happening.

He smiles appreciatively at the models onstage.

Looks like it'll be a real good show. (*To a female model.*) Very professional.

Reza Thanks.

Ali Where's Sabrina?

Reza She's gone backstage to check on the models.

Ali Here's the leaflet, and I picked up that book. It's a bit obsessive asking me to bring it here.

Sab *walks in.*

Ali *Salaam alakum.*

Sab Hi.

Ali I was just saying to Reza, this is a slick show.

Reza We make a good team.

Silence. **Ali** *notices the awkwardness between* **Sab** *and* **Reza**.

Ali I brought the leaflets over for you to see.

He gives one out of the box to **Sab**.

Sab They're really good!

Ali Did Reza tell you about our escapades handing them out this weekend?

Reza I didn't get a chance.

Ali (*to* **Sab**) We drove and walked the whole of London. We handed out leaflets and posters to shops –

Reza Universities –

Ali Fashion colleges –

Reza Community centres –

Ali And in the midst of this we ended up in a museum in Forest Hill. Reza just wouldn't leave.

Reza You enjoyed the exhibits too. The hunting equipment, the giant anaconda –

Ali Which took all of five minutes. Three cigarette breaks later and he still wouldn't leave. I had to drag him out of there after an hour.

Sab *laughs.*

Ali I feel sorry for the girl you end up with, you'll bore her to death.

Reza No, I won't, I'll find a girl who likes the same things.

Ali (*shakes his head*) Women like the finer things in life, they'll want entertainment, excitement, luxury.

Reza That's not every girl's idea of fun. What do you think, Sab?

Beat.

Sab I have to agree with Ali.

Ali *smiles in satisfaction and gives* **Reza** *an 'I told you so' look.* **Reza** *is confused.*

Ali He even bought a book on the whole exhibit which he made me bring here. Reza, if you're not careful, you're gonna end up a geek.

A model shouts from out back.

Model Guys, I need a hand.

Sab *begins to leave but before she can do so overhears:*

Reza Ali, do you mind checking on her?

Ali Sure.

Exit **Ali**.

Reza Are you sure you're OK?

Sab I'm fine.

Reza Why didn't you turn up?

Pause.

Sab I don't know.

Beat.

Reza (*gives her a book*) I hope this will cheer you up a little bit and make up for the fact you missed the exhibit.

Sab You got this for me?

Reza I know it's not the exhibit but I thought it was unfair you missed out because of work.

Sab You shouldn't have.

She hesitates in opening the book.

Reza Don't you like it?

Sab I do, I really do. Thanks a lot.

Reza Are you sure you're OK?

Shades 207

Sab Yeah, this has really cheered me up, Reza.

Beat.

Reza Yeah.

Sab Do you mind if I do take that offer of a lift after all?

Blackout.

Scene Nine

Mark *is watching TV. He is dressed in a cowboy outfit in the living room.* **Zain** *walks in, half dressed and holding up two shirts.*

Zain Which one?

Mark *points to one.*

Zain That one? I wonder what Sab's doing. She's taking ages.

Mark I don't think she's feeling well.

Zain What? She was fine when she walked in. (*Calls out.*) Sab, Sab!

Mark I think we should just leave her to it.

Zain No way. We've had this planned for ages. We're meant to be escaping everything – the nine-to-five, fashion shows. Not after I've gone to all the trouble of buying her a present.

Mark That's really gonna make her want to come.

Zain At least she won't have to decide what to wear.

Sab *walks in*

Zain Aren't you ready yet?

Mark *and* **Sab** *share a look.*

Sab I know we had this planned, but I'm not feeling it. I may just stay home.

Zain Come here. (*He feels her forehead for a temperature.*) You don't seem ill.

Sab I just need the rest.

Zain Is it the time of the month?

Sab *hits* **Zain**.

Zain You go all weird around then. It's not PMT and not a temperature …

Sab I really need to catch up with stuff for the fashion show.

Zain No way – that wasn't the deal. Tell her, Mark.

Mark I'm not getting involved.

Zain You missed the last two nights out – hanging around with that brother seems to have gone to your head.

Sab The next one, I promise.

Zain I got you some pills.

Mark (*laughs*) I love the way you can justify taking pills and not alcohol.

Zain Don't encourage her. She's already jumped back on the wagon and, technically, the Qur'an says nothing about having a few Es.

Mark I thought the word intoxicant covered it.

Sab It doesn't matter, guys. I'm not in the mood.

Zain I bought you a costume.

Sab You bought me a costume?

Zain So you have to come! I'm gonna get it.

Zain *exits*.

Sab He bought me a costume?

Mark Yeah. Why don't you just tell him?

Mark I don't know how you're gonna get out of this without telling Zain – especially with him getting you a costume.

Sab What did he get me?

Mark (*laughing*) You're gonna find out in a bit.

Sab It's not a bunny outfit?

Mark I think you're safe.

Zain *walks in, holding in his hands an immaculately wrapped package with a pink bow round it. He gives it to* **Sab**.

Zain Open it.

Sab *looks at it.*

Zain Screw the wrapping, open it.

Sab *opens the package. She pulls out a jilbab, hijab and a veil – all black.*

Sab You're kidding.

Zain You like it?

Sab Funny, really funny.

Zain Go on, try it on.

Sab No way.

Zain Go on.

He tries putting it on her.

Sab Get off, get off. Mark, tell him.

Mark I'm not getting involved.

Zain Go on, it'll be a laugh.

Sab No way!

Zain Go on. Tell her, Mark.

Zain Go on.

Sab No.

Zain What a waste. (*Looking at* hijab.) Are you sure?

Sab *stares at him. He picks it up.*

Zain Be boring. I always wanted to know what it was like underneath this.

Mark And?

Zain I wouldn't imprison my beauty that way for the sake of any man. I'm going to get my hat.

Zain *exits.* **Mark** *hugs* **Sab**.

Mark It was a little funny. *Beat.*

Sab A little.

Mark Why not just make life easier on yourself and tell him?

Sab Not now.

Mark You have to tell him at some point.

Silence.

You shouldn't have made plans with him today.

Sab I felt bad, especially after I let him down by not going to the exhibition.

The Pussycat Dolls' 'Buttons' begins to play loudly. **Mark** *and* **Sab** *look at each other.* **Mark** *shrugs his shoulders as if to indicate he does not know what is happening.* **Zain** *walks in with the full jilbab on, wearing red heels. He struts as if on the catwalk, does a whirl, dances provocatively in front of* **Mark** *until he moves to* **Sab**, *whom he picks up and begins to dance with.* **Zain** *separates from her and starts to remove the outfit.*

Zain Come on, Sab, how you can resist it?

He strips off veil and throws it to her.

It's good practice for the future.

Sab He's not like that.

Beat.

Zain   He's why you're not coming tonight.

Sab   Like I said, we're behind schedule.

Zain   Do it tomorrow. Tell him you have to cancel. He'll understand.

Sab   He's on his way.

Zain   Here?

Sab (*nods*)   To pick me up.

Zain   You're going on a date!

Silence.

You actually like this brother. (*Beat.*) Tell me this is some sort of horrible Halloween joke.

Mark   It's good for Sab –

Zain   You're so deluded, Sab.

Sab   I'm just working with him.

Zain   So, you're not falling for him?

Sab   You put us together!

Zain   Not for you to fall for him. Are you falling for him?

Silence.

Answer the question!

Sab   Don't be stupid.

Zain   Great, so you can cancel on him.

Sab   He's on his way.

Mark   Zain, leave it. It's not a crime for her to fancy someone. Anyway, she doesn't want to come. We should go, we're going to be late.

Zain   It's a party, it's fucking expected.

Mark   She's made up her mind. We should go.

Zain Why aren't you surprised? (*Beat.*) Why aren't you surprised?

Mark What?

Zain Sab's just confessed to liking someone and you're not surprised, you're not – you knew. You knew about this and you didn't tell me.

Sab It's not Mark's fault. I made him promise not to say anything.

Zain We tell each other everything. We're meant to trust each other.

Pause.

Sab I was going to tell you, I swear –

Zain I can't believe you've got Muslim-girl syndrome.

Sab Fuck off, Zain.

Zain You're the one who's going to get your heart broken. (*Beat.*) Sure, he likes you now because you're all different and exciting, but what happens when you get married?

Sab No one's said anything about marriage.

Zain We both know that's where he thinks it's gonna lead, otherwise he wouldn't be going to dinner with you. Are you gonna give up everything for this guy?

Sab He's not like that.

Zain He's gonna let you wear skirts, club and hang round with *kafirs* like me when you go into his family home?

Sab Things I want have changed. I want someone to come home to too.

Zain Sure, you'll be the bad girl gone good, but in his family, you'll always be the girl who tempted him from someone better.

Mark Zain, that's enough.

Zain Do you want to end up in the same situation as your brother's wife? Thinking you're marrying the guy of your dreams but you end up limited to the whims of the community auntie? Staying married to someone you don't love … because of the neighbours next door?

Sab I don't want to talk about this, I'm gonna get changed. (*She begins to leave.*)

Zain Into your *shalwar kamees*?

Sab Is this how you're going to be?

Zain (*sincerely*) Maybe you're right, maybe he is the exception. You should have said, we could have done it properly – had a dinner party. (*Beat.*) To make him feel comfortable, we could have invited Osama, Abu Hamza, and while we're at it the whole of the Taliban. Then for dessert we could have a nice democratic vote about who they'd stone first, me or you. He's as bad as your fucking brother.

Sab Fuck you. I'm not staying to listen to this shit. This is my damn flat too and I'll invite who I want, *mujahidin* and all. (*To* **Mark**.) Will you let me know when you leave so I know it's safe to come down?

Sab *exits.*

Silence.

Zain Shall we go?

Silence.

You're right. No hurry. We should have a drink here instead.

He gets the drinks carrier bag, opens up the vodka, pours himself a large measure, and another which he hands to **Mark**.

Zain We'll have a couple here – get in the mood. Music, need some music. (*Puts some house music on.*) Cigarette?

He chucks a cigarette at **Mark**, *lights his own, downs his drink, then takes a long drag of his cigarette.*

Zain That feels good.

He begins to bop to the music. **Mark** *watches.*

Zain We should really get into the party mood. You want a pill now?

He continues to dance, gets bored, goes back to **Mark**.

Mark Maybe you should slow down.

Zain We're going to a party. We're meant to be having fun.

He takes a pill. **Mark** *just stares intently at* **Zain** *and drinks.*

Mark You were a little too much, Zain.

Zain I was a little too much.

Mark Why did you have to bring her brother into it? You know she hasn't spoken to him for years –

Zain You're meant to tell me everything, that's what partners do.

Beat.

Mark I know you're scared.

Zain Just leave it, Mark.

Mark I've been where you have.

Zain What, poor little white boy Mark? Did Mummy and Daddy not speak to you for a week, two, three?

Mark This is not about us.

Zain The big leap out the closet isn't a three-week fucking holiday from the family for me – it's a fucking *fatwa*.

Mark You're not the only fucking victim in the village, Zain. You need to lay off Sab, she's not the enemy.

Zain You have no idea what you're talking about!

Mark This is the first time in a long time she's liked someone.

Zain He's not right for her.

Mark You haven't given him a chance.

Zain I know what they're like. All politically correct to the outside world, but in their houses do you think they'd accept people like you and me? If Sab wants to be a part of that world she'll have to change.

Mark That's her choice.

Zain She'll stop hanging about with us.

Mark She loves you, Zain.

Zain Me or him. They always choose their husbands.

Silence.

Mark She's not Nadia.

Zain She'll have no choice.

Mark I know you're scared of losing her, but you can't –

Zain She's one of the few people who has never batted an eyelid. One of the few people I can speak to about you.

Mark You need to support her like she's supported you.

Silence.

You need to give him a chance for her.

Silence.

'I destroy my enemies when I make them my friends.'

Zain I'm off Americans at the moment.

Mark People are not black and white like the printed page of the Qur'an. Just as the words have many shades, so do people. 'We should not judge them as the ink first beholds our eye.'

Silence.

Do you remember writing that?

Beat.

216   Contemporary English Plays

Zain Maybe you're right. Maybe I should give him a chance before I crucify him, but not tonight. We have a party to go to.

Mark And Sab?

Zain I'll apologise to her when she's calmer.

Mark Make sure you don't fall out over this.

Zain Shall we go before he turns up and the pill kicks in? Can you imagine me meeting him high?

They both laugh.

Let her know it's safe to come down.

Mark Sab, we're leaving, babe, and Zain says he's sorry.

The men exit. As the door slams, **Sab** *walks back into the centre of the room and sits on the sofa. She picks up the hijab and looks at it. She puts the cloak and the veil in the bag, but hesitates when it comes to the hijab. She walks to the mirror with it in her hand and tentatively tries it on. She looks at herself in the mirror.*

Blackout.

Scene Ten

Reza's *house.* **Reza** *typing on his laptop.* **Ali** *walks in.*

Ali Why you down here?

Reza Needed the peace.

Ali You missed Friday dinner with the lads.

Reza I know, we needed to concentrate on the fashion –

Ali How come I didn't get a call?

Reza It was a little last-minute. **Ali** *gets out a cigarette and lights it.*

Ali You need to take a break. If I didn't know you better I'd think the cause here was the girl, not Palestine.

A look of guilt passes **Reza***'s face.*

Reza I think she's got something, Ali.

Ali (*shocked*) Something?

Reza Yeah. She's intelligent, funny, passionate about justice in the world. (*Beat.*) She's really quite Islamic.

Ali What are you saying?

Reza I think she's the one. (*Beat.*) I did the *isthi'hara*!

Ali The *isthi'hara*! You only do that when you want to – It's that serious.

Reza I got a good sign.

Ali That's great, that's really great. Did you have a dream, a feeling?

Reza A dream.

Ali Wow. Dream. Nice one. Well, there's no arguing with that.

Reza I want the family to meet her.

Ali You're going to get married.

Reza *Inshallah.*

Ali Does she even like you?

Reza *nods.* **Ali** *puffs harder on his cigarette.*

Ali Have you asked her?

Reza (*shakes his head*) She knows I'm not the kind of guy to get close to her if I didn't see a future; it wouldn't be right.

Ali Right, wow. I can't believe she – I mean, I never would have thought she'd be the kind of girl you'd want to marry.

Reza It's funny what Allah has in store for you.

Ali It's great. It's good news. Have you spoken to Auntie, Uncle, Nazia?

Reza I thought I'd introduce them after the fashion show.

Ali Right. This is good news. Exciting. God, you're so brave.

Reza Brave?

Ali I mean, I don't know how I would bring home a girl.

Reza What?

Ali I mean, *ammi*, all she needs is the tiniest reason to reject anyone. (*Asian accent.*) 'Marriage is not just about two people, Ali.' (*Beat.*) You're lucky your parents aren't like that. Hey, what's with the face? They'll love her.

Reza She's not what they would have imagined.

Ali What matters is what's in here. (*He taps his heart.*) They'll see what you see. (*Beat.*) You just have to introduce her the right way.

Reza Yeah, you're right.

Ali Warm them up to her before they meet. Why don't you invite her to the talk on Thursday?

Reza At the Islamic centre?

Ali Bhaji will be there. Introduce her as your work colleague; let her make a good impression on Bhaj independently. Bhaj will love her for being at the talk when she finds out about the charity work.

Reza That's a great idea.

Ali Bhaj's a good judge of character.

Reza Yeah, she is.

Ali I'll whisper good things in her ear.

Reza Thanks, Ali, you're a real mate.

Ali *waves his hands as if to say, don't be silly.*

Ali I better start organising your stag do.

Shades 219

Reza It's not official yet.

Ali I can still plan.

Reza I'm not gonna get any work done, am I? I'll put this away and be back.

He exits with laptop, **Ali** *is left alone onstage. He lights another cigarette and smokes, deep in thought.* **Nazia** *enters with a tray of tea and biscuits.*

Ali Bhaji.

Nazia I bought you some *chai*. (*Begins pouring into cups.*)

Ali You're a mind-reader.

Nazia *hands* **Ali** *his tea. He drinks it.*

Ali You make a beautiful cup, *mashallah*. If you weren't married, your tea alone would make me propose.

Nazia *laughs.*

Nazia Your tongue is sweeter than sugar. Have a biscuit.

Ali Bhaji.

Nazia Yes.

Ali How's Reza been?

Nazia I've barely seen him these past few weeks – he leaves early in the morning and returns when I've gone home. (*She pats her stomach.*) I get tired easily these days. He's OK?

Ali He's fine.

Nazia Why the question?

Ali I think he's falling for someone.

Nazia Reza! Who?

Ali This girl he's working on the fashion show with.

Nazia Sabrina?

Ali He's spoken about her?

Nazia He mentioned her briefly at dinner. We should book tickets for the show. What is she like? (*Beat.*) Ali, tell me!

Ali She's nice.

Nazia *Alhumdillah!* My little brother has been keeping secrets, that's not like him. He must like her a lot.

She laughs, but sees a worried expression cross **Ali***'s face.*

Nazia What's wrong?

Ali Nothing.

Nazia Don't worry, marriage won't change things between you. It's time he – [*was settling down*].

Ali It's not that, Bhaji.

Nazia What is it? (*Beat.*) Ali?

Ali I'm not sure he's making the right choice.

Nazia *Kyu?*

Ali I don't think I should say this.

Nazia Ali.

Ali Bhaji, I can't.

Nazia *Bole*, I've known you since you were a baby.

Beat.

Ali You have to promise not to tell Reza.

Nazia You have my word.

Ali I don't wish to taint anyone's reputation, but Sabrina …

Nazia What is it?

Ali She hit on me.

Nazia Sabrina?

Ali   I had to push her off me.

Nazia   No.

Ali *nods in shame.*

Nazia   Have you told Reza?

Ali   He doesn't know.

Nazia   You should tell him.

Ali   He won't listen to me.

Nazia   Of course he will.

Ali   I tried to warn him off lightly in other ways. I pointed out she's a clubber, lives with two men, but – (*He shakes his head as if he can speak no further.*)

Nazia   Reza knows all this?

Ali (*nods*)   Perhaps she will change after marriage.

Nazia   I can't believe Reza would like someone like that. I'll speak to him.

Ali   No, Bhaji, then he will know I have interfered. Maybe you should meet her yourself before Reza introduces her to the family.

Nazia   But how?

Ali   She's coming to the talk this Thursday. You can see her then.

Nazia   Thanks, Ali, thanks a lot.

Blackout.

Scene Eleven

An Islamic talk. **Sab** *is facing the audience. She joins in a round of applause, and as she does so looks around. She is clearly nervous.* **Zain** *approaches from* **Sab**'s *blind spot. He is wearing sunglasses. He puts his hand on* **Sab** *shoulder, and she jumps.*

Sab What are you doing here?

Zain You know me, there's no other way I'd like to spend an evening than to be at an Islamic talk. The glamour. Can't keep me away from them.

Beat. They share an awkward silence. Mark told me what was happening.

Sab So?

Zain I thought you might need a friend. (*Beat.*) I know things haven't been great between us, but I wouldn't torture myself like this for just anyone.

Sab Thanks.

Zain Don't be silly. I could hardly pass up the opportunity of seeing you meet the holy crew. This is way too good to miss.

They both laugh.

Sab I'm sorry I never said anything about Reza. No more secrets.

Zain No more secrets? It's gonna be a dull life.

Sab Can you take off those sunglasses?

Zain Why?

Sab I can't see what your eyes are doing.

Zain So?

Sab I can't see what you're actually thinking.

Zain Don't be stupid.

Sab *moves and grabs* **Zain**'s *sunglasses off him.*

Zain I think you should behave. Three o'clock, your boyfriend and entourage are approaching. Smile.

Reza *Salaam alakum.*

Zain *Walakum salaam.* (*Shakes hands.*)

Shades 223

Ali *Salaam alakum.*

Zain *Walakum salaam.* (*Shakes hands, goes to shake hands with* **Nazia**, *but she doesn't.*) *Salaam*, sorry I wasn't thinking. (*He looks at* **Sab**.)

Nazia *Walakum salaam*, no problem.

Reza Bhaj, this is Sab who I have been working with, and Zain, the organiser of the festival.

Nazia *Alhumdillah*, Reza's told me what a good job you're doing for a worthy cause. Awful what is happening in Palestine.

Zain It's horrible. I hope we will be able to help in some small way.

Nazia I'm looking forward to the whole event; we've already bought our tickets. It'll be nice to see what my little brother has done.

Reza Most of the work has been down to Sab.

Nazia Yes, so Ali has told me.

Reza *gives a look of appreciation to* **Ali**.

Nazia I do hope Reza has been doing his fair share.

Sab (*nods*) We make a good team.

Reza *and* **Sab** *smile at each other*.

Nazia Good to know Reza is committed to his charity work as usual.

Ali Did you enjoy the talk?

Sab It was interesting.

Zain (*nods*) Interesting.

Nazia I was surprised by some of the views.

Reza It's healthy to have debate, Bhaj.

Nazia The second speaker was –

Ali Asking women to take off the headscarf.

Nazia It's a bit much.

Zain I thought he had some interesting points. Finally, a *fatwa* not condemning someone to death. It'll be good for our image.

A dull silence. **Sab** *glares at* **Zain**.

Zain I was joking. (*An awkward laugh.*) If the *hijab* is making women targets for violence, then maybe they should consider removing it – for their safety.

Reza Logically his argument makes sense, but it would be nice if there was another way.

Ali It is the sisters who are the victims here; it's the public who needs educating.

Zain If it lets them walk around freely without the fear of a backlash, then they should.

Nazia I could never imagine taking off my *hijab*, whatever the circumstances. It's integral to a woman's identity as a Muslim.

Zain I thought belief in Allah and the Prophet were integral.

Ali There are codes of conduct which we must follow.

Zain Most of these codes of conduct are open to interpretation.

Reza That's why talks like these are so great – they allow people to interpret things in so many ways.

Ali Wearing the *hijab* is a virtuous act.

Zain Not wearing a *hijab* doesn't make you any less of a Muslim than one who does.

Reza No one says it does.

Zain Everyone knows wearing a *hijab* makes a woman virtuous and others less so.

Ali It's a duty.

Zain I thought it was optional.

Reza I guess you guys subscribe to different schools of thought.

Nazia What do you think, Sabrina?

Sab I have a lot of respect for women who wear it, but I think people can be just as religious without it.

Nazia You share a view similar to your friend. How did the two of you meet?

Zain *and* **Sab** *look at each other. They take a little too long to answer.*

Ali You live together, don't you?

Zain We met at university.

Ali I must be mistaken, I thought –

Sab We're flatmates.

Zain Rent is so expensive nowadays, you have no choice but to share.

Nazia Your families don't mind?

Sab Zain's like family.

Reza Bhaji, there's three of them living together.

Nazia So you live with one of your relatives?

Zain We live with another guy.

Nazia It's so strange, I never thought for a second to move out of my family home before I was married.

Reza Sabrina's from Manchester, Bhaji. She can't commute to work. Sabrina's job has really helped us make this show. She's been able to call in a few favours.

Nazia You've been very lucky. I was surprised when Reza told me what you did.

Sab Why?

Nazia It's something that white girls usually do.

Zain *tries to hold back an 'I told you so' look at* **Sab**, *who recognises the hidden dig.* **Ali** *smiles.* **Reza** *is shocked at his sister.*

Reza Bhaji!

Zain I guess we could say that about all jobs once upon a time.

Nazia Of course, you're right. Someone has to make the first step into new territories, but it can be hard for those around you. What did your parents say about your job?

Sab *looks at* **Zain**, *then at* **Reza** *and back to* **Nazia**.

Sab They were resistant to it at first.

Reza But they're fine now. They're coming down for the fashion show, aren't they?

Nazia *looks at* **Sab** *questioningly.*

Sab Yes, yes, they are.

Nazia (*nods*) The hours must be long.

Reza That's a hazard of working in the City.

Nazia I keep saying to Reza, he has to find a job where the hours are shorter. When he gets married he can't leave his wife for hours waiting for him to return.

Sab That wouldn't be ideal.

Zain He might not have to; she might be working long hours as well.

Nazia Mum and Dad are looking for a good girl for him to settle down with. I am sure they'll do a good job. They did with introducing the rest of us to our partners. Just the baby left.

Reza Bhaji.

Sab If you'll excuse me, I'm going to use the Ladies.

A few seconds after **Sab** *leaves:*

Zain Excuse me.

He follows **Sab**, *who's slightly ahead of him.*

Zain Sab, Sab.

Sab *turns around.*

Zain Are you OK?

Sab *nods.*

Zain She was a right bitch. Talk about a pit bull in a headscarf.

Silence.

Sab It was just meant to be a friendly meeting.

Zain Yeah, friendly like Basra. If that's how she's to his friends, you're better off out of it. (*Sees* **Sab***'s face.*) He wasn't the one spouting the crap, I suppose.

Sab He wasn't, was he?

Zain He wasn't exactly telling her to shut up either.

Sab I'm gonna use the Ladies.

Zain Do you want to go home?

Sab I'm gonna get some fresh air.

Zain Do you want me to come with you?

Sab (*shakes her head*) I just need a few minutes.

Spotlight moves back to **Reza**, **Nazia** *and* **Ali**.

Reza Why did you have to say that thing about getting married?

Nazia Why shouldn't I have said it?

Reza It's just a little embarrassing. Makes us seem a bit backward.

Nazia *Chup.* They're Muslim, they understand, and if they think that, don't worry, in a few months, you will barely see them, the conversation will be forgotten.

228　Contemporary English Plays

Reza　Maybe.

Nazia　Maybe?

Reza　I may do some charity work with them.

Nazia　That's good. Who knows, you might meet a girl to marry through it.

Reza　I already have.

Nazia　What?

Reza　I like Sabrina.

Nazia *laughs.*

Reza　Why are you laughing?

Nazia　Because you're joking.

Reza　I'm thinking of introducing her to Mum and Dad.

Pause.

Nazia　I see. How would you explain her lifestyle before she met you?

Ali　Bhaji.

Nazia　Ali, give Reza and me a minute.

Ali　Of course.

He exits.

Nazia　How would you explain her lifestyle before she met you?

Reza　They don't have to know.

Nazia　You'd lie to them?

Reza　No.

Nazia　What else wouldn't you tell them?

Reza　I didn't mean – [*that the way it sounded*].

Nazia　Reza.

Nazia Realistically, if she's to be your wife, she will have to make big changes, Reza. Will she?

Silence.

It is a part of life to be attracted to people, but you must think about what's best for you, your *deen*, your family.

Reza I know, Bhaj, but once you get to know her you'll realise she's similar to us.

Nazia Reza, you're such a decent guy. I could see why any girl would want you, but you can't believe everything everyone tells you. She lives alone with that boy.

Reza They're just flatmates.

Nazia The way he ran after her. It felt like they were …

Silence.

At the end of the day we will trust your judgement. If you think she will fit in with the family, then fine. But you know there are other options. Mum and Dad introduced me to Imran. I couldn't be happier.

Silence.

We have to be the example, Rez.

Reza I value your opinion, Bhaj. *Silence.*

Nazia I hope I haven't said anything wrong.

Reza *shakes his head.*

Nazia If it is destined to be it will be. Do what you feel is right.

Fade out. Spotlight onto **Sab**, *who is waiting outside.* **Ali** *comes out. He looks at* **Sab**. *She ignores him. He lights a cigarette.*

Ali Do you mind?

Sab Go ahead.

Ali *begins smoking,* **Sab** *ignores him, starts to walk away. He offers her a cigarette.*

Ali Would you like one?

Sab No.

Ali How's your evening been?

Sab (*going to leave*) Fine.

Ali I was surprised to see you here.

Sab Were you?

Ali A pleasant surprise.

Silence.

The only thing with work and the time of these things is you never really get a chance to eat, do you?

Sab Not really.

Ali You must be hungry.

Sab I'll eat when I get home. (*Begins to leave.*)

Ali Why wait?

Sab What?

Ali We can go get something to eat.

Sab No thanks.

Ali You seem a little upset.

Sab I'm fine.

Ali Join me for dinner.

Sab I'm not hungry.

Ali We could get to know each other. You'll see I'm really a nice guy, and then –

Sab Then what?

Ali What life brings.

Sab What life brings.

Ali We're both adults. (*He looks at her and stubs out his cigarette.*) Some harmless enjoyment never hurt anyone.

Sab I'm not interested in being your whore.

Ali But you are in being Reza's.

Sab Fuck you!

Ali What's the difference between us? We're the same, him and me. In fact, I'm more likely to give you what you want. Reza is too straight and yellow for that. Why not me? I would treat you well.

Sab You want me to be your wife?

Ali We both know that's unrealistic.

Sab Unrealistic.

Ali Our lifestyles wouldn't be compatible, but there are other options.

Sab *begins to walk away.* **Ali** *stops her by blocking her path.*

Ali I'd treat you well – the best restaurants, the most expensive shops. There's nothing stopping us from enjoying ourselves.

Sab God.

Ali He forgives.

Sab (*stares at him*) You make me sick. You'll have to get your thrills elsewhere. I'm not for sale.

She turns and walks away. **Ali** *is disappointed but recovers quickly.*

Ali You're a dime a dozen. I'll pick you up tomorrow on the street corner.

She ignores him and carries on walking out.

Blackout.

232 Contemporary English Plays

Scene Twelve

Reza *in his office on the phone. He has a laptop in front of him.*

Reza (*on phone*) I've scheduled us to audit the McMinn Enterprises on the thirteenth of this month. We will hold a meeting on – (*Knock at door.*) Come in. (*Back to phone and computer screen.*) The twentieth, great. See you then.

He looks up. **Sab** *stands in front of him. He is visibly shocked.*

Reza Sab. (*Beat.*) What are you doing here?

Sab I needed to see you.

Reza You look … well. *Silence.*

Sab You haven't responded to my phone calls or emails.

Reza It's been manic at work.

Sab You missed the rehearsal yesterday.

Reza Sorry, I picked up the message late.

Sab There's one tonight.

Reza I'm not sure I'll be able to make it. I'm working on this really intense project and I'm not sure if –

Sab Why didn't you ring me when you found out?

Reza I thought I might be able to reschedule. (*Beat.*) I just don't think I can be as involved as I was.

Sab Right.

Reza I'm happy to hand out leaflets, spread the word.

Sab *nods.*

Reza I'll do what I can.

Beat.

Sab You sure have the corporate persona down to a T.

Reza What?

Sab Couldn't you have thought of something more original?

Silence.

Why don't you just say it?

Reza What?

Sab Just say it.

Reza What, Sab?

Sab We both know this isn't about the fashion show. (*Pause.*) You've gone cold on me since … (*Begins to get emotional, then controls herself.*) I just want to hear the words.

Reza What do you want me to say?

Sab That you're scared.

Reza Scared?

Sab Too weak to pursue someone who hasn't had the seal of approval.

Reza It's not that.

Sab It's certainly not some bullshit project.

Silence.

Reza I realised I gave you the wrong impression.

Sab Wrong impression?

Reza That my feelings for you were more than just friends. I thought it was best to distance – [*myself*].

Sab Be a coward and avoid my calls.

Reza No, yes. I just wanted some time to think.

Sab And?

Reza I think we inhabit different worlds.

Sab What does that mean?

Reza I don't think we're suited.

Sab You didn't think that a few weeks ago.

Silence.

Reza We're just looking for different things.

Sab What are you looking for?

Reza Someone, someone.

He looks at **Sab** *as if to say it is she he is looking for.* **Sab** *does not register the look.*

Sab Someone who's a poster girl for Islam?

Reza No.

Sab This is bullshit.

Reza Sab, I'm sorry. *Silence.*

Sab (*struggling with the words*) If I wore the *hijab*?

Reza What?

Sab Would that make it easier?

Reza Sab.

Sab Would it make it easier? (*Beat.*) Would it?

Reza Yes.

Sab If that's what it takes then – [*I'll do it*].

Reza Don't do this.

Sab If I did it, then why not?

Reza Sab.

Sab Why not?

Reza You wouldn't be happy.

Sab I'd do it for you.

Reza It's not that simple. I'm sorry, Sabrina.

Sab What else is there?

Reza You and Zain.

Sab What about us?

Reza How am I gonna explain that?

Sab We're flatmates.

Reza I should have realised how close you were. When my sister said –

Sab But he's, he's – he's just a good friend, trust me.

Reza I always thought my wife would be –

Silence.

Sab Would be what?

Reza Sab, I have to worry about my family's reputation. People would believe –

Sab Fuck them, this is about you and me.

Silence.

We work, Reza, we work.

Reza I can't do it, Sab.

Sab *reaches for him but* **Reza** *walks away.*

Sab So that's it? You're just gonna –

Reza You'll find someone else, someone better.

Sab You're right, it's best I know now, you're just like the rest of them. Too scared to challenge the crowd. Too scared to stand up for more than one version of a Muslim. Too scared to ask me if I've fucked Zain.

Reza (*winces*) Sab!

Sab Would it matter if I had? I wouldn't have cared if you had. I wouldn't have judged you. That would have been the past. I honestly thought you were – (*Laughs.*) More fool me. I don't need this bullshit. You know what's really funny? Ali turned out to be more honest than you. Goodbye, Reza.

She begins to leave.

Reza Sab.

She doesn't look back. **Reza** *looks at the door, slowly gets up, closes the door. Leans against it and closes his eyes.*

Blackout.

Scene Thirteen

Zain *and* **Mark** *in the flat.*

Mark *EastEnders* is on in ten minutes.

Zain So?

Mark They're going to get together.

Zain Why does he fancy her? She looks like a smashed pumpkin.

Mark They're an odd couple.

Zain Like Clive and Thomas.

Mark They're sweet.

Zain That's because you never have a bad word to say about anyone.

Mark They're getting married.

Zain It seems everyone's got the bug. Imagine marrying Clive. (*He shudders.*) I'd rather do Mr Burns from *The Simpsons*.

Mark (*laughs*) It's sweet, they're making a commitment.

Zain Thomas is a gold-digger.

Mark You are so cynical.

Zain He's marrying a corpse. What twenty-two-year-old gay guy goes out with a forty-year-old?

Mark (*laughs*) Sab was worried about being over the hill. I can't believe we're as bad.

Zain It's a dog-eat-dog world.

Mark Zain, do you ever see us – *Beat.*

Zain Us?

Mark You know –

He makes head gestures. **Zain** *looks as him, puzzled.*

Mark – getting married?

Zain *laughs.* **Mark** *is visibly upset by the response.*

Zain You're being serious.

Mark *nods. Silence.*

Zain You and me?

Mark Just forget it, it was stupid.

Zain God, no, it's just that I never imagined – I mean, I never thought I'd ever get married.

Mark *looks upset.*

Zain You know how I feel about you. It's just with everything I never thought –

Mark I can't believe you're giving Sab such a hard time.

Zain What?

Mark At least Sab has the courage of her convictions.

Zain What?

Mark She knew you wouldn't like it; his family might not like her but she still put herself out there, tried to change the status quo. I'm going to get some cigarettes.

Zain *looks shocked as if he can't quite work out what has happened. He recovers a few seconds after* **Mark** *has left the flat.*

Zain Mark, Mark! (*He pulls out his phone and makes a call. He cuts off his phone.*) Great fucking job, Zain.

He walks towards the door and opens it. **Sab** *walks in.* **Zain** *stays at the door.*

Zain Bloody hell, Sab, you scared the life out of me.

Sab Why you standing in the doorway?

Zain Did you see Mark?

Sab On the way in. He said he was heading to the shop.

Zain Did he look OK?

Sab Yeah.

Zain He said he'd be back?

Sab *EastEnders*'s on in a minute.

Zain Did he say he was coming back for it?

Sab I didn't ask.

Zain *stays at the door.*

Sab What's going on?

Zain I've been a fuckwit.

Sab What happened?

Zain We had an argument.

Sab About?

Zain He asked me to marry him.

Sab Seriously?!

Zain *nods.*

Sab That's brilliant.

Zain (*sighs*) I laughed, Sab.

Sab You didn't?!

Zain *nods.*

Sab Poor Mark.

She comforts **Zain**.

Zain I always thought I'd marry a woman.

Sab What?

Zain I always thought this was a phase. When I realised it wasn't, I decided I'd never get married. Imagine doing that to some poor cow from back home. When he said it, Sab, I don't know, it was funny and scary, me marrying Mark. (*Beat.*) That'd mean I'd be completely out of the loop, wouldn't I?

Sab No, you'd still have me.

Zain Something so official – it feels like choosing sides.

Sab It's never that simple.

Zain All I saw was the *dohl* playing, a grand stage and both of us fighting over the wedding dress. Imagine that?

Sab (*laughs*) That'd be one hell of an Asian wedding! (*She is trying to hold back the tears.*)

Zain Sab?

Sab You better make it up with him. He's a great guy, and he's probably one of the few guys who mean it. I want to be bridesmaid.

Zain Hey, we could get married on the same day – you marrying the brother and me Mark. Now that would be the talk of the century.

Sab *can no longer stop the tears.*

Zain Why the tears? Mark and I will be fine.

Sab You were right.

Zain About me being a fuckwit? Hey, I know that may come as a shock, but I'm just mortal too.

Sab *laughs through her tears.*

Sab Reza.

Zain *looks at* **Sab**.

Sab He's not doing the show.

Zain Why?

Sab He thinks we're not suited.

Zain To get married?

Sab His family.

Zain What a typical spineless Asian wanker. You're worth ten of them.

Sab Maybe.

Zain Why are you so insecure?

Sab Everybody needs a hobby.

Zain (*laughs*) One of you is worth a million of the God gang.

He hugs **Sab** *and rocks her back and forth.* **Mark** *walks back in, a six-pack of Stella in his hands.*

Zain Can I have one?

Mark Is everything OK?

Zain Son of a preacher man has just pulled out of the show and –

Sab – dumped me.

Zain Technically you can only be dumped if you've kissed a person.

He squeezes **Sab** *comfortingly.*

Mark What did he say?

Sab We inhabited different worlds.

Mark Stupid fucker.

Sab The most ridiculous thing was he thought that Zain and I were – (*Making a gesture as if to say 'sleeping together'.*) You know.

Zain/ Mark What!

Zain Why?

Sab We live together.

Mark You should have told him Zain was gay. (*Beat.*) I wasn't thinking.

Pause.

Zain (*looks at* **Mark**) You could have told him, Sab.

Sab I shouldn't have had to.

Zain It always the same story. (*Pause.*) Do you want me to send them a copy of one of Sarah Maple's paintings? That'll stir them right up!

Sab (*laughs*) Don't be stupid. (*Pause.*) God, I need someone to present the fashion show with me. I'm gonna have to call people –

Zain (*in mock horror*) Call people, call people, when the perfect man is right here? I was born for the role. I will have more charisma in my little finger than in the whole of preacher boy's being.

Sab (*laughs*) Thanks, Zee. I just wish you could sort out everything else so easily.

Zain You know you can always marry me – I'm allowed four partners –

He reaches out for **Mark**, *puts one arm round him, the other round* **Sab**.

Zain – but being married to Mark and you I think I could settle with just the two.

He kisses **Sab** *on the head. Blackout.*

Scene Fourteen

Reza *in his office, typing.* **Ali** *sitting on a chair.*

Reza   Give me five minutes and we can go.

Ali   You just need to get back to the old routine.

Reza   Yeah.

Ali   Get some fresh air, play football with the lads.

Reza   I'm fine.

A knock at the door.

That was quick.

They laugh.

(*Still packing away.*) Come in.

Zain *walks in.* **Reza** *is surprised.*

Ali   *Salaam alakum.*

Zain *refuses to shakes his hand and does not respond.* **Reza** *turns round.*

Reza   *Salaam alakum.*

Silence.

I'm surprised to see you here.

Zain   I wanted to speak to you.

Ali   We're on our way to *jummah*.

Zain   It won't take long.

Reza   It's fine.

Silence. It drags on a little too long for comfort.

Do you want to speak in private?

Zain   No, he can stay.

Reza   If you're here to speak about the fashion show –

Zain I'm here about Sab.

Silence.

Reza Is she OK?

Zain You shouldn't have led her to believe something could happen between the two of you.

Reza I made a mistake.

Zain You chickened out.

Reza I'll speak to Sab again, make sure she understands.

Zain She understands. She got the message loud and clear. She'll get through it.

Ali She does have you to comfort her.

Reza I'm sorry if I hurt her.

Ali Don't apologise, you made the right choice.

Zain As much as I hate to say it, I agree with him.

Ali Then why are you here?

Zain I came here to set the record straight.

Reza About what?

Zain My relationship with Sab. Sab and I are just friends.

Ali You expect us to believe that? The maths doesn't add up.

Zain Well, we are.

Ali I believe the correct term is friends with advantages.

Zain I'm with Mark.

Ali You brought him here as a witness? Of course he's going to agree –

Zain He's not here. I'm with Mark, not Sabrina.

Silence and confused looks.

Ali You mean you and Mark are – (*Puts his middle finger over his index finger.*)

Zain Yes.

A look of disgust passes over **Ali**'s *and* **Reza**'s *faces, but just as quickly another emotion replaces it.*

Ali B-b-but, b-b-but, but you're Muslim – (*To* **Reza**.) This is worse than we thought.

Beat.

Reza (*to* **Zain**) So, she's never had a re— [*lationship with you*]?

Zain No.

Reza And you're definitely – ?

Zain Yes.

Reza Oh God.

Ali You're so much better without her. Look at who she would have brought into your home. You were spared.

Zain (*to* **Ali**) I can't believe you ever thought Sabrina would go out with you.

Reza What?

Zain You mean he didn't tell you he asked her out?

Reza Ali?

Ali You don't believe him, do you?

Reza Did you?

Ali You know me. *Pause.*

Reza You're lying.

Ali Reza, this is me.

Reza You're lying.

Ali I only did it so you could keep your *izaat*. She was unsuitable.

Zain That's why she had to turn you down twice.

Reza Twice?

Ali You're going to take this *shai'tan*'s word over mine? Do you think he's going to worry about lying when he's committing the worst sin of them all?

Zain I haven't got anything else to lie about. *Beat as* **Reza** *realises the truth of* **Zain***'s words.*

Reza You're meant to be my friend.

Ali Reza, I swear on Allah –

Reza Don't! Don't!

Ali I did it for you.

Reza For me? (*Beat.*) I think you should leave for *jummah*.

Ali Are you coming?

Reza On your own, Ali.

Ali She would have embarrassed you.

Reza Get out.

Ali I did you a favour, you don't know where to box people. She would have made your father's standing in the community –

Reza Get out!

Ali You want to be left alone with him?

Reza GO!

Ali *hesitates, but leaves.* **Zain** *and* **Reza** *are left alone. Pause as* **Reza** *recovers himself.*

Reza I'm sorry.

Zain It's not me you have to say sorry to.

Reza I owe you both an apology. I'll call her.

Zain Don't.

Reza What?

Zain I didn't come here for that. I came here so you'd know the truth. God does not judge according to your bodies and appearance, but He scans your hearts and looks into your deeds.

Reza The Prophet was a wise man.

Zain He was. Maybe if we listened to him we wouldn't be so quick to try and judge each other. I thought you of all people would know that.

Silence.

Reza I've been an idiot.

Zain Sab deserves someone better.

Silence.

Reza Will you tell her I'm sorry?

Zain *nods.*

Zain I think it's time I left.

Reza I'll walk you out.

Zain It's fine.

Reza No one will know anything from me, but as for Ali, I can't guarantee he'll do the same.

Zain That's all I can ask for.

Reza (*nods*) Thank you.

Zain (*surprised*) For what?

Reza For telling me the truth. It couldn't have been easy.

Zain I'm sorry things couldn't have worked out differently for you.

Reza *and* **Zain** *shake hands.* **Zain** *walks to the door, but hesitates and turns back.*

Zain I have to also say –

Reza Yes?

Zain I think it would be for the best if you and your family didn't turn up for the event.

Reza But –

Zain I think she's been hurt enough. (*Silence.*) I'll refund any tickets.

Reza There's no need, it's the least I can do.

Zain (*nods*) So, we're agreed?

Reza *looks at* **Zain**. *Unable to trust his voice, he nods his agreement. Blackout.*

Scene Fifteen

The fashion show. **Sab** *in a long, black, strapless dress,* **Zain** *in a suit.*

Zain (*flicks his collars*) Smoking!

Sab Have you been checking on the models or looking in the mirror?

Zain *coughs, does a twirl, coughs again.*

Zain All's fine and dandy, Captain. (*Salutes.*)

Sab Great.

Pause.

Zain You OK?

Sab *nods.*

Zain Don't be nervous (*putting his arm around her*), cos no one's going to be looking at you even if you do fuck up because all eyes will be on me.

Sab *hits him.*

Zain I do look good. (*Holds his arms out.*) I look good, go on, say it.

Sab (*laughs*) You look good.

Zain The lady had impeccable taste. You going to be OK?

Sab I am the professional organiser here.

Zain Sab.

Sab I'll be fine.

Mark *walks in.*

Mark Five minutes, guys. You OK, doll?

Sab I wish you guys would stop asking me that – makes me feel like I'm terminally ill or something.

Zain Shall we get this show on the road then?

He takes **Sab** *by the arm and twirls her round.*

Zain (*to* **Mark**) See you soon.

Mark I'll be here, getting the models prepped.

Zain Remember to crack open the champagne on our return.

Mark Dom Perignon all the way.

Zain *and* **Sab** *exit.* **Mark** *is left onstage.*

Mark Ladies and gents, let's go.

A girl dressed in a sari gets ready to move onto the stage. A song plays. After a while, we see **Reza** *walk backstage.* **Mark** *spots him and stops him before he can walk on with the models.*

Mark You're a little late, aren't you?

Reza I've come to speak to Sabrina.

Mark She's busy running an event you should have been helping her with.

Reza I'll wait here for her.

Shades 249

Mark I think you should leave.

Reza I need to speak to her.

Mark Not here.

Reza It's important.

Sab *and* **Zain** *return in conversation. They spot* **Reza**. **Sab** *is visibly shaken,* **Zain** *annoyed.* **Reza** *and* **Sab** *look at each other.*

Zain I think you should leave.

Reza Sabrina –

Sab We need to get on with the show. I'm gonna wait by the side of the stage for our cue.

Reza *blocks her exit.*

Reza Sabrina, I'm really sorry for thinking those things, I should have –

Sab It's in the past.

Reza I just want you to know if I could rewind time … I can't believe I ever thought …

Sab You're forgiven, OK. There's no need to feel guilty.

Reza Sabrina, I need to explain. I just want to talk to you and make you see –

Sab What's left to say? You shouldn't have come here.

Reza I've been an idiot. I made a huge mistake.

Sab I can't do this (*She begins to walk offstage.*)

Reza I want you to meet my family. My parents want to meet you.

Mark *and* **Zain** *look at* **Reza** *with respect.*

Sab I'm not gonna be the girl who pushed you off your pedestal.

Reza You don't understand. I've spoken –

Sab You'll find someone better.

Reza I don't think I will.

Sab It's all over with. You were right, we're looking for different things.

Reza Just give me a minute.

Sab I said it's over! Just go. (*Beat.*) Please.

Reza *looks at* **Sab** *and exits. Beat as* **Sab** *struggles with her emotions.* **Mark** *and* **Zain** *look at each other.* **Mark** *walks up to* **Sab** *and puts his arm round her.*

Mark I thought that was pretty romantic.

Sab Not now, Mark.

Mark Why don't you go after him and give him a chance to say his piece? What he did was really sweet.

Sab Mark.

Mark It must have been really hard for him.

Sab I'm going to take my position offstage. You coming, Zain?

Zain Sab. He didn't have to come here to apologise, especially after we told him not to. That's sweet even for a brother.

Mark *smiles at* **Zain**.

Sab Zain?

Zain Admittedly, it was all a little Bollywood, but I think you should go talk to him.

Sab We're in the middle of the show.

Zain I have enough personality to command the stage for both of us. You were holding me back anyway.

Sab Why are you defending him?

Zain Sometimes we make mistakes, Sab. Sometimes, when we should say yes we get scared and fuck things up. Sometimes we don't do the thing we know we should do. He's trying to do the right thing. It's better late than never.

Sab I don't want to go through it all again.

Zain You don't have to. Just hear him out. *Silence. He puts his arm round* **Sab**.

Zain Whatever happens, we'll be right here when you come back.

Sab *begins to leave but hesitates.*

Zain Go on, go!

Sab Thanks, Zee.

Sab *walks off the stage.*

Blackout.

A Day at the Racists

Anders Lustgarten

You start from the presumption that only you are intelligent
and sensitive enough to see how bad capitalist society is.
    Trevor Griffiths, *The Party*

Racism is like a Cadillac. There's a new model every year.
    Malcolm X

For Zena Birch, for all the help and advice.

Acknowledgements

Thanks to Lisa and Nina at Soho; Ben and Lily at Curtis Brown; the Debnath and Rochlitz hospitality, enjoyed across the world; Laurence Lustgarten; Donna Dickenson and Chris Britton; Stephanie Street; Sarah Grochala and Anna Kerth for the Polish; everyone who helped with interviews, sources, readings and comments.

This play is written in testament to the (forgotten) history of British working-class activism.

A Day at the Racists was first performed at The Finborough Theatre, London on 2 March 2010, with the following cast (in order of appearance):

Peter Case	Julian Littman
Driver	Gwilym Lloyd
Polish Lady	Vanessa Havell
Burka Woman 1	Thusitha Jayasundera
Burka Woman 2	Zaraah Abrahams
African Guy	Trevor A. Toussaint
Labour MP	Vanessa Havell
Mark Case	Sam Swainsbury
Clinton Jones	Trevor A. Toussaint
Gina White	Thusitha Jayasundera
Zenobia	Zaraah Abrahams
Tony McDonald	Gwilym Lloyd
Rick Coleman	Nick Holder
Housewife	Vanessa Havell
Journalist	Vanessa Havell

Black Man/Asian Woman *were played by members of the company*

Director	Ryan McBryde
Designer	Mila Sanders
Lighting	Dan Hill
Sound	George Dennis

Characters

Peter Case
Driver
Polish Lady
Burka Woman 1
Burka Woman 2
African Guy
Labour MP
Mark Case
Clinton Jones
Gina White
Zenobia
Tony McDonald
Rick Coleman
Housewife
Journalist
Black Man
Asian Woman

Act One

Lights up on a bus stuck in traffic. **Pete Case**, *a white man in his fifties, is late for work. He is trying to read a book on local history, but his frustration distracts him. A jaunty tune starts up.*

'We came to England through the tunnel last night
(That's right, that's right)
We claim asylum now they're treating us right
(So right, so right)
Oh something tells me, Ahmed, this is the place to be
Cos here we're getting everything and we're getting it for free.

Oh I've got a brand new leather jacket and a brand new mobile phone
Brits they live in cardboard boxes while we get furnished homes
Legal aid, driving lessons, central heating and free bills
Oh we get all the benefits and you get all the bills.'

Pete *looks at his watch. A fat woman in a bright pink jumpsuit in front of him is on her mobile phone, yelling in Polish. We follow what she says on surtitles.*

Woman in Pink Jumpsuit (*into mobile*)   Nie! Tak ci powiedział? A ty co mu powiedziałaś?
(No! He said that? What did you say to him?)

Pete *sighs and checks his watch again. The bus jumps forward, then grinds to a sudden halt again. The driver opens the door.* **Pete** *tries to control his anger. Tune*:

'They drove a lorry from Ikea straight away
(You pay, you pay)
TVs and furniture, it was mostly OK (You pay, you pay)
But flat it wasn't suitable, the council's run by fools,
After crossing fifteen countries we need heated swimming pools.

Oh I've got a brand new leather jacket and a brand new mobile phone

Brits they live in cardboard boxes while we get furnished homes

Legal aid, driving lessons, central heating and free bills Oh we get all the benefits and you get all the bills.'

Pete's *phone rings.*

Pete Yeah, hello?

Two women in burkas plump themselves down on top of him, shoving him along the seat, as they carry on a loud conversation in Arabic.

Burka Woman 1 كلا! هل قال هذا؟ وماذا قلتي له؟
No! He said that? What did you say?
Kalla! Hal qal hatha? Wa matha qulti Lahu?

Burka Woman 2 قال لي أن هاتفه الجوال كان مكسوراً.
He told me his mobile was broken.
Qal lee ana hatifahu aljawwal kan maksooran.

Pete On the bus.

The woman in the pink jumpsuit pulls some smelly-looking foodstuff out of her bag, takes a huge mouthful and shouts into her phone, spraying bits of food everywhere.

Woman in Pink Jumpsuit (*into mobile*) Co powiedział?
Że mu się popsuła komórka? Dupek! Zasługujesz na kogoś lepszego!
(Is that what he said? That his mobile was broken? Arsehole! You can do better than him, you know.)

Burka Woman 1 أحمق! أنت تستحقين رجلاً أفضل منه بكثير.
Arsehole! You can do so much better than him, you know!
Ahmaq! Anti tastahiqeen rajulan afdal minhu bikatheer.

Pete I'm trying to, mate, believe me I'm trying.

An **African Guy** *sneezes violently, wipes his hands on the bus seat, then pulls a thick stack of money from his pocket as he sings along to his iPod far too loud.*

African Guy 'Who the fuck cares
I'm stanky rich

I'ma die tryna spend this shit
Southside's up in this bitch'

*The **Bus Driver** shouts something out of the window. Horns start to blare.*

Pete Because I went to see our useless fucking MP is why. (*Beat.*) Have a guess.

The woman in the pink jumpsuit turns around and removes her top to reveal a sensible suit and blouse. She is now his local Labour MP.

Pete So there's nothing you can do for me?

MP I'm sorry, Mr Case. This is not something over which I have any control.

Pete Even though we've been here however many years …

MP The current method of housing allocation –

Pete Paid our taxes? Done our bit?

MP … is based on objective need, rather than length of residency. The policy has been that way for some time.

Pete And he has an objective need!

MP It's a policy that's intended to favour the needs of families rather than –

Pete He's got the little one.

MP *Large* families, families that would otherwise have / nowhere else –

Pete He's in my front room. He's kipping on the couch in my front room.

MP That is unfortunate, and I'm sure difficult for you, but the policy is geared towards the most vulnerable, those with large families, whom I know you wouldn't –

Pete Large families of who? (*Beat.*) Come on, large families of who? Cos I thought the birth rate in Britain was right down.

Beat.

MP Mr Case.

Pete Speaking.

MP That's not a particularly constructive attitude, if I may say so.

Pete Oh?

MP To bring immigration into the discussion is frankly –

Pete *Me* bring it into the discussion?

MP This borough operates a policy of absolute equality.

Pete You're rigging the system in favour of people from outside the area –

MP Absolute non-discrimination and / equality.

Pete Instead of the people round here who've put the work in!

MP It's something I personally feel very strongly about.

Pete Do you now?

MP I do. As a matter of fact. Yes.

Pete That's nice. Absolute equality. So how come you've got five houses and my son don't have one?

MP I'm not going to dignify that with a –

Pete I forget; did you put in for the moat or the massage chair?

MP I have other constituents who are equally deserving of my time.

Pause.

Pete Know what's funny? (*She shrugs awkwardly.*) I've voted for you lot every time.

Beat.

MP Good. (*Brief smile.*) Thank you.

Pete I've voted Labour in every election since 1974. I dragged my carcass round the factory floor every lunchtime and tea break for a month before every election, getting bums off seats and down the polling station for ya. Even after Kinnock slung me out the bloody *party*, I've kept voting for you.

MP   And I hope we can persuade you to continue to do so.

Pete   You must think I'm a proper mug. Don't you? Go on. At least give me that much. You must think I'm a proper mug.

Beat. The woman digs into her bag, takes a huge bite of the dodgy food and spits it all over **Pete** *as, pulling her pink top back on, she morphs back into the Polish woman.*

Woman in Pink Jumpsuit (*into mobile*)   Myślę, że powinnaś uciąć mu tego jego bezużytecznego fiuta i sprzedać na "Ibeju"! (I think you should chop off his worthless dick and sell it on eBay!)

She turns back away from him. The song continues

'We go to garage to buy nice motor car
(Price is no bar)
Flash BMW cos we've come so far
(Price is no bar)
It costs many thousands, but man oh what the heck
We come back tomorrow and we pay with welfare cheque.'

Pete (*into phone*)   Mark with ya?

'Oh I've got a brand new leather jacket and a brand new mobile phone
Brits they live in cardboard boxes while we get furnished homes
Legal aid, driving lessons, central heating and free bills
Oh we get all the benefits and you get all the bills.'

Burka Woman 1   المهم, كيف سيلعب فريق إنكلترا الليلة برأيك؟
Anyway, how do you reckon England are gonna do tonight?
Almuhim, kaifa sayalaab fareeq ingeltara allailah bira'yik?

Pete (*simmering*)   You're gonna have to speak up, Clint. It's a little noisy here.

Burka Woman 2 بطريقة 3-5-2 وأن يحاولوا الهجوم عن طريق الأجنحة
هذا يعتمد (على عوامل مختلفة) أعتقد من الأفضل أن يلعبوا

Depends, really. I think they should go 3-5-2 and try attack down the wings.

Hatha ya'tamid ala awamil mokhtalifa. A'taqid min alafdal an yala'bo btareeqat 3-5-2 wa an yuhawilo alhujoom an tareeq alajniha.

African guy 'Yeah, I talk the talk, and I walk the walk
Like a Teflon Don, but I run New York'

Pete You told him yet?

Woman in Pink Jumpsuit (*into mobile*) To nie jest Polska, Waleska, nie musisz tkwić w tym gównie!
(This is not Poland any more, Valeska: you don't have to take this shit!)

Drilling. The driver leans on his horn and yells out the window. Horns blare in reply.

Burka Woman 1 سيحدث. سيعيدون لامبارد وسينهار كل شيء مرة ثانية.
تعرف ما الذي

You know what'll happen they'll bring back Lampard and it'll all go tits up again.

Ta'arif ma al lathi sayahdoth. Sayueedoon Lampard wa sayanhar kolla shay' marra thaniya.

Burka Woman 2 أكره فرانك لامبارد هذا.

I fucking hate Frank Lampard.

Akrahu Frank Lampard hatha.

Pete I tried to, mate. Last night.

Pete's son **Mark**, *a good-looking lad in his early twenties, comes on dribbling a football dextrously.* **Pete** *smiles. Suddenly* **Mark** *boots the ball violently off stage and looks away into a mirror, sorting his hair out.*

Pete What is it tonight? D'n'B, R'n'B?

Mark That's very good, Dad. B'n'B's more your line. (*Fiddles with hair.*) Dubstep.

Pete Dubstep? They just make it up these days, don't they? That's not even a word.

Mark Can you let me get ready, please? I'm well late.

Pete Dubstep … Who's going down with ya?

Mark Why? You don't care who I'm kotchin down some club with, do ya? (*Beat.*) Trev and Kamal, and Bolota's gonna meet us down there.

Pete Bolota's the Ethiopian kid?

Mark Eritrean. His mum is.

Pete Close enough.

Mark Cos they both begin with 'E'?

Pete No, smartarse, cos they used to be the same place, didn't they.

Mark You tell me.

Pete I am telling you. They was one country 'til one split from the other. About twenty year back.

Mark I don't think Bolota's been east of Dagenham in his life. Right, I'ma bounce. Don't wait up, you get me?!

Pete What time you getting back?

Mark Here we go.

Pete I'm just saying, be on time tomorrow.

Mark I told ya, I'll go to work from the club.

Pete You know what Clint's like.

The **African Guy** *rises. He becomes* **Clinton Jones**, *a no-nonsense Cockney mate of* **Pete**'*s in painter's overalls who owns the small firm that employs* **Pete** *and* **Mark**.

Clint Where the hell you been? Them walls s'posed to paint 'emselves?

Clint *makes his way over to a housing association flat being renovated. Plaster on the walls; painting and decorating tools lie around.*

Mark When was I last late?

Clint Thursday!

Mark Six months without a sickie, trying to show both of ya I ain't no charity case –

Pete Fair enough. (*He holds up a £20 note.*) Buy 'em a drink on me. Your mates.

Mark I don't need your money.

Pete I know. If you *needed* it, I'd make you earn it. But you've been grafting like a good 'un, I'll buy you and your mates a drink. (*Beat.*) We're strange like that, fathers.

Mark Takes all sorts. (*Beat. He takes the money.*) Ta.

Pete My pleasure.

Mark And thank you for looking after Ella for tonight.

Pete You know I love having her around.

Mark Enjoy it while it lasts, Dad, yeah? Have me deposit soon.

Pete Listen, Mark –

Mark Make sure she gets her juice in the morning.

Pete I will.

Mark And her vitamins.

Pete I have done this before, you know. With you, for a start.

Mark And see how that turned out.

Pete Mark.

Mark Yeah?

Beat.

Pete It's been good having you around, these last few months. It's been good getting to know you again. Don't rush off, whatever happens. (*Pause.*) Look after yourself.

Mark I do, Dad. All day, every day.

He goes over to join **Clint** *at the flat.*

Pete I couldn't, mate. It's your decision, you do it … (*The bus hasn't moved an inch.* **Pete** *checks his watch.*) Look, hang on, I'll be right there. (*He rises and tries to force his way past the women.*) Excuse me. Excuse me. Excuse me. Get out the bloody – *He shoves past them and approaches the driver. The women glare at him.*

Burka Woman 1 هؤلاء الرجال الإنجليز لا يحترمون النساء. أتعلم؟

These Englishmen have no respect for women, you know?

Ha'olaa alrijal alingileez la yahtarimoon alnisaa. Ata'alam?

Woman in Pink Jumpsuit Ej, zasrańcu, może nieco grzeczniej, co?
(Hey, shithead, try to be polite maybe?)

Pete What's going on, mate?

Driver Station Barking.

Pete Do what?

Driver The bus go station Barking.

Pete Yeah, but it's not though, is it?

Driver Excuse me please?

Pete The bus ain't going to Barking, is it? On account of we're just sat here, do you know what I mean?

Beat.

Driver Excuse me please?

Pete *slaps his hands together and inhales deeply.*

Pete Do you know where you are going?

Driver The bus go station Barking.

Woman in Pink Jumpsuit (*into mobile*) عج السائق. هاي أنت!
لا أدري. هنالك شخص أحمق يز

I don't know, some wanker is distracting the drive. Hey buddy!

La adri. Honalik shakhsun ahmaq yuz'ij alsa'iq. Hey ant!

Pete And do you know where station Barking is, old son?

Burka Woman 1 أتركه وشأنه. هو يحاول أن يقوم بعمله!

Leave him alone, he is only trying to do his job!

Itrukhu wa sha'nuh. Howa yohawil an yaqoum bi'amalih.

Driver (*smiling apologetically, palms up*) No.

Someone bangs on the side of the bus and unleashes a torrent of abuse. The sound of a jackhammer. **Pete** *rips the doors of the bus open and storms away. The song*:

'Our friends in Parliament are all on our side
(Cock-eyed, cock-eyed)

Sometimes they talk tough but you know it's a lie
(Cock-eyed, cock-eyed)
Immigration is a good thing, on that they all agree
The only ones who'll stop it are the wicked BNP.

Oh I've got a brand new leather jacket and a brand new
mobile phone
Brits they live in cardboard boxes while we get furnished homes
Legal aid, driving lessons, central heating and free bills
Oh we get all the benefits and you get all the bills.'

The cast turns to the audience and collectively shouts:

'TO STOP ALL THIS NONSENSE, VOTE BNP!'

Pete *heads to the flat, where* **Clint** *and* **Mark** *are wrestling with an oversized cistern.*

Clint Bit more your end.

Mark I've got my end.

Clint No you ain't. (**Mark** *hefts his end up a little more.*) Float valve.

Mark Eh?

Clint How loud was the music in that gaff?

Mark Thass Benga for you! Nasty, *dutty* bass, blood!

He holds out a fist for **Clint** *to bump.* **Clint** *glares at him.*

Clint That was a … one a them questions you ask yourself, Mark. Pass us the fucking float valve.

Mark (*passing him the float valve*) You've got the right hump this morning, dontcha Clint? Big night last night, was it?

Clint No. It wasn't.

Mark Not as big as mine anyway! This one gyal, yeah … (*Points to his arm.*) See that? What are those, mate?

Clint (*not looking*) Stab wounds, hopefully.

Mark Scorch marks! Thass how hot this chick was, you know! Oh my days! (**Pete** *enters.*) Alright Dad? Hear what, you're lucky your little couch ain't got space for two cos it woulda got *bruk* up last night! I woulda rode dat ting like the Grand National! I'm talking about up and over, up and over, you know what I mean?!

Pete *looks at* **Clint** *with a 'You told him yet?' expression.* **Clint** *shakes his head.* **Mark** *starts singing some dancehall tune about hotness.*

Clint You turn off the stopcock on the rising main?

Mark Course.

Clint Course? Says the twat who set off indoor Niagara Falls on his first day. We had geezers turning up in barrels and everything.

Mark Clinton, I've come in and saved *your* arse.

Clint You may have improved but you ain't what you think you are, Mark.

Mark It was Titanic in here this morning.

Clint I've got stuff on my mind.

Mark I had to pull Kate Winslet out the shower curtain. You were miles away.

Clint Get on with your work!

Mark *looks hurt. Pause.*

Pete We lost the Mandela House contract.

Mark What? (**Clint** *busies himself with the cistern.*) Who to?

Beat.

Clint Them Polish fellas that're doing Harrison's.

Mark But they shouldn't even … They haven't got their City and Guilds. Do they have City and Guilds in Poland? You can't get the contracts now unless …

He looks around as if appealing to an invisible referee. **Clint** *bangs his spanner hard against the cistern by way of reply.*

Pete Cheaper bid.

Mark Course cheaper bid, they're not fucking qualified! How can the council give 'em the contract? (*Pause. Neither of them will meet* **Mark***'s eye. He clocks what this means. To* **Pete***.*) *I've* got my City and Guilds. Eight months I spent getting 'em, cos you told me there'd be work at the end of it.

Pete There is / work.

Mark But not here. Come on then, spit it out. I might be thick but I ain't stupid. Mandela House, that's half the order book. (*Beat.*) At least be straight with me, Clint.

Pause.

Clint As it stands, I don't have enough work for three.

Mark Well that's that then.

Pete Hold on –

Clint As it stands.

Pete There's ways / around it –

Clint If things pick up –

Mark Nah nah nah, bollocks. *Bollocks*. The way it is out there right now? Don't take the piss out of me *and* take my job.

Pete He hasn't taken your job. It's not his –

Mark No. But you have. I'm better than you, Dad, don't pretend I'm not. Alright, I was shit when I started, but I've done my courses and I've knuckled down and now I'm better than you. I'm faster and I've got a better eye. It's true, ain't it Clint?

Beat. **Clint** *looks away.*

Pete I need my job an all, Mark.

Clint It was him got you the place here.

Mark I made the most of this, you know? I fucking *hated* being here when I started, I'd've hated anything that wasn't football, but the white spirit in yer eyes and the boredom of it … When you've had thousands of people shouting for ya and then it's just you in a room with a roller and some spackling, it's quite hard to take.

Pete You're making a meal of this.

Mark I knuckled down and I got *good* at it, Dad.

Pete There's other jobs. That Tesco's just opened up.

Mark (*glaring*) Raise my daughter on five pound an hour?

Pete You've almost got yer deposit.

Mark Yeah, what about *rent*?

Pete You can stay with me a bit more, I like having you there.

Mark That's nice.

Pete I can carry you –

Mark I don't want to be fucking *carried*, Dad! (*Beat.*) Fuck it. It don't matter anyway.

Pete There's gotta be a way we can get you into one of these places.

Mark Aw, come on now –

Pete You should have this place. We should be doing up this place for *you*.

Mark It's a *waste of time*.

Pete You been down for it since the year dot, they can't just take it away from ya –

Mark They've changed the rules.

Pete Then they can change 'em back again!

Clint He's right, Pete. They don't care about local people, do they?

Mark I'm gonna leave the country. I've been thinking about it and I'm gonna leave the country.

Pause.

Pete No.

Mark That's what I'm gonna do though.

Pete And go where?

Mark Somewhere hot with a beach, birds in bikinis and drinks with fruit in 'em. Somewhere away from this shithole. (*Beat.*) Gary's in Malaga working on sites and that, he reckons he can sort me out with some labouring work.

Pete In Spain? Do you not read the papers? They're in worse shit than we are!

Mark I'll find something.

Pete Sat in some bar watching Sky Sports, dreaming of home?

Mark I won't be dreaming of home.

Pete What about your football? The fella from the Orient said get your knee sorted –

Mark I'm twenty-three. Nobody gets picked up at twenty-three. There's nothing here for me no more.

Pete What about Ella? What about … me and Ella?

Beat.

Mark I'll take her with me. When I get settled.

Pause.

Pete You know what your problem is, Mark? You've got no bottle. Never have done. When the going gets tough, Mark Case bottles it. Even when you was little.

Mark Is that right?

Clint Mark, I need you to go get me –

Pete Oh yeah, no problem when you was head and shoulders above everybody else on the pitch, you pissed it then, thought you was the best thing since sliced, but when the standard got a little bit tougher, games got a little bit harder –

Mark (*bitter*) I got hurt.

Pete You couldn't hack it. You did a runner, just like you're doing now.

Mark Runs in the family then.

Clint Right, that's it, both of you back to –

Mark The big man, the rebel. What the fuck have you done for the last ten years? A jobbing painter and decorator, takes the bus to work. Embarrassing.

Pete The rest of the world is busting a gut to get over here, climbing in back of lorries and under trains, risking life and limb, and you, you lot can't wait to get away. If it ain't all on a plate, you'd rather do a few Es, get off your heads.

Mark And all that effort, all them strikes done you so much good, ain't they?

Pete You're lazy, Mark. Lazy and weak. (*Beat.*) Where's it gone, the energy, the confidence, the belief we used to have in this country? The only people who's got it now are the immigrants. Where's it gone, Mark? Where's yours gone?

Beat. **Mark** *leaves. Pause.* **Pete** *circles the room.*

Clint Go after him.

Pete D'you know what they told me down the social? You know what they told me?

Clint Go after him, Pete.

Pete I sat there two and a half hours, waiting. Like the United Nations it was. Every language under the sun except English, all at two hundred decibels. I dunno why these backpacking cunts go all the way to India when they could just spend a couple of hours down the DSS. And then the woman calls me in, not being funny but she barely speaks English herself –

Clint Course.

Pete And she gives me the line about criteria and need and points, and in the end she tells me, 'The only way you can get your son on the housing list is to make him homeless.' That's my government telling me that. My own government is telling me I should kick my boy out on the street and then *maybe* they'll think about helping him.

Clint Peter. He's disappointed enough in himself. You can't be an all.

Pete Who says I'm disappointed in him?

Clint Come on, son.

Pete He's got no spark, no *courage* to him now. He's gotta pick himself up, get –

Clint Did you see the way he looked at ya? Like a kicked puppy.

Pete How can he leave?

Beat.

Clint Go on. I can cover it here.

Beat.

Pete What'm I supposed to do, Clint? If he goes, that's the last of Ell I'm gonna see.

Clint Go after him.

Pete I'm gonna lose my son and my granddaughter, both of 'em, just like that.

A young, well-dressed, Asian-looking woman appears alongside him, clutching a stack of electoral materials. She calls herself **Gina White**.

What am I supposed to do?

Gina Hello again.

Pete *turns. They are in his doorway. In his hand he holds the history book he was reading on the bus.*

It's Pete, isn't it?

Pete It is, yeah.

Gina I'm Gina.

Pete Yeah, I remember.

She holds her hand out, business like. He shakes it, somewhat uncomfortable. Pause.

Gina So, have you had the chance to read the stuff I left you?

Pete I haven't, no. Work, you know how it is.

Gina What do you do?

Pete Painter and decorator.

Gina Right.

Pete It was a, what do they call it now? A 'career rebrand', you could say.

Gina Meaning you got fired.

Pete Yeah.

Gina What'd you do before?

Pete Union organiser. (*Nods his head down the road.*) Car factories.

Gina Oh yeah? Interesting.

Pete That's one word for it. 'Outdated' would be another. What's that other thing they want now? 'Transferable skills'? I've got the opposite of that.

Gina What's the book?

Pete Local history stuff. A geek, my son calls me. I've got piles of stuff in here.

Beat.

Pete I'd better get back to …

Gina I could pop back in an hour or two? Give you a chance to look at what I left?

Pete Yeah. No. No. Yeah.

Gina (*smiling*) So yes *and* no?

Pete You're all right.

Gina All right you want me to come back or all right you want me to stay?

Beat. **Pete** *pulls a handful of crumpled leaflets from his back pocket.*

Pete Do you really mean this?

Gina We do.

Pete You really *mean* it?

A Day at the Racists   277

Gina   I do, yes.

Pete   Cos this is like going back in time for me. 'Nationalise public services.' 'End the privatisation of schools and hospitals.'

Gina   They care about big business, we care about ordinary people.

Pete   'No more bank bailouts.'

Gina   They 'can't interfere with the market' when it sends our jobs to China, but they'll bend over backwards for the bankers?

Pete   'Local residence the key for council house allocation.' Nobody's saying this sort of thing!

Gina   We are, Pete.

Pete   My son, right, born and raised in this area, and I went down the social and they've got *nothing* for him, nothing, it's all gone to these immigrants on the basis of greater need. And maybe they have got needs, those people, and good luck to 'em, but *so do we*. And we was here first. Nothing against them but we was here first and more than that, we put our shift in. I've paid my taxes and I put a shift in and I want what's coming. Not to me, because I'm a worn out old bugger, Gina –

Gina   I wouldn't say that.

Pete   But to the people who's important to me. And you look at who's in charge nowadays, the *contempt* they have for working-class people, taking away pensions and healthcare that people've been paying for for decades and then bang, just like that, privatised, gone ... And you can take it from scum like the Tories cos they've always been that way, but from the Labour Party ...

He hesitates for a moment.

Gina   Carry on.

Pete Cos we made the Labour Party, do you know what I mean? Froze our bollocks off on picket lines, went on strike and lived off fresh air and fuck all for six months at a time. And now we've turned to dust in their eyes, ain't we? We're the fucking *problem* now: chav scum, ASBO meat. A source of *laughter*. Prime time TV entertainment. I hate them for it. I bloody hate them for it. (*Pause.*) Sorry. Sorry.

Gina It's fine.

Pete (*hand on chest*) Phwoah. Bloody hell. Sorry.

Gina It's good to hear.

Pete Dunno where that came from.

Gina I agree. I agree with everything you've said.

Beat.

Pete Ah, this is a joke! I used to have proper tear-ups with you lot in the Seventies!

Gina Those were not my lot.

Pete (*Pointing to his cheek.*) See there? That's where one of yours stuck his blade in.

Gina Those were not mine, Pete.

Pete You ask your bosses, they'll remember me. Pete Case, Head Case they used to call me. We was on the national news once, when they blackballed us from the factory. I've been called a 'socialist agitator' by Moira Stewart on national TV, that's my claim to fame. Got the tape somewhere, but it's Betamax, useless.

Gina Join the British National Party, Pete.

Pete I'm not gonna join the bloody BNP when I've spent half me life fighting 'em.

Gina Do you think we should be building council houses for people like your son, instead of 'luxury accommodation' for parasitic tosspots?

Pete I'm not a *fascist*, Gina, I'm not a racist!

Gina Do you think we should cut back on the number of immigrants in this country, who undercut British workers and put them out of jobs?

A Day at the Racists   279

Pete   I don't have a problem with people trying to feed their –

Gina   Do you think we should cut back on the number of immigrants –

Pete   Yes, I do, I do, alright.

Gina   Do you think we should restore our sense of dignity, of community, of pride?

Pete   I'm older than you, Gina. I know what these people are about.

Gina   Do you think anybody, and I mean anybody, in power gives two rancid shits about people like you and me, Pete Case, Head Case? (*Pause. Pete can't look at her.*) Then tell me what are you waiting for?

The sound of children playing. Parents' evening, **Ella***'s school.* **Mark** *and* **Pete** *being shown round by her teacher,* **Zenobia,** *a young, middle-class black woman.*

Mark   Who's this?

Zenobia   That's Mary Seacole, the first black nurse in Britain. She went with the British to the Crimea.

Mark   I went with the British to Ayia Napa meself. Coulda used some medical attention there, no word of a lie. Which one's Ella's?

Zenobia   This one.

Mark   Rah, that is good, you know!

Zenobia   She's talented, your daughter.

Mark   She thinks the world of you.

Zenobia   And a lovely little girl too.

Mark   Always singing your praises.

Zenobia   Well, they do at that age, don't they?

Mark   I can see why.

Zenobia They grow out of it eventually. I'm not that special.

Mark I'd have to disagree.

Zenobia That's sweet of you. Now if you'll excuse me, there are other parents –

Pete So is this the same thing she was doing a few weeks ago?

Beat.

Zenobia No, that was Diwali, Mr Case.

Pete Right. It's just they seem quite similar, you know. To an ignoramus.

Zenobia Not especially.

Pete Easy to muddle up, maybe.

Zenobia That was an Asian festival. This is Black History Month.

Pete OK. Fair enough. (*He looks around.*) Lot of ... lot of ethnic stuff she's getting at the minute.

Mark It's Black History Month, Dad.

Zenobia It's the time of year. Come back at Christmas or Easter, it'll be different.

Pete Other made-up stuff, you mean?

Zenobia Pardon?

Pete When does she study the rest of it?

Zenobia The rest of what?

Pete Her heritage. British history.

Zenobia This is part of British history.

Pete Part of, yes. And I can understand that, why you want to give her all this lot, it's something your generation probably never got.

Zenobia It's not my choice, Mr Case. I don't set the curriculum.

Pete Don't get me wrong, I think it's fair enough. I just think you can go too far the other way, you know?

Zenobia I only teach what they ask me to teach.

Mark What's she missing then?

Pete I told ya, British history.

Mark The empire and all that? You always taught me 'Queen and Country' was bollocks. (*To* **Zenobia**.) He took my school textbook away one time cos it said Wellington won the battle of Waterloo. (*Parody of* **Pete**.) 'Wot, on his fackin own?'

Zenobia *tries to hide a smile.*

Pete I'm talking about her roots.

Mark When he wants cheering up a bit, this geezer pops in the Diana crash tape.

Pete Mark, shut up for a minute. (*To* **Zenobia**.) Her society. What's made her.

Zenobia Isn't this part of what's made her?

Pete Of course it is, I'm not denying that. I'm talking about the bits you've forgotten.

Zenobia I haven't *forgotten* –

Pete See, it upsets me a little bit how people (*to* **Mark**), *uneducated* people, go on like British history is nothing but theft and murder. Because of some chinless wonders a couple of hundred years ago, an aristocracy I've got *nothing* in common with –

Zenobia If you'd come to the previous –

Pete The working-class movement, right, started right down this road! The first independent trade union was here gasworkers, 1867. First Labour MP, West Ham –

Mark Dad, she's five.

Pete And she should know the history of where she's from!

In 1919, the London dockers refused to load arms for the White armies fighting the Russian revolution.

Zenobia And in 1940 they helped load refugee Jews back onto the boats that returned them to Germany. I did history at uni.

Pete Demonstrations against Mosley in the East End.

Zenobia Demonstrations *for* Mosley in the East End!

Pete Why do you have to contradict me?

Zenobia Because things were not, are not, and never will be, all one way.

Pete So she shouldn't get only the black stuff!

Mark (*incredulous*) The 'black stuff'?!

Zenobia With respect, have you *seen* Ella lately?

Pete Why's it matter so much what she looks like?

Mark Dad, lock it off, *now*.

Pete You're shoving her into a box and telling her who she can and can't be, cos of what she looks like! You know what she said to me last week? 'Where am I from? Cos Razana's from Pakistan and Angelika's from Poland and Khalifa's from Somalia, but I'm not from anywhere special.'

Mark Where's all this come from?

Pete I want what's best for my granddaughter.

Mark And she's trying her best to give it to her. Like she was trying to say but you wouldn't let her, if you'd come to the one at Easter –

Pete I was / working.

Mark If you'd come to the one at Easter, you'da seen all chicks and fluffy bunnies and you wouldn'ta gone off on this mad BNP turnout. (*Beat.*) I'm surprised at ya.

Pause.

Pete I've got to go. Thank you for teaching my granddaughter.

Zenobia It's fine. It's my job.

He leaves. Beat.

Mark I've never met that geezer before in my entire life.

Beat. They both laugh a little.

Zenobia It's just, no offence, but I get the same routine from the white parents *every single day* …

Mark I know.

Zenobia 'Why do the kids have to do this black stuff? Why can't they study 'our' culture?'

Mark He's not like that, I swear.

Zenobia 'How long has it been a crime to be white?'

Mark He ain't got no Staff. He ain't coming in with a spider's web tattooed on his face, know what I mean?

Zenobia No, I know, but –

Mark He's a decent man, I promise.

Beat. She smiles.

Zenobia I had one bloke in last week, he'd lost one of his fingers, probably in some bizarre prison ritual or something, so across his knuckles it said LOVE and HAT. (*They break up laughing.*) The worst bit was, he kept ranting on about how bad his kid's spelling was! Inside I was *pissing* myself! Sorry, I probably shouldn't say that …

Mark Nah, nah, it's funny … (*Beat.*) Listen, Ms Williams … I don't know if this is, like … and you can shoot me down proper if you don't … cos I know it probably ain't professional and I don't wanna say you ain't professional, like … cos professional's one of the nicest things about ya … not that it's the only nice thing about ya, I mean –

Zenobia Mr Case.

Mark Mark. Sorry. Probably not the best time to lyrics ya –

Zenobia I'm sorry, Mr Case, but this isn't acceptable. I'm afraid I have to hold you responsible for what happened today.

Mark What?

Zenobia You're going to have to write out some lines for me.

Mark *What?*

Zenobia Got a pen and paper?

Mark (*scrabbling in his jacket for a scrap of paper to write on, he can only find a Rizla packet, which he holds up apologetically*) Yeah, I mean sort of …

Zenobia That'll do. Ready? Oh seven nine four seven, six eight seven three four one. You get that?

Mark Oh yeah. I'm a very good student. When the teaching's right.

Zenobia I'm glad to hear it.

Mark When do I have to hand this in?

Zenobia How about Friday night?

Mark That should work. That should definitely work.

Pete *on the doorstep with* **Gina**.

Gina Why does she have to be one or the other, you mean?

Pete Exactly! I thought you'd understand … (*Beat.*) Cos the thing is, right, if you say anything, you sound –

Gina Sound racist.

Pete And there's no comeback to that, is there? What can you say, 'My best friend is a black geezer'? You sound like a prick. You say anything, you get some social worker who's missed five Baby Ps before lunch round your gaff lecturing you on 'tolerance', like you eat off the floor, you're some kind of animal. (*He stops* *himself. Pause.*) I'm a nice man, really, Gina. Promise. I'm not normally like this.

Gina   Can I come in, Pete?

Beat.

Pete   Ella's just gone to bed. I don't wanna wake her, you know.

Gina   How old is she? Ella?

Pete   She's five.

Gina (*smiling*)   Nice age.

Pete   That's her there, look.

He hands over a picture from his wallet. The photo appears as a poster above their heads: a mixed-race (black and white) photogenic little girl with a happy smile.

Gina   Lovely little thing, isn't she?

She hands the photo back. Pause.

Pete   Who are you, Gina?

Gina   I'm your BNP election candidate.

Pete   Not what are you, who are you?

Gina   How'd you mean?

Pete   Where are you from, who's your family?

Gina   I'm not that comfortable talking about my personal life.

Pete   Well you might wanna get used to it, love. I think a few people might have questions, d'you know what I mean?

Pause.

Gina   My mum's English, Irish if you go back far enough, my dad's Pakistani.

Pete   Big families on both sides then.

Gina   Except neither side wanted the marriage and they cut them off. I have six aunts, seven uncles and thirty-seven cousins, and I've met a total of three of them. I think the isolation was what did for my parents, turned them in on each other.

Pete It's hard when you get isolated.

Gina Is that what happened to you and Mrs Pete? There must have been a –

Pete Carry on with yer story.

Beat.

Gina When I was a kid, we moved around a lot. I don't know if it was for my dad's work or to distract them from hating each other. All I know is I was never at home.

Pete OK.

Gina Right away, wherever we'd land up, they'd have me in one box or another, like you say about Ella, even if it was just the 'reject/don't fit in' box. I won't be put in a box, Pete. You know what lives in boxes? Toys.

Pete Different nowadays, though, innit? I see Mark with his mates, all colours under the sun, they don't even care.

Gina Oh, it's still there, under the surface, trust me. All these little groups, hiving themselves off, marking out their territory so they can get council grants. It's skin deep, this liberal tolerance.

Pete Call me a liberal and I guarantee we'll fall out.

Gina When were you last part of something? When's the last time you lost yourself in something bigger?

Pete Work.

Gina Painting and decorating?

Beat.

Pete Factory days.

Gina When else? The times I've been happiest, Pete, when I've made the most sense, are times of *patriotism*. Diana's death. Last Night of the Proms. The World Cup.

Pete The World Cup is when you've been happiest?

Gina Lost in the group, the heart pumping, something to be proud of. What is anyone *proud* of now, Pete? The answer should be all around us: England. Its pride, its passion, its greatness. The rivers and the hills and the beauty around you.

Pete It's flat as a roadkill sarnie round here.

Gina A thousand years of history and nobody knows who we are any more? But you know that history. You know you're part of something.

Pete I read your new constitution. (*Pulls it out.*) 'The British National Party stands for the preservation of the national and ethnic character of the British people –'

Gina That's me.

Pete '– and is wholly opposed to any form of racial integration between British and non-European peoples. It is committed to reversing the tide of non-white immigration and to restoring the overwhelmingly white make up of the British population.'

Gina They have to say that, don't they?

Pete Do they?!

Gina *For now*, so they don't lose the base. But in the long run, they'll adapt or die. People aren't out and out racist any more, not like they used to be. But they are still patriotic. And sick and fucking tired of spongers, whether it's wanker bankers with their hands out who fuck off to Dubai the moment anyone mentions tax, or bearded freaks with seven wives all claiming housing benefit. We, the British people, the way we are *now*, we've had enough. Whatever we look like, whoever we sleep with, whoever we pray to, the British people have had enough. Kick out the parasites, pull up the drawbridge and let's get on with it. (*Pause.*) Come to the next meeting. (*Beat.*) Please.

McDonald No fucking way.

Pete *melts away.* **Gina** *with the BNP's local organiser, an unreconstructed but not unintelligent racist named* **Tony McDonald***. Suddenly she is all steel again.*

Gina I don't think it's up to you. Orders from above.

McDonald From Rick the Prick, the one-eyed wanker? He can go fuck himself. I'm the regional organiser here.

Gina Which is why I need your help to put the campaign together.

McDonald I already told you.

Gina (*smiling*) Give me a go.

McDonald No fucking way.

Gina What's wrong with me?

McDonald Look at you. You think I can get my members to campaign for that? You think I can get my members out on the streets for a –

Gina Where are you from, Tony?

Beat.

McDonald Where am *I* from?

Gina Yeah. Where's your family from?

McDonald Becontree.

Gina No, *originally*. Scottish name, McDonald, correct?

Beat.

McDonald Celtic warriors. Conquerors.

Gina Immigrants.

McDonald Not as recently as your lot.

Gina We're all outsiders, originally. But we're here now, aren't we? And we both want what's best for Britain.

Pause.

McDonald Fucking European elections. Coleman wins two seats in the Europeans, *two seats* out of seventy odd, and all of a sudden it's 'time for the party to enter the political mainstream'.

Gina You don't see winning seats as an important aim for a political party?

McDonald Not as much as marking your territory, no. Standing up and saying who we are.

Gina I think that attitude may be the reason Rick sent me here, Tone.

McDonald Winning is secondary to staking out who we are, not letting people forget White Britain exists. Always has been. But two seats in the Euros and Coleman, the opportunist cunt, who in my opinion has never been a true member of this party, shits himself, rubs out the fucking Party constitution like it's a pub throwing order, and parachutes in some cocky little half-breed to stick her nose in like she owns the place. Classic Coleman. No local knowledge whatsoever. Anyone knows the first thing about this area knows there is zero fucking chance –

Gina Call me a Paki. (*Beat.*) Come on. Call me a Paki. Get it over with.

Beat. **Pete** *materialises in a doorway, unseen by either of them.*

McDonald Look me up on Stormfront, darling, you'll see who you're dealing with.

Gina Call me a Paki.

Beat.

McDonald Paki.

Gina Can't hear you. Louder.

McDonald Paki.

Gina Again.

McDonald   PAKI.

Gina   BOOOOORRRRRIIING! Is that the best you can do? How old are you, Tony? Fifty, fifty-five? And that's the sum total of wisdom those years have granted you? You should be embarrassed, mate. You want to win this election?

McDonald   Of course I do.

Gina   I will do that.

McDonald   But not at any price.

Gina   See, you might think you're radical, Tony, 'not like all the rest', but really you think like the lefties. All either of you see is my face. They see my face and they tell me about their yoga classes and their challenging Indian gap year. You see my face and you want to stick a pint glass in it. But it's the same thing. I'm here for a reason.

McDonald   Because this is your only chance of becoming a celebrity.

Gina   Because this is the only party that believes what I believe, in the greatness of Britain and of British identity.

McDonald   British identity doesn't include you.

Gina   I could have signed up as 'ethnic outreach officer' for the Tories or Labour. They're gagging for people like me. That would have been the easy way.

McDonald   Wouldn't have *stood out* quite so much though, would ya?

Gina   I could've got onto the lists of 'faces to watch' and had all the Westminster village idiots queuing up.

McDonald   Wouldn't be quite so 'controversial'. Don't think, because I'm true to myself, that I don't know what's going on.

Pete (*entering*)   Always been a step behind the times, aintcha Tony?

Gina   Pete!

A Day at the Racists   291

Pete (*kissing* **Gina***'s cheek, winking at* **McDonald**)   Alright son?

Gina   You two know each other?

Pete   Oh yeah. We go way back.

McDonald   I've seen it all now. The Yanks have a nig-nog president, the BNP have a Paki candidate and Red Case strolls into my office.

Pete (*pointing to his face*)   I told you how I got this? That was Tony's handiwork.

McDonald   You want a matching pair? Then get the fuck out of my sight.

Pete   Can't. Gina invited me.

McDonald   This is your idea?

Gina   It is, yeah. Pete's exactly the kind of person I'm trying to draw into the party.

McDonald   Do you have a fucking clue what you're doing?

Gina   I think so.

McDonald   This Red trash, this Marxist scum, you want him in the *party*? The whole *point* of the party is to have cunts like this in the gutter, flush them out and punish them, let the red blood flow so people can see how weak they are, how weak and feeble are the Yids and the Reds and all the other mongrels and mixers.

Pete   I remember you pissing your pants in the New Cross Road.

McDonald   Scum like this are the reason for the party's existence.

Pete   The Battle of Lewisham, August of '77. Literally pissed his pants.

McDonald   He does not join the party.

Pete   Bricks and smoke bombs raining down and all I remember is this big stain spreading across Tony McDonald's denims.

McDonald (*springs to his feet and into* **Pete**'s *face*) What is your fucking game? What is your fucking game? What is your fucking game? (**Pete** *bristles. They are chin to chin. Pause.* **McDonald** *steps back.*) Who are you trying to kid? A fucking Red and a Paki working for the BNP? You're not even funny.

Gina No, I'm not.

McDonald You're mad if you think this is the last of this.

He storms out. **Gina** *calls after him.*

Gina Give Rick my love! (*She turns to* **Pete**.) That was *amazing*! The look on his face! The way you put him in his place, that was *exactly* what I need –

Pete I'm gonna go home now, Gina. **Gina** (*face suddenly falling*) What?! Why?

Pete Feel a bit sick actually.

Gina You need to sit down?

Pete It was alright when I was winding him up but I think I might puke now. (*He bends over to catch his breath. Pause.*) Look at me. Fucking look at me. I'm actually in the BNP offices. I was actually thinking of joining the BNP.

Gina You *are* –

Pete I may have come down in the world but I ain't sunk that low. See ya, Gina.

He makes to leave. She bars his way.

Gina No. No. Bollocks. Alright, you've run into an old adversary, it's jarred you a bit. You'll get over it.

Pete Gina –

Gina Has anything in the real world changed? Any of the things that brought you here tonight, have they changed?

Beat.

A Day at the Racists 293

Pete Look, it might have made sense, when we was *talking*, when I was reading your stuff in my flat –

Gina And it still does.

Pete But you talk about the real world the real world is people like him.

Gina People like him are a dying breed. I'm the future. *I* am.

Pete Yeah, but ...

Gina Look at me, is that what you're gonna say? Who's the racist now, Pete? 'You're a Paki, you stay with the other Pakis.'

Pete You know I don't –

Gina I thought this country was about freedom, where's the freedom in that? Fuck any system that says my dad can come over here and keep his disgusting Paki ways –

Pete Gina –

Gina That is what they are, Pete! What kind of freedom says my Dad can marry me off to some obese stinking fifty-year-old peasant from his village who signs his name with his thumbprint and tries to stick his cock up my arse on the wedding night? And then my white mother and all her kind tell me it's 'my culture' and I should be *grateful* to have it, because she's too fucking scared and lost and weak to know what's hers and so in her mind she's *brave* for sucking my Dad's dick and getting his passport because she didn't have to, she could've married that ginger IT engineer from Huddersfield and never had the neighbours whispering. Fuck all that.

Pete I'm gonna go home.

Gina Don't go. What made you come in? Once you saw Mr Knuckle-dragger there, you could have slipped back out the way you came. What made you stay?

Pete Wanted to wind him up, didn't I?

Gina Was that all? (*Beat.*) There is a great mass of humanity out there, lost and lonely and afraid, that we can reach. Help me find what the people need and want and dream of. Give them a little of what's been stolen from them and they will be ours forever.

Mark *enters the finished flat. He stares around.*

I can make a real difference in people's lives.

Mark Fucking hell.

Gina But I need an organiser.

Pete No.

Mark (*walks around in some disbelief*) Bloody fucking hell.

Gina A man with experience.

Pete Not me. No. No way.

Gina A man with passion and intelligence, whose passion and intelligence are being criminally wasted as of now.

Mark (*jingles a set of keys*) Bloody fucking fucking bloody hell.

Gina A man who wants to make a difference in other people's lives, and his own.

Mark *does a little dance of ecstasy as he takes in the room.* **Pete** *enters the flat.* **Gina** *watches him.* **Pete** *and* **Mark** *stare at one another. Pause.*

Mark I can't believe we was working on this place and now ...

Pete I know.

Beat.

Mark Here's your bit, look.

Pete How'd you know that was my bit?

Mark Look at the finish on this.

Pete Looks alright to me.

Mark That is a crap finish. You never could finish. If I'd known I was on the list for the gaff, I'd have done it meself.

Pete You weren't on the list.

Pause. They look at one another.

Mark What about the rent?

Pete You'll have to earn it, won't you.

Mark That's my point.

Pete I reckon Clint'll take you back on.

Mark Where's he got new work from?

Pete You'd be doing my stuff.

Mark What are you gonna do?

Gina I want you to run my campaign, Pete.

Pause.

Pete (*to* **Mark**) I'm thinking of taking this job.

Mark Doing what?

Gina Will you do it?

Pete With the council. I haven't decided yet. (*He looks at* **Gina**. *Beat.*) I don't want to do anything public.

Gina It's nothing to be ashamed of.

Pete Not until you've proved yourself. Alright?

Gina There's no reason to hide –

Pete *Alright?*

Gina As you like. Whatever you like, Pete.

Mark Dad?

Pete Yeah?

Beat.

Mark Thank you.

Pete It's my pleasure.

Beat.

Mark I didn't think you had it in you.

Pete Well I do.

Mark You didn't have to do no-one, did ya? I'm not gonna find some poor Somali bird and her three kids under the floorboards?

Pete Connections. The way it works, always has done. (*Beat. To* **Gina**.) You did it.

Gina I told you I would.

Pete I've been trying to get him one of those places for five years.

Gina When I say I'll do something, Pete, I do it.

Mark I thought you give up all that politics stuff from time?

Pete I never gave up politics, Mark. Politics gave me up.

Gina What do you say, Pete?

Beat. **Mark** *looks around the room again.*

Mark Dad?

Pete Yes, mate?

Mark You reckon Clint can sort me out some pink matt cheap?

Pete Why?

Gina Will you do it?

Mark For Ella's room. Don't suppose you fancy giving me a hand?

Pete With my finish?

Mark If you can be arsed.

Gina I want you, Pete.

Beat.

Pete (*to both*) Yes. I'd love to. I would love that.

Lights gradually down.

Act Two

Pete, *smartly dressed, energised, buzzing around with papers in hand.* **Gina** *enters.*

Pete   Right, here's the plan.

Gina   The plan is coffee.

Pete   You know them three tower blocks by the motorway?

Gina   Did you drink it all?

Pete   No party's been up there for going on twenty years. Too scary, lifts are fucked, no-one fancies the smell of piss in their clothes afterwards.

Gina   Look at you! You did drink it all!

Pete   You're going up there this morning. What are you talking about?

Gina   Coffee.

Pete I ain't made any coffee. Why are you talking about coffee?

Gina   Because it's eight o'clock in the morning.

Pete   There's hundreds and hundreds of people lives up there, Gina! How d'you reckon them people are gonna react when they see someone gives a shit about them?

Gina (*smiling, moves across and takes the papers from him*)   If they're anything like me, they're going to be charmed, and just a little scared, by your enthusiasm.

Pete   I'm not the one going.

Gina   Thank you for the suggestion, I think it's an excellent idea. I will get up there as soon as I can.

Pete   You need to get up there now.

Gina   They're tower blocks, Pete, they're not going anywhere.

Pete   It sends a message. It shows no-one's gonna be left behind, that we're here for the people no-one else cares about –

Gina (*smiling, passing him back the papers*) I've got to go somewhere first. Stay here. Keep having good ideas. And try not to explode.

She takes a seat at a table with **McDonald**, *clutching a pint, and the party leader,* **Rick Coleman**, *whose polished veneer cracks at times to let through something very dark.* **Pete** *looks at the papers, hesitates, then strides purposefully out of the door.*

Coleman That was an excellent speech, Gina.

Gina Thank you, Rick.

Coleman Exactly on message. Well done. One or two cracking jokes as well.

McDonald You like a joke, don't you, Gina?

Gina I try to entertain as well as inform.

McDonald Which of us do you reckon is funnier?

Gina I don't –

McDonald Why are blacks like bicycles? Cos they only work with chains on. (*No reaction.*) Here's a good one: bloke goes into a bar with a crocodile. He says to the barman, 'Do you serve niggers in here?' Guv'nor says, 'Course we do, we're not racist.' 'Right then, I'll have a pint of lager and a nigger for the crocodile.' (*Beat.*) Laugh, Rick.

Coleman I tend not to laugh at things I don't find funny, Tony.

McDonald You used to love all that.

Coleman I don't think so.

McDonald Oh, you did. I remember you standing on the bar after NF meetings, roaring out the Yid jokes. 'Why do Jews make the best magicians? Because they –'

Gina Most men are in favour of the burka. It gives you somewhere to wipe your cock after a blow job. (*Beat.*) You've probably heard that one.

McDonald I have, yeah. Different when you tell it though, innit. (*Pause.*) Thirty years fighting for blood and honour, fighting to purge White Britain of the taint –

Gina And failing. Because there's more of us here than ever, aren't there? So on your own terms, you're a complete failure.

McDonald Failure would be to surrender. Which I will never do.

Gina Here's one for you: 'What's the difference between the BNP and the royal family? One's a group of neo-Nazi bigots who hate democracy, the other's the BNP.'

Coleman That's very funny, Gina.

McDonald She's walking down my streets holding my flag like I'm the one doesn't belong here. You any idea how much that hurts?

Coleman You don't altogether understand politics, do you?

McDonald Don't underestimate me, cunt.

Coleman The point of the Party is not to serve as a vehicle for your pathetic little 'blood on the leather' rentboy paramilitary fantasies, Tony. The point of the Party is to operate as a modern political force.

McDonald You're a parasite, Coleman.

Coleman You see, most people don't share your embarrassingly crude reaction to the lies of multiculturalism.

McDonald A worm in the guts.

Coleman Whether that's because of the sheer volume of Third World sewage they wade through on the streets or the Marxist conspiracy in the media, I couldn't say. It really doesn't matter.

McDonald (*to* **Gina**) You trust him, do ya?

Coleman The point is, the British people are too indoctrinated to try to turn the clock back. It won't work. They have ethnics in their workplaces, ethnics in their families. A touch of the tar and all that.

McDonald Do you trust him?

Gina I've no reason not to.

McDonald *laughs a short bitter laugh.*

Coleman But that doesn't mean they aren't angry. What people have done, you see, is they've *codified* their anger. People speak in code now. 'Knife crime' means, 'I'm afraid of black men', 'terrorism' means 'Brown people frighten me'. And they vent their rage over the breakfast table, with their orange juice and the *Daily Mail*, because nobody in politics will take the code to its logical conclusion. Except for us. Six million *Mail* readers and no political party to represent them. That is a very salient fact, Tony, one no nationalist should ignore. Now do you understand why she's here?

McDonald Winning elections is not as important as staying pure.

Coleman If you want to stop mass immigration, you have to achieve power within the mainstream political system. There is no other way.

McDonald Two seats in the Euros and maybe, *maybe*, one in Parliament?

Gina Once I win, people will look at us in a different way.

Coleman Credibility, Tone. The people who want to vote BNP but think it's a waste? The people who vote Tory hoping they'll stop hugging and start hurting? All ours.

McDonald People don't vote *for* anyone. They vote in *protest*.

Coleman We will give them that outlet also. The decision has been taken.

McDonald You'd fuck thirty years of my work, thirty years of my life, for a joke?

Coleman You will give Gina the full extent of your co-operation

McDonald   You don't tell me –

Coleman   Or you will be replaced –

With unnerving quickness **Tony** *picks up his pint and pours the last of it deliberately over* **Gina***'s head. He holds the empty glass close to her face. Pause.*

McDonald   The future isn't here quite yet.

The sound of heavy rain. **Mark** *and* **Zenobia** *in a restaurant. It's not going well.* **Zenobia** *fiddles with her fork. Beat.*

Mark   It's caning it down out there. It's like Katrina with white people.

Zenobia   Mmmm.

Beat.

Mark   I wouldn't say it's been raining a lot, but I was at B&Q today and this old bearded geezer was buying up all the wood. Said he was in a hurry to get to the zoo?

Zenobia   What were you doing at B&Q?

Mark   I wasn't … It was, like, a set-up? For the joke?

Zenobia   Right. Have you got a lot more rain jokes?

Mark   Nah –

Zenobia   Or a lot of other jokes that need a handout in advance?

Mark   Did I do something wrong?

Zenobia   Well, yes, Mark. When you offered to take me out for dinner, I was expecting a little more than Nando's.

Mark   What's wrong with Nando's? Ella loves Nando's.

Zenobia   Ella is five. If I was five, I'm sure I'd love Nando's too. The next time you want to impress a *woman*, you might wanna consider something a bit more upmarket. (*Beat.*) I'm sorry. I'm being a bitch.

Mark   You're not being a bitch.

Zenobia I *am* being a bitch.

Mark Maybe just a little bit.

Zenobia (*slaps him on the arm*) Oi! You're not meant to agree with me!

Mark What's the matter, you don't like fried chicken? You'll get kicked out the black person's union if you don't like fried chicken.

Zenobia You do like to walk a fine line, don't you?!

Mark (*Johnny Cash*) 'Because you're mine, I walk the line.'

Zenobia Ouch. I see how they got all those confessions at Guantanamo now.

Mark See, you've given me an idea there. I'm gonna keep singing until you smile.

Zenobia No.

Mark 'Just one Cornetto!'

Zenobia Shut up!

Mark 'Give it to me!'

She shoves her hand over his mouth. He takes it and keeps hold of it.

Zenobia (*laughing*) Stop it!

Mark There's loads more where that came from. What about that Susan Boyle song?

Zenobia Don't you *dare*!

Mark Nah, I don't need to now, I've had my wicked way with ya. Got you to smile.

Beat. She gradually withdraws her hand from his and sits back in her chair.

So go on then. What's the drama?

Zenobia What do you mean?

Mark It ain't just the peri-peri giving you the hump, is it?

Beat.

Zenobia They want to turn the school into an Academy.

Beat.

Mark I don't actually know what that –

Zenobia They're going to close the school down and reopen it on the waste land between the dump and the sewage works.

Mark What?

Zenobia Flog off the old site for 'executive housing', and rehire the teachers on half the pay, and everything based on test scores, and no time to give the immigrant kids basic English or show the British kids from the shitty estates how to brush their teeth or clean themselves properly.

Mark They can't do that.

Zenobia Read the papers.

Mark Are you gonna stay?

Zenobia Not on that money, with some box-ticker peering over my shoulder all day.

Mark No.

Zenobia It's not worth it, Mark!

Mark They can't just do that!

Zenobia Yes they can.

Mark Who's doing it?

Zenobia The council.

Mark Then stop them. Batter them.

Zenobia 'Batter them', how are you gonna –

Mark I don't know, Zenobia! They're elected, ain't they? Then do what my dad used to do get your lot together, pressure them, get new people in, get it out there what the bastards are up to. If that don't work, go round their houses and set them on fire.

Zenobia Mark –

Mark This is the first time Ella's been happy at school. She loves your class. Why should someone be able to take that away from her? Why should they? (*Beat.*) I'm not educated like you, Zenobia. I don't know how things work or why they work. Who needs education when you're gonna be the next David Beckham? But I'm not, am I? (*Beat.*) I don't want my girl to miss out, that's all. I'm sorry if –

Zenobia Shut up. (*Beat.*) I'm gonna go home now, Mark.

Mark Aw, look, I'm really sorry –

Zenobia I'm going to go home and think about what you said. And maybe make a few phone calls. (*Beat.*) And next time, assuming you're up for a next time?

Mark (*grinning*) I think I can fit you in.

Zenobia Take me somewhere decent?

Coleman *and* **Gina**. *He watches her as she wipes the beer from her hair.*

Coleman Are you alright?

Gina I'm fine.

Coleman You're soaked. Let me help you.

He pulls out a handkerchief and daubs at her brow. Something in his fastidiousness, the care he takes not to touch her skin with his bare hand, says more about the way he sees her than any amount of rhetoric. She realises this and disgusted and chilled, pulls strongly away. They study each other. He puts away the handkerchief.

Coleman I'm sorry about that. I do hope it hasn't put you off.

Gina Nothing I haven't dealt with before.

Coleman Tony, I mean. If you want, I can have him disciplined, brought up before the committee –

Gina I really don't need your protection, Rick.

Coleman I know you don't, Gina. Or I wouldn't have chosen you.

Gina Is that how it worked? I had the impression it was the other way round.

Coleman I'm sure your memory is better than mine. (*Beat.*) One thing on your next speech.

Gina Yes?

Coleman Play up the Islamification of Britain a little more. Shariah law, immigration via the womb. You know, how quickly they breed –

Gina Saw the update on the website, yep.

Coleman I think that'll play very well down here.

Gina I'll consider it, yes.

Beat.

Coleman Well. Duty calls. Is there anything more I can do to help you, Gina?

Gina There is, actually. Cutting out the references to 'Third World sewage' would probably be useful.

Coleman In private conversation, between friends –

Gina You used it in your speech last week. Three times.

Beat.

Coleman What you have to do, you see Gina, you have to titillate them. It's like an erotic film. Do you watch erotic films, Gina? (*Beat.*) I don't, but I understand the principle. You know what they want, they want the naughty stuff. But you don't give them what they want, not up front. You hint at it, you suggest it, but you don't give it to them until they're gagging for it, then … bang.

Gina You told me we would campaign on a positive line.

Coleman It's like fishing. You ever go fishing, Gina?

Gina A positive line about England. What England can be.

Coleman Bait in the water, flick of the wrist. Get it to glimmer. Flick of the wrist.

Gina Bait in the water.

Coleman This *is* a positive line. *You* are our positive line.

Gina Before I signed up to this, you agreed British nationalism's deeper meaning, it's not what you look like, it's where you're from, putting British people first –

Coleman Whatever their colour. And I stand by those ideas one hundred percent, every one of them. The ideas of the future.

Gina Then why are you – ?

Coleman They're not a very sophisticated electorate, the great British public. They don't adjust to change very well.

Gina You're not giving them the chance.

Coleman It's quite a complicated argument. Confused people tend not to vote.

Gina Then make it clear what –

Coleman Having you as our candidate makes it clear, surely?

Gina Not if you keep undermining me, no.

Coleman Once you're in position, we can roll out the more sophisticated stuff.

Gina You told me –

Coleman (*losing patience*) I also told you there were certain things you might have to swallow. If you wanted the high profile the Party can offer.

Pause.

Gina Fine.

Coleman Anything else you want to raise? Might as well get it on the table now.

Gina Nothing.

Coleman Sure?

Gina Sure.

Beat.

Coleman Good. Then I'll see you before the election, Gina.

Pete *leading a community clean-up day, collecting rubbish from a local estate. He puts a couple of things into a black plastic sack. A middle-aged housewife comes out of her door and watches him suspiciously.*

Housewife What do you think you're doing?

Pete Evening, madam.

Housewife Never mind madam, what d'you think you're doing?

Pete Community clean up. Helping make the area look like it used to.

Housewife Who are you, council?

Pete Not council, no.

Housewife I bloody thought not, they're effing useless, council.

Pete Tell me about it.

Housewife Waste of bloody taxpayer money. Ain't seen council round here for donkey's.

Pete That's Labour for you.

Housewife I hope you're not expecting us to pay for that.

Pete Course not, Madam. Community service.

Housewife Oh yeah. What'd you do then?

Pete Not that kind of –

Housewife My old man's out on one a them now. A hundred and twenty hours for a knock-off DVD player, don't seem worth it really.

Pete We provide a community service, I mean.

Housewife Who's we?

Pete (*pulling out leaflets and handing her one*)   Compliments of the British National Party.

Housewife Get off ! You're never BNP!

Pete We are.

Housewife BNP's never done sod all round here apart from stand on the High Street gobbing at Pakis, excuse my French.

Pete That's in the past.

Housewife (*examining leaflet*)   Who the bloody hell's that on there?

Pete Gina is our candidate in the election.

Housewife But she's a – !!

Pete You get any more problems, graffiti, ASBO kids, you give us a bell on that number and we'll see what we can do for you.

Housewife You're never BNP.

Pete And I hope in return we can count on your vote on May 6th.

Housewife You keep this up you might. (*Beat.*) Don't suppose you fancy popping in for a cup of tea?

Pete That's lovely, but I can't.

Housewife He won't be back for a bit, the old man. (*Beat.*) Ain't been back for a couple a nights. I don't –

A Day at the Racists

Pete I've got to get on. Thank you though.

Beat.

Housewife Another time.

Pete Yeah.

Housewife Ta for clearing that lot up. Right eyesore it was.

Pete It's my pleasure.

She disappears back into the house, muttering to herself.

Housewife (*muttering*) Bloody BNP clearing up the streets, dunno what the world's coming to …

Pete *carries on his work, putting a couple more things into the bag.*

Clint *walks past.*

Clint Fucking hell, look who it ain't! What you doing here?

Pete (*hurriedly stuffing leaflets back in his pocket*) Clinton! Alright son! This ain't your normal way home.

Clint Nah, had a shufti at this gaff they want me to put in a bid on.

Pete Anything good?

Clint Not worth my while. Where the fuck you been? Tash thought we might have fell out or something, she ain't seen you for so long.

Pete Yeah, sorry about that.

Clint Nah, it's all good, busy people, busy people. So's this it then? The new job?

Pete It is, yeah.

Clint Clearing up rubbish and that?

Pete It's community outreach, mate. This is just one part.

Clint It's good you're getting your hands dirty, anyway. Most of them council bods couldn't tell one end of a shovel from the other.

Pete   No.

Clint   Effing useless, council. Waste of bloody taxpayer money. Still, least they got you out here.

Pete   Yeah.

Clint   Step in the right direction.

The **Housewife** *comes back out, head down, reading the leaflet.*

Housewife   Here, I wanna ask you summink ... (*Catches sight of* **Clint**.) Fucking hell! You got them an all??!!

Pete   It's not a great time.

Housewife   Darkies an all!

Clint   Who the fuck are you calling –

Housewife   Sorry love, I didn't mean it in a racist –

Clint   What other fucking way – ?

Pete   Just call the –

Housewife (*to* **Pete**)   How long have you lot – ?

Pete   Just call the number on the leaflet and they can answer any queries, alright?!

Beat. She turns and stomps back into the house, muttering again.

Housewife (*muttering*)   Pulled the rug right out from under my feet, that has. Dunno what the world's ...

Clint   Bitch. Like she's never seen a black man working for the council.

Pete   It's not the council.

Clint   I'm not, but she don't know that ... That's got me right fucking ... You know what I'm like, you pulled me off fellas in the factory nuff times.

Beat.

Pete I'm sorry, Clint.

Clint Not your fault, is it? (*Beat.*) Fuck it. Let's go for a pint. There's this mad job I got offered the other day. I know you'll say knock it on the head, specially after that, but it's tight as a gnat's arse at the mo –

Pete I can't, mate.

Clint If I wanna keep Mark on, I've gotta find –

Pete Another night.

Clint Fair enough. Come round for dinner then. How's next Tuesday?

Pete Yeah, good, yeah.

Clint Sorted. Good to see you, old son. We'll have a proper chinwag and you can catch me up on the rest of what you're doing. (*Beat.*) I'm glad for ya, mate. You look happy.

Pete I am happy.

Clint Good. You deserve that. You're worth more than some decorating job, Pete.

Pete Thank you, Clint.

Clint See you Tuesday. *He starts to make his way off.*

Pete Clint?

Clint Yeah?

Beat.

Pete You're a good mate.

Clint Always. (*Beat.*) See you Tuesday.

He leaves. **Pete** *carries on with his work.* **Gina** *enters.* **Pete** *brightens.*

Pete You got the message then?

Gina Yeah.

Pete Good day? I've had a good day.

Gina Long day.

Pete Where were ya?

Gina What's all this?

Pete I told ya, it's the Pete Case master plan.

Gina Picking up rubbish?

Pete Why do people think that's all … This is politics, Gina. The theory and the ideas, that might mean something to us, but to people out here, this is what politics means. Go see some panel beater and discuss the appropriation of surplus labour, you get a bang in the face. Tell him how to get a week's more holiday, he's right there with ya.

Gina The factories are closed, Pete.

Pete But the principle's the same. In the last words of the immortal Joe Hill, 'Don't Mourn. Organise.'

Gina Who?

Pete Who?! Joe Hill was leader of the Wobblies, American union mob, turn of the last century. He got stitched up for murder by the bosses: they stuck him in front of a firing squad and shot him. His absolute last word was 'Fire!' I like that.

Gina Me too.

Pete 'Don't Mourn. Organise.' Useta think I'd have them words on my gravestone.

Gina (*smiling*) What d'you think you'll have now?

Pete (*grins*) I'm not thinking about it right now, Gina. Have a gander at this lot.

He passes her several lists of names.

Gina What are all these?

Pete   Sign-up lists.

Gina   You got all these in one day?

Pete   Going back tomorrow.

Gina   You diamond!

She gives him a big hug.

Pete   I had my doubts when I started, but it's you on the leaflet. The number of people who don't wanna take one and you show 'em your picture –

She kisses him deeply. He hesitates, then responds. They kiss for a while.

Gina   Come to mine.

Beat.

Pete   I don't –

She kisses him again.

Gina   Come to mine.

Pete   Alright. Yes.

She smiles. Beat.

Gina   You're something, you know.

This moves him – how long has it been since someone told him this?

Pete   You're ... more than I let myself expect.

She takes his hand and they start to leave.

Gina   I did have one idea. About what you just said.

Pete   Go on.

Gina   The thing everyone mentions, apart from housing, is education. How their kids don't get enough time in school cos the immigrant kids need basic English.

Pete I've heard the same, yeah.

Gina What about a campaign 'Local Children, Local Schools' something like that? Saying it's not racist for people to want equal treatment, it's what they deserve.

Pete Sounds good.

Gina Couple of photogenic local kids on the posters. (**Pete** *nods in agreement.*) I was thinking of Ella for one of them.

Pause.

Pete I dunno, Gina.

Gina She's perfect. She's pretty, she presses all the right buttons …

Pete Black but not too black, you mean.

Gina Don't be silly. (*Beat.*) We can use that photo you've got in your wallet.

Pete I'd have to ask Mark.

Gina Of course. I'm sure he won't mind though. After what we did for him?

Beat.

Pete She liked you, Ella.

Gina I liked her.

Pause. He hands over the photo.

Pete Look after her.

Gina I will. (*Beat.*) Come on then. Or have you changed your mind?

They leave, his arm around her.

Mark *out on the streets with* **Zenobia**. *They are handing out leaflets.*

Zenobia Stop the Academy!

Mark Scrap the Academy!

Zenobia Axe the Academy!

Mark Er, knock the Academy on the head!

Zenobia Refute the Academy!

Mark Sod the Academy!

Zenobia Repudiate the Academy!

Mark Bollocks to the Academy!

Zenobia/Mark Fuck the Academy!

Mark Let's go home now.

Zenobia Not until we've got rid of this lot. You've got loads more left than I have! Go on, get that man there.

Mark *approaches a white man walking quickly. He holds out a leaflet.*

Mark Excuse me, mate, it's about this new school they wanna build –

White Man Got no kids, mate.

He disappears.

Zenobia (*imitation*) 'Excuse me, mate!'

Mark What? Easier for girls, innit.

Zenobia And why's that?

Mark You got certain assets.

Zenobia Yeah. A brain. (*She approaches a black man.*) Hello sir. Did you know that the new Academy school will be weighted in favour of Muslim children?

Black Man What? They get everything, don't they?

Zenobia (*handing over a leaflet*) There's a concerned citizens' fightback meeting, next Thursday, Town Hall?

Black Man Ta for that, darling. I'll take a look, yeah.

He walks off reading it.

Mark You can't say that!

Zenobia Sssssh. (*She approaches an Asian woman.*) Hello madam. Did you know –

Asian Woman Very sorry, can't stop.

Zenobia The new Academy school will be weighted in favour of Christian children?

Asian Woman No-one told me that.

Zenobia (*handing over a leaflet*) There's a concerned citizens' fightback meeting, next Thursday, Town Hall?

Asian Woman Thank you. I never heard that, are you –

Zenobia If you pop along next Thursday you can find out more.

Asian Woman I'll certainly try, thank you.

She leaves.

Mark You're right out of order! You can't be telling 'em lies to get 'em to come!

Zenobia Once they get in the door, they'll find enough to piss them off.

Mark Yeah, that the reason they came was bollocks!

Zenobia The head of the Council is a director of the developers! How fair is that?!

Mark That don't mean –

Zenobia So we have to be goody-goodies while they stitch up the 'independent' decision? Do you want Ella's school to survive or not? (*Beat.*) Mark, on its own the truth is not gonna be enough for us to win. We have to give it a little helping hand.

Beat. He puts his hand on her hips. She does the same to him.

Mark   Created a monster, didn't I?

Zenobia   A flesh-eating monster.

They kiss. Eventually she lets him go.

Zenobia   Go on. I know it's the Arsenal game tonight.

Mark   You sure?

Zenobia   On yer bike. Slacker.

Mark   See you at mine later?

Zenobia (*grinning*)   I'll think about it. (*He leaves.*) Scrap the Academy! Block the Academy!

McDonald *appears. He watches her.*

Pete *in the office, listening to the radio with growing concern '... with reports of attacks on the Asian community in which at least one man has been hospitalised. Some have linked the violence to a new campaign by the British National Party, advocating discrimination by local schools against immigrant children.'*

Pete   It's not *against* anyone, it's *for* us …

He turns, cup of coffee in hand, and almost walks into **Clint**, *who is carrying a bag with his decorating stuff.* **Clint** *drops the bag. They stare at one another. Long pause. The radio goes on 'In a recent poll, 62% of whites said they agreed with the policy, and almost half said it would make them more likely to vote BNP in the upcoming general –'.* **Pete** *switches off the radio. Beat.*

Clint (*grabbing bag*)   No, fuck this.

Pete   Clint, stay –

Pete *grabs* **Clint**. **Clint** *violently shoves him away, sending his coffee mug flying.*

Clint   Get your hands off me! Don't you fucking touch me, you traitor! You *traitor*!

Clint *shapes to punch* **Pete**.

Pete It's me, it's me, it's me ...

Clint *slams his fist into his palm. He doesn't know whether to run, hit or cry. Pause.*

Clint Thirty seconds. Thirty fucking seconds you *cunt*.

Pete It's housing. It's hospitals. It's schools. That shit where they're gonna close down your little one's school, Ella's school, we'd never allow that.

Clint We.

Pete Yeah, we. You and me and the people that've put the fucking graft in, whatever their colour.

Clint Colour already.

Pete I don't give a fuck about that, you *know* I don't. But *we are here*, we've been here generations and how come that don't count for anything?

Clint Listen to yourself.

Pete I have *nothing* against the new people. But the ones what's put their time in, we are *owed* something.

Clint You know what you sound like?

Pete It's different with Gina. She's not gonna let them go back to –

Clint You sound like the bosses. 'Do yer time, stand in line, don't you get ahead of the man in front cos he's been here longer.' You sound like the bosses, Pete.

Beat.

Pete It's only what's fair.

Clint You're going after the wrong people. It ain't those down the bottom taking from us, it's them at the top.

Pete How many times've I heard you going on about 'fresh off the boat Africans'?

Clint Yeah, cos of something in the fucking *Sun*, but I'm talking about... (*He makes a big frame gesture with his hands.*) You was the one showed me. How we'd be squabbling so much over a few crumbs, management'd drive by in their new Bentleys and we'd let 'em go. Divide and rule. This is the same thing, mate. (*He repeats the gesture, starting small and opening his hands wider. Beat.*) You was the only one treated me as a straight up human my whole first year at school. I'll never forget it.

Pete I don't want nothing to come between us, Clint.

Clint Then you shouldn't have joined the *BNP*, Pete! (*Beat.*) Why didn't you tell me?

Pete Cos I knew it'd be like this. That you wouldn't understand.

Clint Why wouldn't I understand?

Pete Look at ya. You're alright.

Clint How the fuck am I alright? I'm that fucking brassic I was seriously thinking of putting in a tender on the BNP offices! (*He screws up a piece of paper and throws it at Pete.*) You can stick that where the sun don't shine.

Pete New car.

Clint So fucking what?

Pete Nice extension on the house.

Clint And? I haven't worked for it?

Pete Foreign holidays.

Clint You of all people should know I've worked for it.

Pete I've worked too! I've worked too, and where's all that for me?

Clint I ain't took it.

Pete But I ain't got it!

Clint Are you jealous of me, Pete?

Pete Of course not.

Clint Are you *jealous* of me, is that why you're doing this?

Pete I want something of my own! (*Pause.*) You're the people I'm doing this for, Clint. You and me and Mark. Locals.

Clint (*softly*) Where am I from? (*Beat.*) Where am I from, Pete?

Pete Dagenham.

Clint Originally.

Pete Hornchurch.

Clint What does it say on my passport for place of birth, dickhead? What woulda happened to my folks and me if your lot had been in charge then? You're telling me we shouldn't be here, Pete. (*Beat.*) They was always gonna go back to Yard, my folks. Always 'Nex' year, nex' year we reach.' But we chose to stay. When you *choose* a country, you choose being less than you should be. You choose eating other people's shit, washing their streets and emptying their toilets and having them question your right to everything you get. You eat that shit for the sake of your children. He had a degree, my dad, you know that?

Pete I didn't, no.

Clint Engineering degree. He had a degree and he drove a bus. Never complained about it. It's the way it was. (*Beat. With deep sadness.*) It's divide and rule, old son, it's the oldest trick in the bloody book. You're so much smarter than me, how come you can't see that?

Pete I don't know what else to do. What else can I do, Clint?

Clint I don't know. (*He picks up his bag.*) Don't come Tuesday.

He leaves. **McDonald** *approaches* **Zenobia**. *She goes to hand him a leaflet.*

Zenobia Hello sir, did you know –

Another white man, wearing a balaclava, emerges from the shadows. They flank her. She falters. Beat.

A Day at the Racists 321

McDonald What you doing?

Zenobia I'm ... it's a campaign ... against the –

He rips the leaflet from her hand. She gives a little involuntary gasp.

McDonald Let's have a look then.

Zenobia Don't –

McDonald Sssh. I'm reading. (*Beat.*) This looks like shit.

Zenobia No, it's –

McDonald Are you saying I can't read? Cos I'm reading this and it looks like a load of nigger-loving, mongrelising shit. 'Protect the rich diversity of our community.' (*He tears up the leaflet with deliberate slowness.*) But I don't like the rich diversity of our community. I want all the rich – interesting choice of word, seeing how much you lot sponge off the fucking state – diverse parasites to fuck off back where they come from. Can you explain to me why this *isn't* a load of mongrelising shit, darling?

Zenobia *can hardly speak from terror.*

Zenobia I ... please ...

McDonald You see, this is the thing with coons. They're very chatty when they've got the whip hand, but get 'em one on one and they generally struggle. (*He pulls out a large hunting knife and opens it slowly.* **Zenobia** *starts to hyperventilate. To* **Zenobia**.) Did you know it's scientifically proven that blacks are on average fifteen to twenty per cent less intelligent than white people?

Zenobia I ... I ...

McDonald She can't even speak. You're pulling your average right down, love.

Zenobia (*whispering*) I'll call the police ...

McDonald *puts the knife close to her cheek. She shrieks. The other man holds her fast.*

McDonald I want you to give whoever you're working for a message. (*Beat.*) The message is, 'Fuck off you spear-chucking African cunt. This is the white man's country.' Can you remember that? (*Beat.*) Then I'll give you something to help you.

He runs the point of the knife gently down her cheek, then suddenly cuts the straps of her top so she has to clutch it humiliatingly to her. She hunches in on herself, face averted, as **McDonald** *deliberately folds up the knife, puts it away and as the two men leave, pats her on the head. She is left in a tearful, shell-shocked, terrified heap.*

Pete *makes his way to his front door. As he puts his key in the lock,* **Mark** *appears out of the shadows. He clutches several documents and a can of beer. He is considerably drunker than he realises, but the alcohol fuels not sloppiness but a tight, focused rage.*

Pete Jesus, you nearly gave me a heart attack! (*Beat.*) What are you doing here?

Pause.

Mark Good night?

Pete It was alright.

Mark Where'd you go?

Pete To this woman's place, as it goes. Why?

Mark Quite late back.

Pete Yeah, time got away from us, you know.

Mark But you had a good time, yeah? That's the important thing. As long as you had a good time, Dad.

Pete What are you doing here, Mark?

Mark I brought you a bit of reading. Cos I know what a thinker you are. 'Countering the Smears', by the British National Party.

A Day at the Racists 323

Beat.

Pete I was gonna tell you but I didn't know how.

Mark Question 'Why do you disapprove of mixed marriages?' Answer 'We believe in human diversity, and in preserving the individuality of different ethnic groups.' (*Holding the can out.*) Beer?

Pete Come inside.

Mark 'Environmentalists are always keen to preserve unique animal species in the wild, so why shouldn't the same principle apply to people?'

Pete Why don't you come inside, son, eh?

Mark *crushes the can and slings it away with such ferocity that* **Pete** *jumps a little.*

Mark Two of your environmentalists attacked my girlfriend with a knife tonight.

Pete *What*?! Is she alright, is she – ?

Mark No. She's not. And when she sees *this*, she's never gonna talk to me again.

Mark *holds up a BNP campaign poster showing* **Ella***'s face, with 'Local Children, Local Schools' written above it along with 'Vote British National Party'. Pause.*

Mark Question: 'Do you accept or deny that blacks and Asians born in Britain are totally British?' Answer: 'Blacks and Asians born here are *legally* British, but they are not *genetically* British. Species – *species* – which move into a new area and become established are called colonisers.'

Pete Come inside and I'll try to explain –

Mark MY DAUGHTER IS NOT A SPECIES. (*Beat.*) Tell me what Ella is, Dad.

Pete She's my granddaughter.

Mark Some science mishmash? A freak experiment gone wrong?

Pete She's my granddaughter who I love very, very much.

Mark How can you read this and look at her the same way?

Pete Listen to me –

Mark How can you expect me to let you touch her?

Pete I don't do any of that.

Mark Then what do you do?

Beat.

Pete They've done things for me.

Mark What've they done, Dad?

Pete You don't need to know that.

Mark I think I do.

Pete They've give me a job –

Mark Fuck off.

Pete A sense of purpose, a reason to get up in the bloody morning –

Mark FUCK OFF.

Pete Your flat! They gave me your flat! I got your flat from them, Mark, OK? (*Pause. Mark sways for a second, seems on the verge of falling over.*) Come inside.

Mark You stupid old man. You stupid clueless old man. What did it cost you, Dad?

Pete Nish, it's a council gaff.

Mark You don't know the price of fuck all, do ya? What did you have to do for it?

Beat.

Pete I'm organising the election campaign.

Mark (*holding out poster*) You *organised* this?

Pause. **Mark** *pulls another can out of his pocket, drinks and looks away. Long pause.*

Mark D'you think less of me cos I didn't make it as a footballer?

Pete What?

Mark Do you think less of me because I didn't make it as a professional footballer?

Pete Why are you asking me that?

Mark (*looking away again and drinking*) There's an answer.

Pete No, of course not.

Mark Are you ashamed of me, Dad?

Pete *Ashamed* of you?

Mark Are you ashamed of me because I'm a failure?

Pete You're not a failure, Mark.

Mark I didn't make it, I'm a failure, simple as.

Pete It weren't your fault you got hurt.

Mark (*sharp*) No-one is talking about fault.

Pete You're not a failure, Mark.

Mark You are though. You're like an old toy you remember was brilliant when you was a kid, but then you get it out the attic and it's gone dusty and cracked and rubbish. Tell me I disappoint you.

Pete You don't disappoint me, Mark.

Mark Tell me, Dad. Say it. Say I disappoint you. (*Beat. Raging.*) *Say it*! I'm a failure. I had our future in my hands and I pissed it away, I shoulda had you in a nice big house in Epping or Loughton but I failed, I'm a fucking useless failure of a cunt.

Pete Mark –

Mark You think that everything I've done has been a mistake, that Ella is a mistake, a warped twisted little fuck-up –

Pete Please, son –

Mark Couldn't even get that right, had to embarrass myself and embarrass you, that I'm not your son, Dad, not the way you wanted him to be. Tell me that's what you think of me.

Pause.

Pete (*gently and full of love*)   That's not what I think of you.

Mark Then why have you *done* this?!

He pulls out the keys to the flat.

Pete Don't leave the flat.

Mark Give me some fucking respect at least! Stay in *that*?

Pete I worked for that flat, Mark.

Mark Are you really that thick to think, *really* that thick to think, that if we did mug 'em all off, the immigrants and the asylum seekers and whoever else, if we did put 'em in vans or shove 'em behind barbed wire or send 'em off to the fucking abattoir, that after all that there'd be more left over for people like us? Are you stupid? Didn't you learn nothing from all them days on the picket line?

He throws the keys at **Pete***, turns and runs away.*

Pete Mark! MARK!

Sounds the breaking of glass, the wailing of car alarms, shouting, pitched battles in the street. An assault voices taunting, pleading in a foreign language, scuffling, muffled blows. A terrified cry for help. The sharp crack of head on stone. The wail of a siren and the sounds of running feet.

In amongst this, the radio cuts in and out. '... prepares for the general election, pollsters are predicting a first ever parliamentary seat for the British National ... escalating violence continues to plague ... three more assaults on Asians, including on an eighty-seven year old ... say they wish to interview members of the BNP on suspicion of incitement ...'

Backstage at **Gina***'s election press conference. The bustle of TV cameras and expectant journalists out front.* **Gina** *in a smart suit with* **Coleman***.*

Coleman Nervous?

Gina Not really. You?

Coleman Am *I* nervous?

Gina Yes, Rick. Are you nervous?

Coleman I have done this a few times before, Gina.

Gina Then you've nothing to worry about.

Beat.

Coleman So the Islamification of Britain, the cost to the welfare state –

Gina I know what I'm going to say.

He looks hard at her. Pause.

Coleman I won't be able to stay for the election itself.

Gina That's fine.

Coleman Got to get back up North.

Gina That's absolutely fine.

Coleman So it's all in your hands, Gina. If it goes wrong.

Beat. A low whistling the tune of 'Camptown Ladies'. **McDonald** *appears.*

McDonald (*singing*) 'Don't Unpack, You're Going Back, doo dah, doo dah. Don't Unpack, You're Going Back, doo de doo da dey.' Sing it with me, Rick.

Coleman You're barred.

McDonald (*to Gina*) Your big day.

Gina What do you want?

Coleman You are no longer a member of this Party.

McDonald I thought you might like some input on your speech.

Gina Thoughtful.

McDonald I think a lot.

Gina Of Hitler with his cock out, I expect.

McDonald I think about purity. How the littlest drop of filth spoils it, makes it worthless. My job is to preserve the purity of England for generations yet unborn. That means a long, lonely job of elimination. And nobody likes the exterminator, nobody loves the ratcatcher. But at the end of the day, most people, if they're honest, they're glad he's out there all the same. (*Beat.*) I want you to resign.

Gina And why would I do that, Tony?

McDonald I want you to go out and say it was all a big mistake and you got in over your little shit-brown head.

Gina But I'm not going to do that.

McDonald How many more of your people do you want to get hurt?

Gina They are not my people.

McDonald Because I can arrange that.

Gina I'm sure you can.

McDonald Not just before the election but afterwards too. Every day another three, four, five, ten Pakis go down.

Coleman Oh dear.

McDonald (*explosion of rage at* **Coleman**) FUCK OFF. FUCK OFF. FUCK OFF. (**Pete** *enters, unseen. Calmly, to* **Gina**.) It won't

A Day at the Racists 329

be hard. The anger is out there. I just have to direct it. (*Beat. A note of urgency.*) Are you listening to me?

Gina No, Tony.

McDonald It won't work, Gina. Look at the streets out there.

Gina That'll pass, when you do.

McDonald People don't want to mix.

Gina They already have. They will more. Your world is gone, Tony.

Beat.

McDonald Look at you. You can't keep discipline, you can't keep your people safe. What the fuck can you do?

Coleman Get attention. Thanks to you. (*Pause.* **McDonald** *is thrown.*) When she started, Gina was a bit of a joke. The Asian bird standing for the BNP, a snigger for the ruling classes. Now, she's for real. Look out front: TV, broadsheets, tabloids. Because of her, people have an opinion of us they've never had before: Reforming. Courageous. Electable. The only thing those people used to think about the British National Party was that it was full of people like you. The people we are now seen to be purging. So thank you, Tony. Well done. I couldn't have choreographed it better myself. Because it's not the policies that's got the attention. It's not even the novelty brown girl – no offence, Gina, you know what I mean. It's the violence.

Beat. **McDonald** *snarls.*

McDonald Clever.

Coleman You can always rely on a little bit of violence to tickle the jaded palate of middle England. And where would we have found such a compliant group of inbred, Paki-bashing knuckle-draggers without your help?

McDonald You clever cunt.

Coleman It's just a shame you can't stick around to enjoy the fruits of your labours. But on the bright side, you've helped make the BNP a mainstream political force. So if you love the party like you –

McDonald *grabs* **Coleman** *in a headlock and punches as* **Coleman** *flails his arms uselessly.* **Pete** *lunges out of the shadows and inflicts a terrible rage-fuelled beating on* **McDonald***, eventually dragging him to the door, throwing him out and turning to face* **Gina** *and* **Coleman***, who adjusts his suit and tries to regain his dignity. Pause.*

Coleman My God. What a man. What a man. Who is this, Gina?

Gina This is Pete Case.

Pete Don't.

Gina Pete is my election co-ordinator.

Coleman Gina told me about you, Pete. What a fantastic –

Pete *grabs* **Coleman** *by the cheeks with a single strong hand, squeezing his mouth closed. Eventually he lets him go. Pause.*

Coleman What can I say? It's a contact sport, democracy. (*He straightens his clothes one last time and makes for the exit.*) I'll be waiting, Gina.

Coleman *leaves. Pause.*

Gina I didn't know –

Pete Yes you did.

Beat. She can't refute it.

Gina Come out there with me, love. I'm going to do something wonderful.

Beat.

Pete You've still got my picture.

Gina What picture?

Pete The one of my granddaughter. Can I have it back?

A Day at the Racists 331

Gina Now? I'm about to do the biggest event of my life –

Pete I'd like my picture back.

Gina I don't have your picture on me, I –

Pete *presses his hand into* **Gina**'s *face and mashes it back and forth, driving her to the floor where she sits open-mouthed with shock.*

Gina (*like a hurt little girl*)   What did you do that for?

Pete Who are you?

Gina My name is Gina White.

Pete No it ain't. Your dad was Pakistani, you said. Not many Whites in the Karachi phone book, are there? What's your proper fucking name?

He takes a step towards her.

Gina Begum. My birth name is Hafsana Begum.

Pete Why are you doing this, Hafsana Begum?

Gina Does it matter?

Pete Course it matters, it –

Gina What difference does it make? It's all bollocks, the explanations, the *reasons*. It matters what I'm *doing*.

She scrambles to her feet. Beat.

Pete Is that all this was? A way to get attention?

Gina No

Pete Is that all I was?

Gina I want you to come out there with me.

Pete My son won't talk to me. My best mate won't talk to me.

Gina It'll pass, when –

Pete No it / *won't.*

Gina When I win. When all this gets washed away.

Pete You're just like all the rest.

Gina When I make things *clear*.

Pete Using us and moving on.

Gina Trust me, baby. Please.

Pete I believed you.

Gina Keep believing me.

Pete What about the people that got hurt?

Gina Gandhi tried non-violence. He got shot. I'm going to win.

Pete And that's all that matters?

Gina This is about more than you and me and a couple of Pakis getting a slap now. All the things you believe in, the things you want your society to be – how else are you going to make them happen? How else are you gonna make the world you want to see?

Pete Not through you.

Gina Then *how else*?

Beat.

Pete Do you care about me, Gina?

Gina Yeah. I do.

Pete Then don't go out there.

Pause.

Gina Don't make me do this.

Pete You care about me, don't go out there.

Gina I've gone through too much, Pete.

Pete *You've* gone through … You put my granddaughter on a BNP poster knowing people would get hurt.

Gina I've gone too far now.

A Day at the Racists 333

Pete For me, Gina. Stop this for me.

She kisses him. He doesn't respond. Eventually he pushes her away. Pause.

Gina I've got to go.

Pete See ya then. Hafsana.

Gina It's a waste. It's such a waste. (*Beat.*) Call me. Any time. Please.

She leaves. Hubbub outside. **Pete** *stands rooted. Long pause. He strides after her.* **Gina** *at the press conference with* **Coleman**. *Journalists facing them. Flashing bulbs.*

Gina Dignity. History. Togetherness. A British nationalism based on Britain's greatness, not on skin colour or place of birth. What makes me different from the rest is that I have *faith* in the British people, black, white, brown, all of us. Anyone that's here now and wants to be British first and foremost, I salute you. I believe that once you get the dead weight off your back, you'll make this country *Great* Britain again.

Pete *stands up at the back of the room.*

Pete Liar.

Gina But that is what it requires you have to be British first and foremost. No more special treatment. No more subsidies for mosques where hatred of Britain is –

Pete What about the violence?

Gina It's a choice you have to make. I made it.

Pete Like you chose to have those people beaten up?

Journalist Could you shut up please?

Gina *starts to falter.*

Gina I am … the future of … the future of British politics –

Pete Explain the violence, Gina.

Journalist Can we get this guy out of here?

A security guy moves over and takes **Pete** *by the arm. He resists and raises his voice.*

Pete I can show you Gina White deliberately –

Gina Pete, don't …

Coleman We know this man.

Pete Deliberately caused the violence in our streets –

Coleman This man has a long-standing grudge against the / British National Party –

Pete To raise her profile –

Gina Please …

Pete And to get you here today.

Journalist And how do you know that?

Pete Because I'm her campaign manager. I organised the whole thing. Everything that's happened out there, every beating, every attack, it was all done through me.

The light narrows to a beam on **Pete**, *then blacks out.*

Mark *and* **Clint** *working on another flat, wrestling a cistern into place.*

Mark So the stepdad chases the kid off and the kid's all upset and crying … Next day, the dad hears this massive racket coming out the old granny's room –

Clint Here we go.

Mark So the stepdad goes in and what does he see but the kid grinding away on top of the granny, who's having the time of her life. And the kid looks up, sees the stepdad and goes, 'Not so fucking funny when it's *your* mum!'

Amidst their laughter, **Pete** *enters. He stops near the door. The laughter fades. Pause.*

Pete That's nice work, that. (*Beat.*) Nice finish. I never could get that right.

Pause. **Clint** *rises.*

Clint I'll leave you two to it.

Pete I came to see both of you.

Clint I'm not the one you need to sort things out with, Pete.

Pete I need to talk to you, mate. Please.

Clint I don't have anything to say to you.

Clint *leaves. Pause.*

Mark It's funny, he ain't shut up about ya for the past week, in that weird way of his.

Pete Every compliment sorta half a criticism, you mean?

Mark You know the one. Out the corner of his mouth, 'Least he stopped the fucking BNP bird.' 'Least he done the right thing in the end.' (*Beat.*) Give him time.

Pause.

Pete I went in the pub last night and nobody would talk to me. Lifted their pints and turned their backs. Half of 'em cos they think I did what I said and the other half cos they think I didn't.

Mark Finally managed to unite the community then.

Pete I'm a stupid, stupid fucker, Mark. (*Pause.*) How's Zenobia?

Mark She's alright. (*Beat.*) She gets flashbacks. There's a proper word for it.

Pete I'm sorry to hear that.

Mark Yeah.

Beat.

Pete Her campaign's going well, looks like you might win.

Mark Yeah, we are. I can see why you used to do it now. It's beautiful, as it goes.

Pete I'm very, very proud of you. I hope you know that. (*Beat.*) Are you two – ?

Mark Rocky.

Pete Where are you kipping, Mark?

Mark Mate's place.

Pete With Ell?

Mark It's only for a bit.

Pete Come home, son.

Mark I can't, Dad.

Pete I miss you round the place.

Mark I really want this thing with Z to work.

Pause.

Pete Yeah. OK.

Beat.

Mark I can't look at you in the same way. I really want to, I keep trying, but I can't.

Pete I'm not any different than –

Mark I know what you thought you were doing, and I know why, and I love you for that –

Pete Mark, I –

Mark And I know what you did to try and make it right, she lost because of you, but I don't feel the same way about you. (*Beat.*) Something in here has shifted or gone cold and I'm trying to make it warm up again, I am, but it won't.

Beat.

Pete You're my only son.

Mark And I don't know if it ever will and that terrifies me, Dad, it makes me feel sick. I want it to come back. I'm waiting for it to come back. (*Beat.*) Will you wait with me?

Beat.

Pete I don't have a choice, do I?

Mark I'm sorry, Dad.

Pete You've got nothing to be sorry about.

Pause.

Mark I need to fetch Clint. We're behind as it is.

Pete Can I see Ella?

Mark In a bit. (*Beat.*) Do us a favour? Don't be here when he gets back.

Mark *makes to leave. He places a hand on* **Pete***'s shoulder. Pause. He leaves.*

Pete *stands alone, staring out. He pulls out his phone and stares at it. Lights gradually down.*

The Westbridge

Rachel De-lahay

The Westbridge was first performed at The Bussey Building, Peckham Rye on 3 November 2011 as part of the Theatre Local Season, with the following cast:

Andre	Ryan Calais Cameron
Audrey	Jo Martin
Soriya	Chetna Pandya
Marcus	Fraser Ayres
Georgina	Daisy Lewis
Saghir	Paul Bhattacharjee
Ibi	Ray Panthaki
Old Lady	Adlyn Ross
Sara	Shavani Seth
Boy	Samuel Foray
Director	Clint Dyer
Designer	Ultz
Lighting	Katharine Williams
Sound	Emma Laxton

The play subsequently transferred to the Royal Court Jerwood Theatre Upstairs, London, opening on 25 November 2011.

Characters

(in order of appearance)

Andre – *sixteen years old, Black British*
Audrey – *Andre's mom, Jamaican*
Soriya – *in her twenties, mixed race White-Pakistani*
Marcus – *in his twenties, mixed race White-Afro-Caribbean*
George – *in her twenties, White British*
Ibi – *Soriya's brother, late twenties*
Saghir – *Soriya's dad, Pakistani*
Old Lady – *Pakistani*
Sara – *sixteen years old, British Asian*

The play is set in Battersea, south west London.

Act One

Scene One

Andre *walks into his house. Night. Light gets flicked on and we see* **Audrey** *sat at the table.* **Andre**'s *shocked to see her.*

Andre Rare! Soz I'm late.

Audrey And you think that's the magic password that will get you upstairs?

Andre I said I'm sorry.

Beat.

Audrey Carry on, yeah? You just carry on.

Andre *kisses his teeth.*

Andre Yeah yeah.

Andre *walks past her.*

Audrey You know what? Get out!

Andre What?

Audrey You hard a hearing? I've had enough.

Andre And where do you expect me to go?

Audrey Now, how's about to one of your croneys' houses?!

Andre What are you on about 'croney'?!

Audrey – or wherever the fuck it is you are when you're not in here night after night!

Andre You know where I am! I was at Tyrone's house!

Audrey You think I'm stupid? You think I never call Tyrone's house?

Andre No one don't answer the phone over there –

Audrey Same way you don't answer your mobile?!

Andre It was on silent!

Audrey And when you seen the missed calls?

Andre I never had any credit.

Beat.

Audrey I moved us from that estate to give you a chance, ya hear? And every night you have me walk back up there looking for you.

Andre You walked up to Westbridge?

Audrey Oh, yes.

Andre And?

Audrey Ya blind? Ya nah see what a gwarn up there?

Andre Not really, I was at Tyrone's.

Audrey Funny that. When my man locking up shop, tells me how a bag of mans were in there not long earlier. One on bike, fitting your description.

Andre So? We went shop.

Audrey You and five boys Shirley let sit up in her house 'til all hours?

Andre No. I was at Tyrone's and we bumped into the rest of the mans outside the shop, innit?

Audrey I swear to Jesus! You tell me you were at Tyrone's one more time, I will kick your head through that bloodclart wall!

Andre Differently! I was at Tyrone's! Fucking phone him! 'Bout you wanna kick mans' heads in! Go on then! Dare ya! Feh!

Audrey Oh, so you're a bad man now? Now you've been walking 'pon street all night?

Andre Walking stre— I'm not gonna tell you again! I was at Tyrone's!

Andre *turns to exit when we hear a banging on the front door.*

Audrey   Get upstairs!

Andre   Who the fuck's that?

Audrey   I said get upstairs!

Banging again. **Andre** *stays.*

Asian Man   Open the fucking door you piece of shit!

Audrey   Move from me door 'fore I call the police!

Asian Man   You think I haven't called them already? That fucking piece of … ! Open up!

Audrey *quickly reaches for her mobile phone.*

Audrey   Andre get upstairs!

Asian Man   Oi! Open now or I kick down bloody fucking door!

Audrey (*on phone*)   Police.

Andre *picks up a heavy ornament off the table and stands near the door ready. We hear the sound of sirens outside. The man kicks the door out of frustration.*

Asian Man   I will fucking kill you!

We hear a softer knock on the door.

Voice   Hello? Open up! It's the police!

Andre   Mom?

Audrey *hangs up her mobile, looks at* **Andre** *who lowers his arm with the ornament.*

Audrey (*to* **Andre**)   You were at Tyrone's all night.

Andre   I was!

Beat.

Audrey   Coming!

Audrey *goes to open the door. Lights.*

Scene Two

George *and* **Soriya***'s kitchen.* **Soriya***'s making breakfast.* **Marcus** *enters from outside carrying a box.*

Soriya That was quick.

Marcus Nah, this is the last of what was in my car.

Soriya Oh, then where the hell have you parked your car?

Marcus Over on the red route. Not risking it after last night.

Soriya 'Cause god forbid anything happen to your baby!

Marcus Shut it you! You making breakfast?

Soriya Yeah, but don't panic, there's enough for all of us.

Marcus No. I was thinking we could go out to eat.

Soriya Oh. Where?

Marcus How about the French café by the bridge you always stare into?

Soriya But what about this?

Marcus Keep it for George.

Soriya You say that like she won't insist on coming with us.

Marcus OK, then put a plate over it. I'll have it for lunch.

Soriya OK.

Marcus Sorted! And then I can go straight from breakfast to grab the last few boxes. Sort out everything here. Clean the place from top to bottom and then before you return from work hunt down the most beautiful roses for your bedside table.

Soriya Aw … lilies.

Marcus What?

Soriya I like lilies, not roses.

Marcus Why piss on it?

Soriya 'Cause you're being too cute.

Marcus I know!

Soriya Alright! You're not that cute.

Marcus Well that's just simply not true.

Soriya Fool! We gonna jump in your car then, if you're shooting straight off after?

Marcus Well, since they've locked off the entire road, no.

Soriya They've blocked off the road?

Marcus Police tape all the way down to the Westbridge estate.

Soriya From last night?

Marcus Must be.

Soriya Welcome to Battersea, eh?

Marcus Ha!

Soriya Oh hun. We can't go out for breakfast. If they've closed the road, the whole bridge will be chokka. It'll take you twice as long to drive anywhere.

Marcus You think?

Soriya Yeah, you'll want to get started now whilst the roads are quiet.

Marcus Ah man. Ok, we'll just have to do breakfast there at the weekend.

Soriya It's a date. Do you reckon you'll be all in today?

Marcus Can't see why not.

Soriya *smiles.*

Marcus What?

Soriya Nothing.

Marcus Weirdo!

Soriya Weirdo yourself!

Marcus *goes to kiss* **Soriya**, *but stops on hearing* **George** *enter.*

Marcus Ah, look who's up.

George Well there's an image I don't need before breakfast.

Soriya Morning to you too!

George How do you look like that?

Marcus She didn't twenty minutes ago.

Soriya Oi!

George No shouting. Head hurts people.

Marcus I wonder why?

George Hey! We tried to come home, didn't we Si? No taxi would drive this way. So we just had to stay –

Marcus And drink?

George … right.

Soriya Here!

Soriya *gives* **George** *a plate of breakfast.*

George I love you.

Marcus Ah, man. That does look …

George Good! Are the sausages –

Soriya Grilled not fried.

George And the tea?

Soriya Fennel 'which helps suppress the appetite'.

George Not that that's why I drink it.

Soriya Of course.

Marcus You do know you guys are defeating the point of a hangover breakfast?

George Well, when you do it as often as we do –

Soriya Did!

George Right ... you have to start making cutbacks. Want some?

George *offers* **Marcus** *some of her tea.*

Marcus Share the tea but not the food eh?

George Drink the tea, you won't need the food, eh.

Marcus I'm cool, I'm gonna get going.

Soriya Let me quickly make you something to take with you?

Marcus Nah, I'm good. I just remembered there's stuff in storage at my mom's I need to grab as well. I just wanna get in. Then, I'll eat.

George Isn't your mom's just over on the estate?

Marcus Yeah, but I need to do one more trip to the old place.

George That's handy though.

Marcus True.

George Well at least there's one benefit to having that eyesore as our view.

Soriya George!

George What? Marcus knows I'm kidding! The architecture's clearly stunning.

Marcus Like an ant farm?

George I never said that!

Soriya Busted!

George You helping Marcus pack today?

Soriya No. Took a bit of lieu time this morning but should really be hitting the office soon.

George   Why? What did the office ever do to you?

Marcus   Ha!

Soriya   Did you just laugh at that?

George   He can't help that I'm a comic genius.

Marcus   And, I'm gone. Call you later.

Soriya   Make sure.

Marcus   See you.

Marcus *exits.*

George   Bye!

Soriya   OK, genius –

George   You can call me George.

Soriya   Right … the bank called again for you this morning, George.

George   What?! They're completely abusing the fact they have my direct line –

Soriya   That you never answer.

George   That they shouldn't expect me to answer, since I could be at work.

Soriya   They write your monthly statement. I think it's fair to assume they know you don't work!

George   It's harassment! No? Bullying! I could probably sue!

Soriya   I doubt it.

George   Well, little Miss Public Relations, had you chosen a proper Indian career, like lawyer, we'd probably have a few more answers here, wouldn't we?

Soriya   I told them I'd get you to call them back.

George   No! Shalln't!

Soriya Why not?

George They're just badgering me for their overdraft money –

Soriya You still have your overdraft? George! You left Uni five years ago!

George Well I wasn't able to ask Mummy or Daddy for anything! I was being independent! Remember?

Soriya And doing so well!

George Well once Marcus is all in, I intend to pay them back fully.

Soriya Good.

George Though that does remind me …

Soriya No!

George I haven't even asked you yet!

Soriya And yet still I feel the answer will be no!

George But I have a date with one of the football players we met last night.

Soriya Already?

George Hey, he had a hot body and spoke four languages.

Soriya Fair point …

George He wants to meet me at Bluebirds later … I'll tell you all the goss …

Soriya You're forgetting, I don't want to know the goss.

George Fine I won't tell you but obvs I have no intention of letting him pay!

Soriya Why not, he's probably loaded!

George I'm an independent woman!

Soriya Shouldn't you be independent with your own money?

George I got you a present with my own money.

George *pulls out a wrapped book.*

Soriya That you clearly can't afford.

George Love me, bestest bestest frwend in the whole wide world.

Soriya Fine! Twenty quid till the end of the month when I expect the rest also!

George Twenty? Babes! That won't even cover a main with tip.

Soriya Well luckily for you, you're on a diet.

George Fine.

George *takes* **Soriya***'s money*

George Now Dad's gone, don't suppose you fancy a tea on the balcony with a cigarette?

Soriya Oi! And no! I quit!

George Course you did! And how is that twenty box from last night?

Soriya Pipe down!

George He leaves the toilet seat up, you know?

Soriya Who?

George Who do you think?

Soriya He does not! Besides you have your en suite.

George I'm just saying … I saw the toilet seat, up.

Soriya George, you're still OK with him moving in, right?

George Of course.

Soriya OK.

George Though if you keep smiling manically like that …

Soriya I'm just … happy.

George Good.

Soriya Can I open the present now?

George Yes!

Soriya *tears open the package. She's confused. Lights.*

Scene Three

Newsagents. The shutters are still down as though closed. **Marcus** *enters. The shop owner,* **Saghir***, is sat behind the till watching him.*

Marcus Hey. You alright?

Ibi (*o/s*) Oi! Dad!

Saghir *looks off to where* **Ibi** *is.*

Marcus Was just in the area so thought I'd pop in. Weren't too sure if you were open though.

Saghir *returns his attention to* **Marcus***.*

Marcus Can't believe how dead it is round here.

Ibi (*o/s*) Dad! Come! Listen!

Marcus Ain't seen the Westbridge this deserted since everyone thought the Sheerin kids got swine flu.

Ibi (*o/s*) Icy! *Joldi!* Quick!

Marcus Remember that? Bless 'em.

Ibi (*o/s*) Hello!

Marcus (*noticing the paper*) Ah, is this talking about the trouble last night? Kids eh?

Ibi (*o/s*) *Abba!* Come!

Marcus Like they've got nothing better to do with their time.

Ibi (*o/s*) Dad! Now!

Saghir (*to* **Ibi**) Damn it boy, some *kala* boy! Wait!

Beat.

Marcus, *unsure how to react, continues to browse the shop.*

Marcus If you, erm, need to run back quickly, I'm OK to watch the shop for you for two secs.

Saghir *remains seated.*

Ibi (*o/s*) It's on the news! *Aa ja!* Come! Just look!

Saghir *stands.*

Saghir I'll be two seconds. Thank you.

Marcus Cool.

As **Saghir** *exits,* **Marcus** *wanders around the shop and then decides to select a drink.* **Andre** *pulls up on his bike, allows his bike to fall to the floor and enters the shop.*

Andre I thought that was you! Wa gwarn stranger?

Marcus Little Andre! Cool?

Andre *clocks the expensive watch on* **Marcus**'s *wrist.*

Andre Yes, big man! Is that you though?

Marcus Don't watch me.

Andre *reaches to the neck of* **Marcus**'s *cardigan to check the label.* **Marcus** *shrugs him off.*

Marcus Or touch what you can't afford!

Andre What? You think mans like me don't own bare Stone Island already? I was just checking it's real!

Marcus Wrenk! You're lucky I don't knock you out for that comment!

Andre What? You wanna go blow for blow? Come then!

Marcus Funny!

Marcus *reaches for his wallet to pay for his drink and pulls out his car keys at the same time.*

Andre Nah bredrin! That's how you're going on? Coming back down sides-in a TT blud?! Oh no!

Marcus It's a car. Standard.

Andre Nah! Soz mate! Tyrone's' Corsa is 'a car'. That is a … ah … I beg you let me ride it?

Marcus You're not even serious. **Andre** Just around the block?

Marcus I swear you've started smoking the same stuff you're selling.

Andre Yo! That's bait! How can you try reel off facts like that and how you don't know who's about?

Marcus Shut up! No one ain't listening! And you think people round here don't know about you and your little mad self already?

Andre Mans like me is a business man. Standard!

Marcus Yeah, yeah.

Pointing at his bike.

Marcus And is that the company car?

Andre Ah, piss take. 'Low you, man.

Andre *goes to exit and notices they are alone in the shop.*

Andre Hold on …

He picks up two packets of crisps and puts them in his pocket and then reaches for a car magazine. He turns to exit but is pulled back on his hood by **Marcus**.

Marcus Uh uh.

Andre *kisses his teeth and replaces the magazine.*

Marcus And the crisps.

Andre *reaches in his pocket and pulls out one of the packets* *of crisps and chucks them down.* **Marcus** *puts them back in the correct place.*

Marcus Now gwarn, get!

Andre Yeah, yeah. In a bit.

Andre *picks up his bike, pulls out the second crisp packet, opens them and starts to eat.* **Marcus** *sees and* **Andre** *smiles a big grin at him before riding off as* **Saghir** *re-enters.*

Andre Laters!

Marcus Right. I better shoot but I'll take this and the packet of crisps for the youte.

Saghir What else did he take?

Marcus He didn't take anything just the crisps that I said I'd get him.

Beat.

Saghir Fine.

Silence as they exchange payment and change. **Marcus** *exits and* **Saghir** *stays fixated on him as he leaves.*

Scene Four

At a bus shelter outside the Westbridge estate. **Soriya** *is sat reading a newspaper.* **Andre** *cycles up behind her unnoticed and reads over her shoulder.*

Andre If it isn't the girlfriend.

Soriya Oi! Shit.

Andre Wa gwarn sexy?

Soriya Are you kidding?

Andre Ah, what? Did I frighten you?

Soriya Approach me again like that again, yeah, and you'll understand 'frightened'.

Andre What?! You're the one caught slipping. You're supposed to know who's near you at all times. You're from south, remember?

Soriya Well I apologise for lowering my guard on my commute to work.

Andre Yeah, well let that be a lesson.

Soriya Can I give you a fashion lesson about wearing hoods up?

Andre Bruv! What you talking about? Girls love this.

Soriya Erm, who exactly?

Andre Well, you for starters. I can see that smile behind your eyes.

Soriya Oh right ...

Andre What? I lie?

Soriya You see what you need to see.

Andre I'm shocked you're even travelling to work on your own after last night.

Soriya Why?

Andre Are you silly? Look at this dump!

Soriya Do you know what happened?

Andre Man like me was in bed sweetheart, week night and all.

Soriya Course you were.

Andre But I'll wait with you until the bus comes, though, if you're feeling prang?

Soriya You know what? I think I've got it.

Andre You don't normally come this way in the morning, do ya?

Soriya And who are you? Neighbourhood watch?

Andre Would you like that?

Soriya Well since I know you no longer live around here, wouldn't really affect me would it?

Andre Who told you that?

Soriya My dad mentioned you'd moved in next door to him.

Andre Is it? Well luckily for you I've still got my one cotch round here.

Soriya I'm sorry?

Andre By the garages, on Westbridge.

Soriya A garage?

Andre Nah. Don't get it twisted, yeah. It's cranked off, warm. Got my flat screen TV in there …

Soriya You're doing alright.

Andre Heated swimming pool. You should come round, you know. I'll give you the tour.

Soriya Well ain't I lucky?

Andre You could be.

Soriya Well I guess I could swing by when you're on your way back from school. Help you with your homework.

Andre Don't be dizzy, do I even look young enough to be in school, though?

Soriya Yes.

Andre I can't help being blessed with this handsome baby face.

Soriya Oh dear.

Andre Nah I'm ramping! I ain't even ashamed. I'm in school, rah!

Soriya Just running a bit late?

Andre Nah, on a real, if you want me to go, maybe, for you, I will.

Soriya Gee. Thanks.

Andre But don't say I didn't warn ya, when I come out all qualified as a doctor and shit and you regret settling for Marcus when you did!

Soriya So you're gonna be a doctor yeah?

Andre Why not? It's not just for your firm you know!

Soriya Alright!

Andre Or, I wouldn't mind doing what Marcus does still. Running my own ting.

Soriya Good for you. Might help if you went school a bit more frequently mind –

Andre Yeah, maybe. Saw Marcus just now.

Soriya Yeah?

Andre He's moving in with ya ain't he?

Soriya Yes dad! Is that OK?

Andre So you're proper gonna marry him and shit?

Soriya Mind your own!

Andre Do you reckon you're gonna get married in a church or a temple?

Soriya Erm ... what?!

Andre What? That must be the first thing you'd think of – two different peoples marrying and that.

Soriya Well ... we'll see I guess.

Andre I think you should get married in a temple. On an elephant and wear a sari thing like that Pussycat Doll video! Fit!

Soriya OK. Deal!

Andre So what they saying, then?

Soriya Sorry?

Andre *indicates towards her newspaper.*

Andre Talking about last night?

Soriya Oh right, yeah, kinda … it was allegedly to do with some girl getting attacked.

Andre That all it says?

Soriya Pretty much. Bag snatch I reckon.

Andre Weird, ennit?

Soriya What?

Andre Just stuff kicks off round here all the time but this … just … dunno … feels different.

Soriya Does it?

Andre *shrugs. His phone vibrates. He stares at it for a while before deciding to ignore it.*

Soriya That's not very nice.

Andre I'll call her back later.

Soriya A girl? Interesting …

Andre Nah, not like that.

Soriya Yeah, yeah.

Andre Ah, look how sad you look.

Soriya You expect me to believe you don't have a girlfriend? A pretty little face like yours?

Andre So you're admitting you fancy me then?

Soriya Don't avoid the question!

Andre What? Gal? I got a whirl a gal! But someone special? Now that would be telling.

The Westbridge   363

Soriya   OK …

Andre   Now you don't avoid my question.

Soriya   Why don't you ask me when you've finished medical school?

Andre   Please! You'll be past it by then!

Soriya   Thanks!

Andre   Anyways, in a bit choong ting!

Goes to cycle home.

Soriya   Oi! School!

Andre   Ah yeah, yeah, 'low me. 'Low me. I'm gone!

Turns and cycles in the opposite direction. Lights fade.

Scene Five

Saghir's *house.* **George** *enters carrying a camera and tripod.* **Ibi** *is sat alone in the living room.*

Ibi   George?

George   Surprise!

Ibi   You are aware it's still morning!

George   Hilarious! Do you plan on giving me a hand?

Ibi   Sorry. (*Stands to relieve her of some equipment.*) What's all this?

George   Well, I've got Marcus constantly in and out the flat and so figured I should give him some space and maybe try to find a productive way to spend my day. Then I thought how better than to sort out my portfolio.

Ibi   I'm sorry?

George   For my modelling.

Ibi Right. And you need me to … ?

George Well, I need someone with a good photographic eye to take a headshot of me. No make-up, hair scraped back and two side profiles.

Ibi What for?

George One of the big agencies may be interested in taking me on for commercials. They just want to see some basic shots, my studio ones were too touched up. Anyway I should have sorted this out ages ago so I'm going to do it today.

Ibi And I'm … ?

George Gonna be Mario Testino!

Ibi Of course. You remember I never went ahead with those evening classes, right?

George But you wanted to. And that want is really half the skill.

Ibi Right … and what makes you think I don't have anything better to do?

George Please. You're never at the shop on Fridays so we all know you were sat here watching 'Loose Women' and when you heard the door, you changed it to 'Sky News' to style it out. Put MTV on!

Ibi (*indicating the news*) They're talking about the drama that must have kicked off by yours last night? Over on the estate?

George Big fucking surprise! MTV!

George *starts putting on make-up.* **Ibi** *starts setting up the camera.*

Ibi I thought you said no make-up.

George Yeah. I'm gonna do 'no make-up', make-up. Natural beauty shining through with the aid of Chanel and Mac. Shush!

Ibi OK then … How's everything with you, anyway? Marcus all moved in now?

George As we speak. And they are so in love!

Ibi I detect a hint of jealousy.

George You can't really be jealous of those two. They're a little bit perfect for each other. If anything it's inspiration to go out there and find the same.

Ibi And are you?

George Well, I'm dating! It's a step forward!

Ibi Good! You'll get snapped up in no time. He's coming round here tonight. Gonna meet us for the first time.

George Marcus? I can't believe she's blagged avoiding that for so long.

Ibi I think me marrying Umra didn't help.

George What did that have to do with anything?

Ibi Dunno. Just got the impression she was worried 'cause I'd chosen such a traditional path her choice seemed more … out there!

George Ha! Is that what you think? Maybe if you guys lived in Pakistan! Your choice is so much more out there than hers! Not even Saghir married of his race let alone going through with an arranged marriage! Freak!

Ibi Aw! Look at us. Bonding!

George Besides Si could do whatever she wants. She is the favourite after all.

Ibi Favourite?

George Sorry to say! Order's Soriya and me joint first, then you.

Ibi Oh so even you come before me despite not even being in the family!

George Not in the family? How dare you! I have my own key?

Ibi Oh my. What was I thinking?

George Unfortunately everything you can do ... I do better. Saghir realises this. I think you need to too. Where is he, anyway?

Ibi At the shop. Just dropped him off.

George Already? I thought your uncle did mornings?

Ibi Well I kinda thought it'd be better if we were all in all day, today, in case there was trouble again. Plus I wanted to do the audit on the Mac rather than hard copy, but as soon as dad saw Facebook, well, he weren't much impressed.

George Oh, dear.

Ibi He clearly doesn't trust I can multi-task.

George Aw! Were you dismissed?

Ibi Hurts more when it's your own family.

George Like their style.

Ibi It was too quiet anyway and there's still two of them so ...

George Fair enough. And where's Umra?

Ibi Upstairs.

George Wow! You have her on a tight leash!

Ibi What?

George I'm joking.

Ibi Well don't.

George Oh my god Ibs. Chill!

Ibi I am chilled.

George Wow! You've so changed. Si was right.

Ibi How have I changed?

George You used to be so fun, and up for a laugh and now ...

Ibi What? I'm not interested in you mocking my wife?

George Mocking her! What the hell? Ibi, it's me! I thought we were friends?

Ibi So did I.

George What's that supposed to mean?

Ibi George man. You only come round when you want something! Internet won't work. Car's failed its MOT. I'm like a stand-in boyfriend to you. But that has to stop. I got married for fuck's sake!

George Yes, I know! I had to watch, remember?

Ibi I just don't think we should be as close as we were. It's inappropriate.

George Inappropriate? For you to have female friends? Are you just making this shit up now? The Qur'an according to Ibi?! And as for 'I only visit when I want something', what about the time when you were having second thoughts about the whole marriage thing? Who got out of their bed in the middle of the night to come talk to you?

Ibi To 'talk'? Really? Face it George, you were just scared you were gonna lose me.

George Lose you?! I never had you! And even if that was true, I still came! Still went to the wedding! Welcomed your 'wife' home! And sat back and watched you play happy families with someone knowing I could have done a hell of a better job!

Ibi You! You think you could have done a better job? Your biggest concern in life is 'does my lipstick match my handbag'! Boy do you know what I'm looking for in a wife.

Beat.

George Right.

George *exits. Lights.*

Scene Six

Newsagents. **Saghir** *is sat behind the counter alone reading the local newspaper.* **Audrey** *enters in her nurse's uniform.*

Audrey Oh, hi.

Saghir Hello.

Audrey You good?

Saghir Yes. Tired, but you know …

Audrey Yeah … I'm surprised you're open to be honest.

Saghir Well, they don't pay you to close.

Audrey True … Just got to pay a quick visit to one of my old ladies at 33, and she asked me to get some milk.

Saghir Work as normal, huh?

Audrey Yeah. I'll just take this. It's only for tea.

Saghir You must be tired too, no?

Audrey No, no. I'm fine. Thanks.

Saghir OK.

Audrey This today's?

Saghir Yes.

Audrey Talking about last night?

Saghir Barely. Blaming an 'alleged assault'.

Audrey Well I guess they can only report facts.

Saghir Right.

Audrey I'd better take this as well. Find out what actually happened.

Saghir Look, I need to ask you …

Audrey I just want to pay for this, thank you Saghir.

Beat.

Audrey Fine. I'll leave it.

Saghir We have to talk about it at some point.

Audrey There's nothing to talk about.

Saghir I wasn't intentionally eavesdropping but –

Audrey With your face pressed to the window you heard a lot, yeah?

Saghir I live next door. Come on.

Audrey What do you want me to say?

Saghir That's a nice neighbourhood. Quiet, you know?

Audrey No, I don't think I do.

Saghir Things like last night … they don't know how to react.

Audrey Last night was a misunderstanding.

Saghir I have a daughter.

Audrey What's your point?

Saghir I just want to understand the truth.

Audrey I have a feeling if I tell you the truth you'll be terribly disappointed.

Audrey *puts down the newspaper and milk and turns to exit.*

Saghir Audrey! Your things! Come! Don't be silly.

Audrey It's fine. I'll tell her after last night you were clearly too stressed to open.

Audrey *exits. Lights fade.*

Scene Seven

Inside an empty garage on the Westbridge estate. **Andre**'s *mobile phone rings as he kicks a ball against the shutter. He answers it.*

Andre What?!

Yeah well it's not you who had po po at his yard last night is it?!

Sara!! Do you know what your dad said?! Rape! My mom had to hear that!

No, I stuck to the story, but they ain't buying it and I'm wondering if you're thinking about speaking up and telling the truth anytime soon?

Sara!! Your dad tried to kick down man's door? How does he even know where I live?

You know what?! Go suck out!

Marcus *enters.* **Andre** *hangs up his phone.*

Marcus Someone's in a good mood.

Andre What you doing here? *Indicating the ball.*

Marcus Could probably hear you from the street with that?

Andre And? Feel free to leave. Not really up for talking, yeah?

Marcus What? You're in my cotch asking me to leave?

Andre Gassed! This ain't been your cotch since you dipped, fam.

Marcus Erm, please point out what you put in here, then we'll talk.

Andre Fine. I'll leave.

Marcus Jeez, what's the matter with you?

Andre *picks up his ball.*

Marcus Andre!

Andre *goes to exit.*

Marcus You stole my cotch and couldn't even get a new sofa? Ya tramp!

Andre Dickhead!

Marcus Eeediot!

Andre Prick!

Marcus Wallard!

They both burst out laughing.

Marcus Who was on the phone?

Andre Some stupid gal!

Marcus You must like her if she's making you screw that hard.

Andre No gals worth dramz.

Marcus (*messing his hair*) Aw. It's like the start of a poem.

Andre *shrugs him off, drops his ball and continues to kick it against the shutter.*

Marcus Oi! You don't know about discretion?

Andre Huh?

Marcus How many other people know about this place?

Andre Don't be silly, no one. This is just somewhere for me.

Marcus Then why don't you try keeping it like that?

Andre *stops. Then starts to pass the ball from foot to foot.*

Marcus You not go school today?

Andre Funny.

Marcus Ah! Watch when I see ya mom!

Andre When you see my mom, tell her I said 'hi'.

Marcus What's going on?

Andre What? Mom asked me to leave so I left. Rags.

Marcus What? When?

Andre Last night.

Marcus Why?

Andre What do you mean 'why'?

Marcus You're sixteen and your mom asks you to leave?

Andre Yeah …?

Marcus You get a girl in trouble?

Andre Shut up!

Marcus Well what did you do?

Andre You know what … 'low you. You sound like leng. You've fully changed you have.

Marcus And?

Andre And that means you lose your privileges of talking to me on a lev's.

Marcus Cool! Good luck at the home!

Andre, *frustrated, takes his ball and kicks it hard.*

Marcus Oi! What's gwarnin?!

Andre *ignores him and goes back to repeatedly kicking the ball against the wall. Eventually* **Marcus** *intercepts.*

Andre I can't wait 'til I'm eighteen!

Marcus Is it? Which part? Paying taxes or losing your summer holiday?

Andre I just can't wait to leave these sides. It's fucking dry!

Marcus Ain't nothing wrong with round here.

Andre Please. That's why you ducked off?

Marcus – and happily came back!

Andre Course, now! You're all loved up ... living with gal ... earning big money ...

Marcus Big money? Where do you see big money?

Andre Don't panic I ain't looking to rob ya!

Marcus Listen to you!

Andre Don't think I ain't capable!

Marcus I know you ain't!

Andre Ya dickhead! Mans like me's a sniper!

Marcus Mans like you is homeless and I'm guessing scared.

Andre Scared? I'm not a youte. Just gotta get on with shit innit? Look after number one from now on.

Marcus By living here? I wouldn't recommend it. Gets kinda chilly, still.

Andre Don't be stupid.

Marcus Then where are you gonna stay?

Andre Hostel tonight. Gotta be in at nine.

Andre *shrugs. Starts kicking the ball again.* **Marcus** *pulls out a £20 note from his wallet.*

Marcus I'm starving. Run chip shop for me and get yourself something?

Andre Yeah?

Marcus Chicken and chips and a Rubicon. Get what you're getting and keep the change.

Andre Sick!

Andre *picks up his bike and goes to cycle off.*

Andre I never did nothing you know.

Marcus Look, you better hurry, chip shop closes after lunch.

Marcus *watches* **Andre** *cycle off. Lights fade.*

Scene Eight

Outside the flat. An old Asian lady is carrying bags. **Soriya** *follows.*

Old Lady You live here?

Soriya Yes, upstairs. I'll help you if that's OK?

Old Lady Oi! *Holi!* Slowly! There are eggs in there.

Soriya Sorry, right. What number are you?

Old Lady 3 – so you're at the top you say? You're the one that moved in the black fellow?

Soriya Erm yes. Yes I suppose I did.

Old Lady Huh!

They walk in silence.

Soriya Right is this you?

Old Lady I'll have it from here.

Soriya OK cool. Have a nice day. **Soriya** *goes to walk off.*

Old Lady You know, it's seeing you with him that gives these boys these ideas. You know, the trouble last night?

Soriya I'm sorry?

Old Lady Asian girls should be for Asian men.

Soriya Oh.

Old Lady But then people see you with him and they want to try for themselves. See what the fuss is about. Why make a fuss? Everyone lived perfectly happily round here together before you young ones try to integrate and confuse things.

Soriya Right ... OK ...

Old Lady Don't you try just appease me because I'm old ...

Soriya I wasn't ...

Old Lady I know what I'm talking about.

Soriya OK.

Old Lady And now that poor little girl was raped. Three or four times, they are saying.

Soriya What? Who's they?

Old Lady Oh ... of course ... a little Asian girl gets raped by some black boys – just opposite, on the Westbridge, under your nose ... I would turn a blind eye too. Hope you have a lovely rest of day.

The **Old Lady** *enters into her flat leaving* **Soriya** *outside speechless. Lights fade.*

Scene Nine

The flat. **Marcus** *is in the kitchen eating chips.* **George** *enters holding her laptop.*

Marcus Oi! Trouble! You hungry?

George I can't eat that? Few things you'll need to learn about me if we're to be roomies. No carbs. No dairy. No sugar. I'm allergic.

Marcus To all three?

George Had an allergy test done at Neal's Yard.

Marcus Which means?

George For starters I'm more sensitive to the vicious side effects of wheat than most.

Marcus There are vicious side effects to wheat?

George Oh god yeah! My stomach sticks out and gets all bloated, I become fatigued ...

Marcus Right ... Do you reckon there are starving people in third world countries who have to turn down a loaf 'cause of wheat allergies?

George I think I see where you're going with this. But it's a real serious problem!

Marcus Of course.

George Oh and another tip. Was that you that tried to throw Lily Donaldson in the recycle bin? Because *Vogue* goes on the shelf, only *Grazia* gets thrown. Soriya would most definitely key your car for that!

Marcus What's the difference?

George *opens her laptop to upload her pictures.*

George Between *Vogue* and *Grazia*? Oh lord. I want this to work, honest I do …

Marcus Oi! Seriously! Enlighten me!

George To be honest Marcus, it would seem you were beyond enlightening.

Marcus If I tell you you're looking painfully thin in those pictures will that help?

George Wow! The boy learns quick! *Vogue*'s thick, *Grazia*'s thin. Apart from that, how you settling?

Marcus Good good. All unpacked and about to go to the dad's.

George Dun dun dun!

Marcus Serious …

George Well, Soriya's family's so safe! Grew up with them. They're like my second family, since my first was often quite … busy.

Marcus I guess I'm just worried they'll not think I'm good enough for her.

George You have your own business. That's pretty impressive.

Marcus Well you know …?

George Oh … because you're … (*whispers*) black?

Marcus Wow! You're as direct as Si.

George Well don't worry, you can totally play that down! You're half white too remember! And you should be proud of that! The other side's just a … blip.

Marcus That's … beautiful.

George (*laughs*) Dude, you're not a new idea to them! She's talked about you for like a year. They know all about you already!

Marcus Do they?

George Totes. And she met your folks right?

Marcus My mom, yeah, last week.

George *hums wedding march.*

Marcus Think we're just gonna try living together first.

George That's your thoughts. But what do you think the dad will be thinking? The dad that's literally just watched one child get married …?

Marcus Yeah but that was arranged right?

George Still an agreed marriage. Everyone will be wondering where this is going …

Marcus Well …

George Dude. I'm totally messing.

Marcus Ah man. You just mind I don't sprinkle breadcrumbs in your mouth whilst you're sleeping!

Soriya *enters.*

George Someone's back early! Part-timer!

Soriya Someone really needn't have bothered today.

Marcus How comes?

Soriya They had to let everyone who lived this way leave early to ensure we got home OK.

George Cushy!

Marcus *gets up to greet* **Soriya**.

Soriya I'm exhausted!

George From half a day? Pathetic!

Marcus What's up?

Soriya People! People are ... crazy!

George Tea?

George *jumps up to put the kettle on.*

Soriya Did you know that *Asian women were for Asian men only*?

George Hear hear!

Marcus Number 3?

Soriya She said something to you?

Marcus She mumbled something when I was moving some stuff in the other day.

Soriya You're joking.

Marcus No 'thanks' for the fact I waited for her to pass me on the stairs. Her, taking them one at a time, me holding a large box labelled books!

Soriya Ah babes ...

George You should have told her you're not Asian. Your mom's white, with blonde hair! That would have shut her up!

Marcus Your mom's blonde?

Soriya Have you only just met George?

George Don't panic. I told Saghir the same about your mom. Emphasise the positive, remember?

Marcus … thanks.

Soriya Ignore her.

Marcus I am.

George Here!

Soriya Thank you.

George Marcus?

Marcus No I'm gonna hop in the shower before we have to go.

Marcus *exits*

Soriya Did they say anything on the news about the girl that was attacked on the Westbridge last night?

George Babes, you know I don't watch the news!

Soriya I know! As soon as the words left my mouth I thought, 'Why bother?'

George So what happened? Anyone die?

Soriya Girl got raped.

George Shut up! How do you know?

Soriya Old lady downstairs told me.

George Oh, well then it must be true!

Soriya Oi!

George Si. Please. She blatantly saw us in tiny little dresses last night and is now playing the prude.

Marcus *re-enters.*

Soriya You OK?

Marcus No hot water. Just put the boost on.

George Oh sorry. I completely forgot! I've just run a bath.

Soriya Well they're not expecting us for now, so there's no rush.

George Though you do want to get there quite early.

Soriya Because …?

George You're meeting me for drinks later, remember?

Soriya Oh … right … yeah …

George Marcus got dinner. I get drinks.

Soriya Yes woman who has no money.

George You promised! Besides I don't have a date anymore. He cancelled.

Soriya What?

George Don't! I'll cry. I'm going to soak myself to a prune then later we are going out.

George *exits.*

Marcus So the 'I get dinner, she gets drinks' thing. Is that gonna be the arrangement every night?

Soriya We just need to get her a job or a boyfriend. Or even just a pet.

George (*o/s*) I heard that!

Soriya (*quietly*) She'll be fine. She's just a bit lost at the minute.

Marcus What you looking at?

Soriya A cook book.

Marcus What?!

Soriya I'm making an effort!

Marcus Oh, stop! *Reggae reggae* recipes?

Soriya Well, you always say that's what you eat when you and your friends go out.

Marcus We also eat Chinese and Italian.

Soriya Well I'd like to learn how to cook it.

Marcus Do I have to learn how to cook curry?

Soriya Carry on yeah and you won't have a girlfriend to cook anything for.

Marcus Sorry. When did you get it?

Soriya George got it for me. I think she was taking the piss but there's some good dishes in here.

Marcus Like … ?

Soriya Steak, peppers and tomatoes with ackee and mushrooms.

Marcus Well I don't like ackee or mushrooms but mmm, sounds yum.

Soriya You know what, it's not even for you.

Marcus Good.

Soriya Good.

Marcus So who are you cooking it for?

Soriya George. That girl has spent most of her life in the Caribbean and slept with most of the cricket teams, she'll get this.

Marcus Good.

Soriya Right.

Marcus Well, I'll leave you to it.

Soriya Anyhow I cook this, this weekend, and you don't eat any …

Marcus … you haven't actually threatened me yet.

Soriya Seriously Marcus!

Marcus Of course I'll eat it, just might make myself a portion of chips to go with it rather than the ackee.

Soriya Then it's just steak and chips.

Marcus What's wrong with that?

Soriya I'm trying to do something nice for you.

Marcus Si, you don't have to … If you wanna cook, cool, but cook something you want to eat.

Soriya But some of these sound nice.

Marcus Fine then.

Soriya And it'd be nice to eat something you grew up eating.

Marcus What like … (*reads*) rice and peas or festivals? Babes, that's not me.

Soriya What? You don't like it?

Marcus No … cook it. I'll love it.

Soriya I'm not gonna cook something you don't like.

Marcus OK …

Soriya So, what would you eat? If you were in a restaurant?

Marcus Just chicken and rice.

Soriya Like … (*reads*) creamy coconut and mango chicken?

Marcus No …

Soriya OK, well can you throw me a bone?

Marcus I don't know, Si, just chicken.

Soriya You're as clueless as Ibi and dad! (*Continues reading.*) Oooh this actually sounds quite nice.

Marcus So you've decided?

Soriya Well you like it don't you?

Marcus But it's for everyone?

Soriya Babes, George will pick at whatever I cook her, it's for you.

Marcus Honestly Si …

Soriya Just say thank you and shut up. It won't be a regular occurrence.

Marcus ... thank you.

Soriya Would you mind if I called your mom to ask her for a bit of help?

Marcus What?

Soriya Well, I don't have to.

Marcus Why do you need to?

Soriya I don't. It's fine. It actually looks quite simple.

Marcus No, of course. Yeah call her.

Soriya Thanks. I've just never made stuff like this before. And George will be hopeless.

Marcus Si ... my mom's white.

Soriya I know. We have met.

Marcus You're not getting it. My mom's white and my dad left. She didn't cook this stuff. The house I grew up in was as white as George's.

Soriya Oh hun, no one's house is as white as George's.

Marcus Seriously.

Soriya Ok. So your mom would cook ... ?

Marcus English stuff. Roasts, spaghetti ...

Soriya Spaghetti? Very English.

Marcus Leave off!

Soriya OK ... that's fine.

Marcus I know.

Soriya I just assumed ...

Marcus I know.

Soriya So would you rather a roast? On Sunday?

Marcus Fine.

Beat.

Marcus I'm sorry. I'm just over being embarrassed about not knowing that world. It's not me and I get that. I just need you to, too.

Soriya I do.

Marcus Do you?

Soriya Marcus!

Marcus Nah, it's just for me, not having my dad around, I didn't go without, you know? I mean I always just kinda looked at Jamie like … I don't know …

Soriya No, I get that. And he felt the same …

Marcus You think?

Soriya He gave you the lease. To his baby. Of course he did.

Marcus He just taught me so much, you know? And I'm not even on about work stuff. Like he taught me … bwoy … how to be a man, I guess. He didn't need to be black to teach me that. I don't know … it's like I'm realising what's important and what matters and I'm kinda like 'low all the other stuff.

Soriya I do understand Marcus.

Lights.

Scene Ten

Front of **Saghir** *and* **Audrey**'s *terrace house.* **Audrey**'s *pottering in the garden.* **Saghir** *is home from work.*

Audrey Saghir. Hi.

Saghir Hello.

Silence as **Saghir** *finds his keys.* **Audrey** *continues gardening.*

Audrey You finished early.

Saghir They made us close up, just in case.

Audrey In case what?

Saghir Same as last night.

Audrey What?

Saghir Well people are still angry and no one wants to tell them anything, so what can we expect?

Audrey *returns to gardening.*

Saghir Looks good.

Audrey Yeah?

Noticing a hanging basket between their two doors.

Saghir This smells wonderful.

Audrey If it's in your way –

Saghir No, no, I like it. Honestly.

Audrey Right …

Saghir Look. About –

Audrey Just so you know, the rosemary and thyme just help yourselves.

Saghir Ah. Yes. Thanks

Audrey Better than that dry supermarket rubbish.

Saghir Yes.

Audrey And cheaper. I mean there's plenty of it.

Saghir Thank you. I'll tell my boy's wife.

Audrey Oh right? Yeah, she'll love it if she likes cooking.

Saghir Yes. It looks very nice.

Audrey Yeah, well, don't take much does it? Got those bulbs off the high street, dirt cheap and if they take, well … it's nice innit?

Saghir Yes.

Audrey You're right. It is so quiet here.

Saghir I only meant people here are more likely to think –

Audrey Yeah. Exactly. It allows you to just think …

Saghir It's just how rumours spread –

Audrey Yeah … feels a bit like, I don't really belong here …

Saghir OK, that's just nonsense –

Audrey The whole street probably thinks … well, I thought I'd make the garden look good you know. Show what kind of neighbour I am.

Saghir Look Audrey –

Audrey Though, then I look over at yours. You just pave it over. Kill any sign of life for the extra parking space. And it's the same out the back! But no one will look at you like you're not welcome here.

Saghir No one looks at you –

Audrey Though you'll argue a patio can be good too – right?

Saghir Right …

Audrey Perfect for summer barbecues –

Saghir Yes –

Audrey Not that you be eating meat.

Saghir We eat meat.

Beat.

Audrey God, it's so quiet.

Saghir Yes.

Audrey   We're sorry, OK? I'm sorry, about the disruption last night.

Saghir   I just wanted to understand correctly.

Beat.

Audrey   I asked him to leave.

Saghir   Your boy?

Audrey   For the best.

Saghir   Right ... so he did ... yeah ...

Audrey   Saghir, I'm so sorry. I completely forgot, I have left food on the cooker.

Saghir   Right.

Audrey *goes in. Lights fade.*

Scene Eleven

Saghir's *house.* **Ibi**, **Soriya** *and* **Marcus** *finishing dinner.* **Saghir**'s *seat is opposite* **Marcus**'s.

Soriya   Oi! Big head – pass the bliming rotis!

Ibi   Twenty-seven years of this!

Soriya   Twenty-five! Please don't age me.

Ibi   Wow! Feels so much longer!

Ibi *and* **Marcus** *laugh.*

Soriya (*to* **Marcus**)   Don't laugh!

Ibi   You're such a bully. (*To* **Marcus**.) You see what you could get lumbered with? I say run now, while you still have the chance!

Saghir *enters from the kitchen with more food.*

Saghir   I still can't believe I served you in the shop today. Funny, eh?

Marcus Yeah.

Soriya I still can't believe you didn't recognise him, Dad.

Saghir Ssh, eat the paneer.

Soriya He has the memory of a fish, don't be offended.

Marcus It's fine. He was busy.

Soriya You should have introduced yourself.

Marcus He was busy, Si.

Soriya Doing what?

Saghir Soriya! Less chat more eats, hey?

Soriya Where was chacha-ji?

Saghir Doing stock take.

Ibi That I helped prep!

Saghir Huh!

Soriya I told you to introduce yourself.

Ibi Like your style Marcus, zone her out! Then you can move on!

Soriya Please! Like he could do any better!

Saghir *exits with more plates.*

Ibi Modest this one! Stick with me Marcus! I can introduce you to some nice Asian women!

Soriya Er ... how exactly? You couldn't even find yourself one! (*To* **Marcus**.) I told you it was arranged, didn't I?

Ibi Don't say it like that!

Soriya Like what?

Ibi Like we're one of those weird Asian couples that had never met until the wedding night!

Soriya You hadn't!

Ibi She's such an exaggerator! We'd met! Please don't think we're backward.

Soriya Why would he think you were backward?

Ibi 'Cause some people do!

Soriya Who?

Ibi You!

Soriya I think you seem like you were *made for each other*!

Ibi You're such a knob! I'm half Pakistani and proud!

Soriya I'm half Pakistani and proud. I just didn't feel the need to marry a freshie to prove my loyalty!

Ibi Oh my god! Shut up! (*to* **Marcus**) She's not a freshie!

Soriya (*to* **Marcus**) Ask him if she speaks English.

Marcus Erm … I gonna just stay out of it.

Soriya Or better yet, where she is at this 'family' dinner?

Ibi She's tired.

Soriya Often tired, ain't she Ibs? I wonder what I could read into that.

Ibi Only when you come round sis, read away!

Soriya It's probably for the best anyway. I mean all the interpreting becomes boring after a while.

Ibi She speaks English, knobface!

Soriya Not to me she doesn't, fanny 'ole!

Ibi Soriya's the only one in the family who thought she was above learning Punjabi.

Soriya I was too busy getting into Cambridge –

Ibi Where everyone else in the family managed to get into after learning their mother tongue!

Soriya Our mom's white! Moron! Do you see why I put off this dinner for so long?

Ibi She's so easy to wind up! I'll teach you the tricks!

Soriya And FYI, I did not think you were backward. Just shocked such a beautiful girl actually agreed to marry you!

Ibi Hurts, Si! Hurts!

Soriya Only joking, munchkin!!

Saghir (*re-enters*) Soriya, shhh! You're so loud. She's like this at home, huh?

Marcus Bubbly is the word I like to call it!

Ibi Now there's a polite word!

Soriya Shut up!

Marcus Saghir. You need a hand?

Saghir (*exits*) No. No thank you.

Soriya Ah! You're such a kiss ass! I love you!

Ibi Kiss ass? How did you get a first?

Soriya How did you get a wife, 'knobface'?

Ibi Argh! It's like arguing with a child. God Marcus! You've got your work cut out!

Marcus *gives* **Soriya** *a kiss.*

Ibi Oh, Dad! Quick! Public displays of affection!

Soriya *kicks him under the table.*

Soriya And he says I'm the child?

Ibi Dad! Don't worry about anything else. Think I'm gonna be sick!

Soriya Jealousy. Pure jealousy!

Saghir (*enters*) Shhh shhh! You're all so loud!

Soriya Isn't my dad adorable? Forgetful, but adorable!

Soriya *grabs and wiggles* **Saghir***'s cheeks.*

Saghir Get off!

Ibi Dad! Sit down! Come on. Relax! Before it all gets cold.

Saghir Yes yes! Everything OK?

Soriya Perfect.

Saghir (*to* **Marcus**) How you getting on?

Marcus It's amazing, thank you. You're a talented cook.

Soriya Ha! Don't be fooled! This is the work of Miss Pakistan! These two don't know where the kitchen is!

Saghir Soriya! Ssh! Everybody, eat! Please.

Saghir *serves* **Marcus** *more food on to his plate.*

Marcus Thank you.

Saghir So … erm … well … how you finding living in the flat then Marcus? With George and her silly dieting.

Ibi Ha! She's a nightmare. She sticks pictures of Abercrombie models on the biscuit tin then asks you *if you think they eat biscuits* when you try and get one.

Marcus That could probably be useful!

Ibi I mean it's the ultimate girlie flat! They read fashion magazines and watch programmes about next top models. You sure you can handle it?

Soriya How would you know, Ibs? I can't remember the last time you came over to visit *me*?

Ibi Funny.

Saghir Soriya shh.

Marcus I have enough box sets of *The Wire* to balance things out.

Ibi Nice.

Marcus And literally just got the last of my stuff in today, but very happy. I used to live on Westbridge as a kid didn't I, so the area's home really.

Ibi Oh my god, did you guys hear that a woman got attacked right by yours yesterday, over on that Westbridge?

Marcus Attacked?

Ibi Yeah. They mentioned it briefly on the news earlier.

Saghir (*serves* **Marcus**) You eat fish?

Marcus Thank you.

Ibi What happened again?

Soriya They just said 'alleged attack of a female'.

Marcus Like rape?

Soriya Well ...

Ibi Awful, innit?

Soriya If it happened.

Ibi They saying who the girl is?

Soriya Not on the news.

Ibi Someone 'round here will know. Dad, come on. You're usually good for the details. Did you find out who it was?

Saghir Erm ... Ashan's daughter Sara. Let's eat now, huh?

Soriya Sara?! She's like sixteen!

Saghir Yes. Roti?

Ibi Was raped?

Saghir Attacked.

Ibi Which means?

Saghir Pass me a glass please.

Soriya Attacked by who?

Saghir Possibly one of the little boys from that estate, Ashan said. Glass.

Ibi They don't know who?

Saghir They're not certain.

Marcus Do police have anyone?

Saghir No. They questioned people but … no one.

Marcus Jeez.

Ibi You know who don't you?

Saghir No. They haven't proven anything yet.

Soriya Who was it?

Saghir Nothing is definite.

Ibi Dad!

Saghir I won't say!

Soriya Anyone we know?

Saghir No, no! Don't be silly. Now please eat.

Ibi Textbook round here though ain't it?

Soriya Not rape Ibi, no.

Ibi No, I meant trouble happening and no one knowing anything.

Soriya You sure that's not just you? I mean you don't strike me as the most informed person in our neighbourhood.

Ibi What you on about? I kept an eye on hash tag Westbridge as soon as I heard the first siren. I'm informed.

Soriya I don't think married men your age should be on Twitter.

Ibi Ouch!

Soriya (*to* **Marcus**) Bet your little groupie friend would know more.

Marcus Nah, doubt it.

Ibi You have a groupie Marcus?

Soriya A male groupie! I pretend it doesn't bother me but … I'm keeping a close, careful eye!

Marcus Ha. Ha. Ha. Funny! No, one boy I used to mind when I was little has decided I've grown up and become his Superhero!

Soriya Sounds gay, doesn't it?

Ibi The word 'Superhero' isn't helping!

Marcus Alright!

Marcus *starts to cough.*

Soriya OK, don't cry we were only kidding.

Ibi Told you she was a bully.

Saghir You alright?

Marcus (*coughing*) Yeah. Yes. Sorry.

Ibi That dish has chilli in it.

Marcus (*still coughing*) Yes it does!

Saghir Pani?

Ibi Water?

Marcus Thanks.

Saghir (*pouring water*) Soriya! Go get the yoghurt!

Soriya Is it too hot?

Marcus (*coughs*) No, no, it's …

Saghir I should have made him a sandwich.

Marcus *shakes his head.* **Ibi** *reaches to get the yoghurt.*

Ibi Here. Put this on the side. It helps.

Marcus Thanks.

Soriya   He's being dramatic.

Saghir   You OK?

Marcus   I'm fine. Thank you.

Saghir   You sure?

Marcus   Yes. I'm gonna go refill this, though. Through there?

Saghir   I'll get it.

Marcus   Don't be silly. I've got it. Thanks.

Marcus *exits.*

Ibi   So Dad? What do you reckon?

Soriya   Shut up! And Dad! How can you not recognise him? You look so rude!

Ibi   Si, Marcus didn't seem to care.

Soriya   Dad?

Saghir   Soriya, ssh! I'm eating.

Soriya   Did you serve him today?

Saghir   I can't remember.

Soriya   You're so rubbish!

Saghir   I can't be expected to remember every goddam *Kala* boy that comes into the shop Soriya. Now drop it. I'm eating.

Marcus *re-enters.*

Marcus   Think my mouth has started to calm down.

Soriya   Good. You done sweetie? I'm kinda stuffed.

Marcus   You kidding?! Don't be fooled 'cause I had to top up on a little H2O. I still haven't tried the fish yet.

Soriya   I'm really tired though, and there's still a bit of unpacking to do.

Marcus   Si, I did it all.

Soriya You did your stuff hun, but there will be stuff I need to sort to make more room.

Marcus Oh, OK.

Saghir Soriya …

Soriya Sorry Ibs.

Ibi Si, stay and let Marcus finish his plate at least?

Soriya You've finished haven't you hun?

Marcus Erm … yeah.

Soriya Plus I've got to go meet George. She's gone to some gallery thing and probably shouldn't travel home on her own with everything that's going on, so …

Marcus Well it was lovely to meet you both.

Ibi You too Marcus.

Saghir Yes.

Ibi And you're gonna need to meet Mom next. Her birthday's next month. You going up Si?

Saghir Stupid woman! Move all the way to bloody Birmingham! For what?

Soriya Work Dad! No point asking questions you already know the answer to! Yeah, definitely. Just need to sort out a weekend off so it's worth the travel!

Ibi Cool, well let me know

Soriya Right. See you Dad.

Saghir OK.

Marcus Thank Umra for the beautiful cooking for me.

Ibi Will do. See you guys.

Soriya See you.

Marcus Bye.

Marcus *and* **Soriya** *exit.* **Ibi** *pulls out his mobile phone to check his Twitter account.*

Ibi How nice was he, eh Dad?

Saghir *doesn't answer and instead stands to clear the table.* **Ibi**, *oblivious, plays an uploaded video. We hear the following voiceover while video footage of the Westbridge appears.*

Voiceover The details of the horrific gang rape of a fourteen-year-old Pakistani girl have been flying through Facebook, and thank god, 'cause no one else wants to talk about it. Calling it an 'attack'. Come correct. No less than seven black, Afro-Caribbean males were said to have been involved in the most horrendous sexual attack ever heard. The victim has failed to come forward due to her fear of being deported for being an illegal immigrant and based on that police are reluctant to investigate further. It's the perfect excuse for them not to care, again. If you care, we're calling for all fit and able bodies to attend a protest at the Westbridge Estate at 9 p.m. tonight to voice our disappointment in our justice system! Follow '@Westbridgeprotest' for all updates. Do not let us down! We cannot let these rapists win! We will not be silenced!

Saghir Ibi! How can you listen to this bloody stupid nonsense?!

Ibi They're talking about the attack.

Saghir Who are? Sara's an 'illegal immigrant'? Come! Talk sense please!

Ibi *silences his phone. Lights.*

Scene Twelve

Bar. **Soriya** *and* **George** *dressed up. Tipsy. Sat on chairs at bar.*

George Your dad said what?!

Soriya Yep!

George Awkward!

Soriya It was horrible.

George He has a point though.

Soriya George. No.

George Babes. Just because you're doing the dirty with him doesn't mean your dad should be able to pull him out of a line-up before a proper introduction. Fair's fair Si.

Soriya It was just hearing my dad say that word when Marcus was in the next room.

George I would have had to laugh!

Soriya OK. Clearly you're not listening!

George Oh, lighten up! Ibi must have helped you out?

Soriya Oh, Ibi thought it'd be an appropriate time to talk about rape.

George Just in general? Nice.

Soriya He thought this would be the best time to remind Dad, in case he'd forgotten that, oh, yes … Marcus is a black guy, and from the Westbridge estate … the same estate where a young girl apparently got raped by lots of black guys …

George Oh, babes.

Soriya See? Not funny!

George Ibi's a knob!

Soriya Ibi is a knob.

George That's why he had to buy his wife off the Internet.

Soriya I like that you're clearly over all that though …

George I keep looking at his profile picture of the two of them.

Soriya Oh. Dear. God.

George I think she's actually prettier than me which is bloody annoying since I'd bet good money she doesn't wear any make-up.

Soriya She is younger than us.

George When did we get so old?

Soriya When did you manage to get back on to the wife?

George Fine! I hope Marcus wasn't too pissed we left him all alone on his first official night in.

Soriya If he's even stayed in.

George Bless him. So come on then … what's he like?

Soriya Marcus?

George Yep! In bed?

Soriya What on earth has made you ask that now, after all this time?

George Well, for starters, I think it's important we decipher if he's truly worth all this drama, plus, I need to know if this new living arrangement will affect my sleeping pattern.

Soriya Have you ever heard us before?

George That bad eh?

Soriya No!

George Ooooh! And … ?

Soriya And what?

George Don't act dumb! He's not black. He's not white. Which way did he luck out?

Soriya George!

George What? No one's listening.

Soriya Shut up!

George It's huge isn't it? I want measurements!

Soriya No!

George Not in inches, just is it ... (*she makes hand gestures*) ... here? Bigger?

Soriya I'm not telling!

George It's tiny isn't it? God bless his blonde-haired mom diluting the genes pool!

Soriya His mom's not blonde and he is not tiny!

George Ah! You lucky bitch!

Soriya I know.

George Show off!

Soriya Well, it's nice to remember I've got someone to show off about.

George OK. You're not allowed to talk anymore.

Soriya Even if my dad doesn't see it that way.

George Bore off!

Soriya I just saw myself being with him forever, you know?

George Seriously! Stop talking!

Soriya Did you see that?

George What? You shagging Marcus's big dick forever?

Soriya I really don't think that's what I asked!

George No! But 'little miss perfect having doubts' was too dull to hear!

Soriya Oi!

George Oi yourself! You love him, he loves you! End of!

Soriya Is it?

George OK, clearly you've forgotten who you're talking to! You're gonna have to save all this wank Dear Jane rubbish for your emotionally in touch friends who have nothing better to do than over-analyse unnecessary things. Me? I'd rather live a little.

Soriya George! This is my life ...

George – that is wonderful! So stop fretting! Saghir has never managed to fully influence you before and look how proud he is. That's what you need to remember. And if you fuck up, well, at least you can say you enjoyed the ride.

Soriya Yeah, maybe. Wow. That was quite profound for you.

George Another mastered skill.

Soriya Almost as strong as your accessorising.

George Si!

Soriya What? I'm kidding.

George Well don't. He already thinks I'm a bimbo!

Soriya Who?

George Ibi.

Soriya And we're back here.

George I just sometimes think if I never dropped out ...

Soriya He graduated with a third! After contesting!

George At least he graduated!

Soriya Don't do this ...

George Yeah ... Well how about getting me a new focus then, eh?

Soriya Erm, why are we out please?

George Nice try. You and I both know the only reason you agreed to come out was to get away from those protesting hooligans on our doorstep!

Soriya Well whatever the reason ... I'm thinking hot rich banker.

George Interesting! Seen any potentials?

Soriya Well him at the other end of the bar hasn't taken his eyes off you since we arrived – wearing a suit ...

George *turns round to look.*

Soriya Subtle, George! Subtle!

George He's white?!

Soriya Let's broaden the pool a bit eh?

George Yeah. Fair point! He's kinda cute. Do you think I've lost weight?

Soriya … yes …

George OK. Switch seats with me so I can get eye contact.

George *and* **Soriya** *switch seats.*

George Can't believe you're pushing me towards a white guy.

Soriya Your fault! Unfortunately you can't be trusted with anyone else since you accused some poor innocent in a robe of being a terrorist this evening.

George I didn't accuse him! I was very careful not to accuse!

Soriya Why don't I believe that?

George OK! Firstly, you weren't there!

Soriya Thank god!

George And secondly, religious people are just freaks! So, I actually had every right to be wary whether he was Muslim, Christian … or a fucking Hare-krishna. Besides, it's not like I got off the tube. Now that would have been an accusation.

Soriya You're so considerate.

George Right? I didn't even switch seats. Because I understand, I have to be seen to be cool with it!

Soriya I wish I saw your face when he got off the next stop jamming to his iPod! Oh the guilt!

George Oh babes – there was no iPod. That was my first clue. Who sits on the tube content with their own thoughts? No *Metro*, no music. It's freaky.

Soriya But you do see you were wrong?

George Well ... he didn't blow up *that* tube, no ... but, have you caught the news this evening? I mean who's to say what line he went on after.

Soriya I'm thinking we would have heard.

George Yeah yeah! OK, I was wrong! I admit it! I'm a terrible person who'll go to hell. Happy?

Soriya Ecstatic.

George And it's not a colour thing. It's a religious thing. If the boy on the tube was black or white doing the same thing I still would have freaked –

Soriya But still remained seated!

George Dude. Being called a racist is not cool. I'm white. I don't get away with it as easily as you do.

Soriya I have no idea why Ibi didn't just scoop you up!

George OK! That's mean!

Soriya Sorry.

George Well I was actually thinking about that ...

Soriya George ... No.

George I just think he needs to know how I –

Soriya He knows how you feel.

George No. It's always said in game play. I just need to tell him straight so he can do with it what he will but at least he'll know, for certain.

Soriya And what do you think he's gonna do? Is he gonna leave her? They just got married!

George No ...

Soriya George, honestly, for your sake ...

George You know, I have lost weight. This feels huge.

Soriya What?

George *makes eye contact, smiles and waves at banker off stage. She then stands to go over to him.*

George OK then … your job's done. See you at home, OK?

Soriya Please! I'm not leaving you here. After what happened last night?

George What happened last night? Nobody bloody knows. I've heard so many different versions.

Soriya Well whatever the truth better to be safe than sorry.

George Ugh! You're like Mary fucking Poppins you. Right. Back in a bit.

Soriya George. With Ibi … Promise me you won't.

George I'm going to talk to the banker aren't I? What more do you fucking want?

George *exits. Lights fade.*

Act Two

Scene One

Night. **George** *and* **Soriya** *walking home. Tipsy. Stopped outside Dallas Chicken.*

George   Slow down!

Soriya   Hurry up!

George   I am wearing £700 Jimmy Choo python-skin gladiator heels! They are not designed to be walked in!

Soriya   Course they are! How can they expect you to spend seven hundred quid on a pair of shoes and have money left over to catch a taxi?

George   Ugh! Why couldn't Daddy buy me a flat nearer to the goddam tube!

Soriya   I'm starving!

George   I'm tired!

Soriya   Keep up!

George   Why didn't we catch a cab again?

Soriya   'Cause you couldn't afford one and I didn't want to embarrass you by paying for you … AGAIN!

George   This is dangerous you know. You're risking our safety. A girl was raped!

Soriya   Oh suddenly now you're concerned!

George   And there was a protest on tonight.

Soriya   Pipe down! That would have finished years ago!

George's *ankle gives way and she lets out a scream.*

Soriya   Oh! What now!

George I think my ankle's broken!

Soriya You and those goddam shoes! If you don't get up now I'm gonna leave you here!

George Fuck off! Leave me to get gang raped by all those little shits over there?

Soriya Shh! Will ya!

George Well, help me up!

Soriya *tries to pull* **George** *up but* **George** *ends up pulling* **Soriya** *down.*

Soriya I thought you'd quit the carbs?

George I'm sorry. Do you not enjoy having a roof over your head?

Soriya Spoilsport!

Soriya *gets back to her feet.*

George Sssh! What was that?

Soriya What?

George I can't believe they touched a fourteen-year-old girl? It's pathetic!

Soriya Fourteen?

George It's all over my BBM!

Soriya What? Sara's not fourteen!

George Who's Sara?

Soriya You're not even trying!

George I am! Pull harder!

Soriya I'm too weak! As if Dallas Chicken is the only place open. Come on let's just do it! It'll be our little secret!

George *finally rises.*

George No! Are you kidding? I want that place closed down! It's a health hazard. They should open a Simply Food M&S but that lot (*points to Westbridge estate*) keeps it in business!

Soriya You're such a snob!

George And you're a ghetto queen that brought the hood rat into my bachelorette pad.

Soriya Marcus is not a hood rat. He's from Clapham!

George Clapham Junction! There's a difference!

Soriya And where do you think you live?

George South Chelsea?

Soriya Hate to break it to you, SW11, same as those from the chicken-eating estate.

George Ugh! My parents really really hate me don't they?

Soriya Luckily you have me!

George I love you. Even if you are from India!

Soriya – Africa!

George How is that again?

Soriya Do you just never listen to me?

George Oh! Sorry, yeah. I love you even if you are from Africa!

Soriya And I love you even if you are from Battersea.

George South Chelsea!

Soriya How is that again?

George I'm divorcing my parents.

Lights.

Scene Two

*Outside **Saghir**'s house. **Audrey** is next door scrubbing graffiti off her wall. **Saghir**'s coming home. There are broken bottles all on the floor which have clearly been thrown at the house.*

Audrey You have fun telling everyone what my boy did?

Saghir Are you OK? Is everything OK?

Audrey Gwarn man! Everything's criss. No more than a failure of a mother like me deserves. Eh?

Saghir Look you should be inside. Leave this for the morning. They might come back.

Audrey And have everyone round here see this? **Saghir** I'll get my broom and sweep up the glass. **Audrey** No bother with that.

Saghir Shush!

Saghir *goes inside and returns with a broom and starts sweeping up the broken glass from smashed windows.* **Audrey** *continues to clean. Silence.*

Saghir That stupid protest should never have been allowed to happen. They didn't even know what they were speaking of. Making up more facts to stir up more hatred, you know? So many stupid Muslim boys being angry but not really sure why.

Audrey That girl, the one that …

Saghir Sara?

Audrey Yes. She dropped all charges her dad put against him. Police came round today to tell me in case I wanted to bring Andre home. 'Now why would I want to go and do a silly little thing like that?' I told them! She was probably just scared. Or humiliated … just wants to forget.

Silence as they continue to clean.

Audrey He denied it you know. Over and over, but I could see in his face he was lying. I know my son. Him just like him dad!

Tells me he don't smoke weed, when I can smell it. Him went school, when his teachers asking me to bring in his sick note … I hear him, at police station saying the same lie over and over. Him was at him '*bredrin's yard*'!

I called up his friend and Andre did come round but must have left about half nine. He didn't get in 'til gone twelve. That's three hours. And your son, your Ibi, outside the shop locking up tells me he did see him with a group of mans … so you see? I just know.

Audrey *returns to cleaning the wall. Silence.*

Saghir I never tell no one about your son. No one's bloody business.

Audrey *pauses. Continues to clean.* **Saghir** *continues to sweep. Lights.*

Scene Three

Outside the flat. **Soriya***'s being sick.*

George I told you not to eat that chicken but no! Soriya always knows best! My pores are so blocked from just being in that place! I can actually feel them!

Soriya *gags again.*

George I'm not even certain it is chicken that they sell! I mean you have to question how they can sell meat for so cheap!

Soriya Oh my god! Shut up and hold back my hair or something useful!

George Ah babes! You know I'd love to! But I really don't deal very well with vomit! You know if I get any closer to you I'll end up joining in.

Andre *cycles up.*

Andre Good night?

George Shouldn't you be in bed?

Andre Er ... Shouldn't you have a job?

Soriya Oh god. I think I'm gonna die!

Andre Urggh! I can actually see whole chips in your sick. Did your mother never teach you to chew your food?

George Ew! Right that's it! I'm going up! Hurry up!

Soriya I'll follow.

George *hesitates.*

Andre It's cool. I'll wait with her until she done.

George Si! Be quick!

Soriya I will.

George *exits.*

Soriya Tell me you have a tissue or something on you?

Andre *pulls out a screwed-up piece of tissue and hands it to her.*

Andre I swear on my life it's clean.

Soriya Thanks.

Soriya *goes to walk and then decides to sit instead.*

Soriya Now I'm reckoning that that lamp isn't moving, it's just me drunk, but I still feel the need to check ...

Andre It isn't moving! Hadn't you better go inside now?

Soriya Ugh! Not until my stomach stops churning. I don't know if Marcus is up there or not and if he is, best he doesn't see me like this.

Andre Must be nice to have someone waiting for you though.

Soriya How comes you're out this late?

Andre What you expect me to miss the action? It's all kicking off. I knew it would from when some dickhead tried to broadcast that stupid message on BB.

Soriya   Will your mom not be wondering where you are?

Andre   I don't live at home.

Soriya   Oh. So where do you live?

Andre   At one hostel. It's cool though. No one to nag me …

Soriya   You don't get a curfew?

Andre   Long gone. You just clock in and show your face and then dip off, after hours, when it'd be rude for them to knock your door. You alright?

Soriya   Yeah. The fresh air's helping.

Andre   Look, I've gotta dip. You better go in. Peoples are still carrying on nutty trying loot up people's house and that.

Soriya (*to herself*)   Shit! Dad's shop.

Andre   What?

Soriya   Nothing. Where you going?

Andre   Gotta go buck my bredrin.

Soriya   You know what people round here are saying?

Andre   What?

Soriya   The girl that was attacked, was raped, was gang raped by some kids off that estate.

Andre   What do you reckon?

Soriya   I asked Marcus if he could guess who it might be, you know, 'cause he lived there.

Andre   Time ago!

Soriya   I know, but still. And then I thought, if anyone's gonna have answers, it would be you. But Marcus made me promise not to ask.

Andre   Answers to what?

Soriya   To who did it.

Andre So you ra think it happened?

Soriya He said, some shit just kicked off at home and you had to leave. Why would your mom make you leave home Andre?

Andre So if you knew I wasn't at home already, why ask? Kinda snidey, ennit?

Soriya Curious to what you'd say.

Andre What are you getting at?

Soriya Just odd isn't it? You get kicked out the same night a girl got raped on the estate.

Andre Are you serious?!

Soriya Look, I'm just asking …

Andre No you're not! You're accusing! You dizzy little bitch!

Soriya Erm, excuse me! Watch your mouth!

Andre Nah! You watch yours! True say I thought you was cool but now? 'Low you man! You're as dumb as that stupid little flat mate of yours. Chasing after black man and Indian man like she don't see what goes. How long have you known me for now, eh? And what about Marcus? He used to babysit me when I was a youte.

Soriya That was a long time ago. People change!

Andre Ah, seen. There you go again. You know what, fuck you!

Soriya I'm not saying it was you. But I do find it hard to believe when you're out here night in night out that you don't know more than the scraps of information they're feeding us.

Andre Soz babes. I don't associate with rapists. Not my style ya get me?

Soriya So a girl was definitely raped? Well that's something.

Andre Shut up! How many times have you cut through the estate late at night? Huh? And how many times have you felt scared? Never! You really think you could be walking through estates in Bow or Hackney with that same feeling of ease? These streets don't belong to no rapists.

Soriya That's a very sweet outlook hun but unfortunately …

Andre Don't 'hun' me! The reason you don't know nothing is 'cause there's nothing to know. You think some little girl got raped? Where is she then? The girl don't exist. It's just a story some messed-up person started so they could cause a lot of dramz.

Soriya People don't make up stories like that! Not about rape. It's too …

Andre Shut up man! Yes they do. They hear a little something and retell it to suit their needs. 'Cause if a young Asian girl gets raped by a young black boy or worse, boys, then all Indian people round here have ammunition to say what they really think about their black neighbours! They can say they hate the way man like me smoke weeds on street corner, not thinking about the fact I ain't causing no harm to no one …

Soriya Don't flatter yourself darling, no one cares that much.

Andre That little blonde thing upstairs has proper rubbed off on you. And it's vice versa! Don't get it twisted. You think black women round here, hard-working black women want to see one of the few sharp, intelligent, and I'll ra say it, handsome, black men shacked up with a paki?

Soriya Oi!

Andre Ah. Did that sting? Don't pretend you haven't clocked on to that any ways. They would all love to see you married off to some distant cousin from back home. Then they'd be happy for you.

Soriya You know what you're boring me now …

Andre Ah. My bad. You want entertainment. Shame, 'cause I only deal with facts, like Indian girls like cock same as everybody else! Black cock even. But then you already know that, don't you? Yet when I say it, you're thinking even more I did it, aren't you? How about if I put my hood back up, like how I know you love it. Does that fuck with your head even more? Are you now certain I did it? How about if I step towards you in a way and walk just standardly how black guys walk? Now what you thinking?

Soriya Get away from me.

Andre You so think you're a part of this here world. And yet you wanna make those sorts of comments. And you think making them with a black man on your arm makes it OK? You can't be racist, can you, if you're fucking him at night? He ain't even black sweetheart. You need to realise. One baby with you and that gene's gone!

George *re-enters.*

George Oi! What's going on?

Andre Silenced.

Soriya Hey George. Go back upstairs.

George Si?!

Soriya I just need to swing by my dad's, quickly! Get back inside. I'll call you when I get there.

Soriya *turns to exit.*

George Oi! Si! Don't be silly. You've been drinking you can't drive!

Soriya *exits.*

George Si! Get in! It's dangerous! Si! Come on! I'll call you a cab! (*To* **Andre**.) What the hell?

Andre *shrugs his shoulders.*

George You were supposed to be looking after her! Excellent bloody job!

Andre She's too ... drunk.

George Yeah, she is!

George *turns to exit and hears a commotion coming from the direction* **Si** *went.* **George** *tries to call* **Soriya***. No answer.*

George Well now what you gonna do?

Andre What?!

George I swear if anything happens to her ...

Andre How is this my fault?

George She has to be in her car by now. The red route's only there. Quick! Come upstairs! See if we can see her.

Andre *follows reluctantly behind* **George**. *Lights.*

Scene Four

Saghir's *living room.* **Saghir**'s *sat reading a newspaper.* **Ibi** *enters.*

Saghir Hello?

Ibi Just me.

Saghir Where's Umra?

Ibi She stayed at Amira's.

Saghir You not supposed to stay overnight?

Ibi I saw the news and thought I'd better check you were OK. Have you just got back from the shop?

Saghir No, they made us close earlier.

Ibi Is it?

Saghir ... it is.

Ibi Nah, I was calling. Seen next door's house?

Saghir Yes. We cleaned up most but then figure save the rest for morning.

Ibi And all down the high street, over to Westbridge? There's kids and police everywhere. You pulled the shutters on the shop yes?

Saghir Of course. Ask me stupid bloody questions.

Ibi OK. Cool.

Saghir Waste of bloody time coming back, hey?

Ibi Well no, it's fine. Peace of mind knowing you're alright.

Saghir Yes, yes. And you'll pick Umra up in the morning?

Ibi Well no, she wanted to stay with Amira tonight as they're going to some market in the morning but I said I'd go meet them in the evening for food plus I've got us tickets to see *The Lion King* tomorrow so we still get to do something nice.

Saghir *Lion King*?

Ibi Yes.

Saghir Who do you think she is? American tourist? Don't be stupid! Rubbish show, plus Alijan and the boys are coming over from Greenford tomorrow. They want to meet the lovely Umra. So do they come here or do we all go to Amira's?

Ibi Dad! No! It's booked!

Saghir Ibi. Umra wants to see family. Not silly Disney shows she won't even bloody understand! Why do you think she's always with Amira, huh? *Lion King*? Ha!

Saghir *is engrossed in the paper.*

Ibi Fine I'll see if I can sort a refund.

Ibi *goes to exit as* **Soriya** *enters.*

Ibi Hey sis!

Saghir Soriya?

Soriya Hey Dad? Can I crash here tonight?

Saghir It's after bloody midnight. What are you doing out?

Ibi You look a fucking mess sis.

Saghir Ibi!

Soriya Thanks! I'm tired and I just wanna go to bed.

Saghir You OK?

Soriya Yeah, I'm fine Dad. Just tired.

Saghir You shouldn't be out driving with all these idiots about!

Soriya Dad ...

Saghir I'll go upstairs and make up the bed.

Saghir *exits.*

Ibi What's up?

Soriya I told you. I'm tired.

Ibi And I'm telling you knobface, you're lying.

Soriya Do you think everyone hates the fact that me and Marcus are together?

Ibi Who's everyone?

Soriya Neighbours? Friends?

Ibi Insignificants you mean? Why would you care?

Soriya Just an old lady said something to me tonight, about how maybe we don't belong together.

Ibi People have been saying that for years! And there's a word for them!

Soriya Sensible?

Ibi Have you and Marcus had a fight?

Soriya No. Just since Sara was ... people have been a lot more forthcoming with their opinions on mine and Marcus's relationship. I'm getting tired of defending it.

Ibi Well don't. I don't defend me and Umra to anyone.

Soriya Yeah, but you're weird ...

Ibi I know.

Soriya I wish I was as confident about me and Marcus as you are about you and Umra.

Ibi Yeah, but that was easy for me. Everyone around us were splitting up, divorcing. Mom and Dad, friends from Uni. The only people I knew in long stable relationships were those that married for practicality rather than love. The love will come and I just have to trust that.

Soriya You don't think Mom and Dad should have got married do you?

Ibi I think Mom made a lot of sacrifices to be with Dad. How could you not eventually be bitter when you see it's not being returned?

Soriya When you told me you were marrying her, I was so worried for you.

Ibi And now?

Soriya I don't know. She's obviously beautiful and sweet and kind but …

Ibi Sounds like an alright package to me.

Soriya Where is she?

Ibi Amira's.

Soriya You see?

Ibi What? She not allowed to have friends now? You moved your boyfriend in with your best friend. Could have got your own place but, no.

Soriya That's different.

Ibi Is it?

Soriya You're married.

Ibi So we have to spend every waking minute together?

Soriya Newly married.

Ibi I'm just giving her her space. She's a lot younger than us. I can't even imagine how overwhelming it must be. Like going to study abroad but having to lodge with a family.

Soriya She did agree.

Ibi I know and like me she knows she's made the right choice. That doesn't mean you don't get scared from day to day. It's a journey, like any other. I guess I just want to iron out a few of the pot holes for her.

Soriya Make sure she knows how lucky she is.

Ibi And how lucky I am. She makes me feel safe and loved and I can't wait to start a family with her.

Soriya It sounds almost perfect.

Ibi Nothing's perfect Si.

Soriya I get told me and Marcus are.

Ibi That's a lot of pressure.

Soriya Yeah. I feel like I've been so happy with Marcus as long as others have been happy for us.

Ibi And now?

Soriya I just want to be happy for myself.

Ibi Makes sense.

Soriya Dad didn't love him, did he?

Ibi Dad will love whoever you love.

Soriya He loves Umra.

Ibi God! You sound jealous!

Soriya No. Just happy to see you so …

Ibi Yeah.

Soriya I'm sorry for always being a dick!

Ibi Please, I'm used to it!

Ibi *hugs* **Soriya** *and makes his way up to bed.*

Soriya *is left alone on the sofa. Lights fade.*

Scene Five

The flat.

Sound of crowds of people below.

Andre   She answering her phone yet?

George   No! Do you think it's too late to call the landline?

Andre   Not if you're stressing.

George   I'm just scared 'cause if she hasn't gone there then I'll cause them to panic.

Andre   'Low it then! How pissed was she?

George   Well she was sick …

Andre   You girls man … and you wonder why things happen.

George   Yes child!

Crowds get closer. **Andre** *spots a bag of weed on the table. Smirking, he picks it up and shakes it in front of her.*

Andre   Tut tut tut!

George   Put it back.

Andre   Girls like you make me laugh yeah.

George   I'm not the same customer as the little skag heads you sell to on the estate, yeah?

Andre   Er … actually love … you are.

George   Put it back.

Andre   If you think I'm looking to rob you why invite me into your house?

George Because it's manic out there.

Andre Please! I'm a big man. Anyways, I betta dip.

George What?

Andre I've gotta go.

Andre *turns to exit. We still hear the shouting outside.*

George No. Wait. Stay with me please. Just until Marcus or Si comes back?

Andre You'll be fine. How many floors up is this?

George It's not that. I'm just scared.

Andre Oh, OK.

Andre *is shocked by the request for help but agrees to stay. Sound of breaking bottles and shouts happen louder.* **Andre** *sits down opposite* **George**. *They have nothing to talk about. Suddenly a brick comes through the window.*

Andre Shit! You OK?

George Erm … yeah.

Andre Nah they're taking the piss!

Andre *exits. Lights fade.*

Scene Six

Outside **Saghir**'s *house,* **Soriya**'s *smoking.* **Marcus** *enters.*

Soriya Fuck!

Marcus Whoa! Sorry to scare you? What's up?

Soriya Nothing. I'm fine.

Marcus And smoking again apparently …

Soriya I never said I'd quit, I said I'd cut back. And I have!

Marcus OK. George called. Said you were upset? You OK? You coming home?

Beat.

Marcus Si…. ?

Soriya I don't think this is a good idea.

Marcus What?

Soriya Me and you?

Marcus What?!

Soriya I want out.

Marcus Are you serious?

Beat.

Marcus Look. What's up?

Soriya Nothing.

Marcus You're OK?

Soriya Yes. No. I don't know!

Marcus Look, you're starting to freak me out here.

Soriya I'm sorry it's just …

Marcus Just what?!

Soriya Do Asian people and black people belong together?

Marcus What?

Soriya Name one successful mixed-race couple.

Marcus There's loads!

Soriya Name one! Someone with a successful marriage under their belts.

Marcus Are you fucking kidding me?

Soriya No. I need you to help me 'cause I have all these thoughts swimming through my head and I desperately want you to stop them.

Marcus   If two people love each other that's enough.

Soriya   Really? 'Cause my parents loved each other and they couldn't make it work. I'm guessing your parents did and they didn't manage to stick it out ...

Marcus   We're not my parents or your parents. We're different.

Soriya   Why are we? What makes us so special? Everything we have in common is in line with our age. We like the same music, the same films, but that's it. We've grown up in completely different cultures, different worlds and I just worry they don't mesh together all too good.

Marcus   Ah for fuck's sake! My mom loves you and your dad likes me. They're our worlds! Meshing!

Soriya   No. Our parents are respecting our choices. I'm sure if they could make the decision for us they wouldn't wish this.

Marcus   Wish what? Us to be happy? God forbid!

Soriya   I'm not like you, OK? I'm not cool with who I am! I grew up my whole life being so grateful I was raised with my dad. People stare at me when they can't place where I'm from. They know I'm not white but after that they get stuck. When I'm with my dad they understand. We're Asian. I have an identity. And I love it. I love everything that comes with it. I love belonging to a large family that bickers over the dinner table. I love getting dressed up to go to our many relatives' weddings. I love Dad forcing us to watch crap soaps on ARY when we have dinner round his despite all the protests to just put *EastEnders* on ...

Marcus   And nothing will change that.

Soriya   I'm scared you'll change that.

Marcus   Are you taking the piss?

Soriya   No I'm upset 'cause I've just realised I don't think mixing races works.

Marcus What?

Soriya I know it's a horrid thing to say, but it doesn't mean I can stop thinking it.

Marcus And if we were to last and go the distance ... you don't wanna find out? It shouldn't be about colour or heritage but love and compatibility outside of 'our dads were raised in the same city'. It's a weak link!

Soriya I'm gonna have an arranged marriage.

Marcus Oh my fucking god?! What the fuck?!

Soriya Not right away but it's what I want. I want to have Pakistani children for a Pakistani husband. I don't want my children to be as confused as I am.

Marcus You're underestimating yourself completely. You'd be an amazing mom. You don't think I see that in you? Why do you think I wanna be with you?

Soriya I'm sorry.

Marcus And what about your mom? When your children see she's white? They'll know they're mixed and you'll still have to explain to them. Your neighbours' comments have got through ...

Soriya Don't be stupid. Just things are different now.

Marcus Now what? Now some girl got raped?

Soriya It's got nothing to do with her.

Marcus I find that hard to believe. We were fine. Better than fucking fine. Great. And then some nigger rapes a paki and suddenly –

Soriya A what?

Marcus You know what I mean?

Soriya A paki?

Marcus Fuck off! I didn't mean it like that! George says it all the time!

Soriya It's not the word it's the tone, the context! Everyone knows that!

Marcus Same as nigger?

Soriya Exactly!

Marcus But me saying that didn't offend you!

Soriya You didn't say nigger.

Marcus Yeah I did.

Soriya Well I wouldn't hear that, would I, it's not offensive to me.

Marcus It's not offensive to me either.

Soriya Well good for you.

Marcus 'Cause I know I'm not that. Some wasteman that hangs around the estate doing all sorts with girls, now *that* accusation seems viable. Same way you're not a paki.

Soriya That word shouldn't be used to describe anyone.

Marcus I know and I'm sorry. It's just. I'm angry. I can't help but think about some young girl, your dad's friend's daughter, who's sat at home, whilst all this is going on and refusing to come forward.

Soriya She might be scared.

Marcus She might be exaggerating!

Soriya How can you say that? She was raped. Gang raped.

Marcus We don't know that. It just said 'attacked'.

Soriya To be honest, that's not even the issue anymore. *Beat.*

Soriya How could we ever have thought this could work?

Marcus This what? We were made for each other!

Soriya Erm – I think a lot of people would disagree with that. If we were really made for each other wouldn't you be Asian or me black or anything other than Asian?

Marcus What kind backward talk is that?

Soriya Backward? What do we even have in common?

Marcus We ... we ... like the same music, films ...

Soriya We're so different and you don't see it!

Marcus And you do?

Soriya Yes!

Marcus Since when?

Soriya Since now!

We hear sirens in the distance.

Marcus God! Tonight's ridiculous. Please can I get you home, safely? George is alone in the flat. We should go back, check she's cool and then talk.

Soriya I'm gonna stay here tonight. We can talk some more in the morning. Fresh.

Marcus OK. Well can I stay here with you?

Soriya No. You should check on George. Tell her I'm sorry for running off. I'll be home in the morning.

Marcus Soriya ...

Soriya Night.

Marcus What I said about the girl ...

Soriya It's not even the issue anymore.

Soriya *exits into the house. We hear more sirens. Lights.*

Scene Seven

Outside the Westbridge. **Andre**'s *walking alone pushing his bike alongside him.* **Audrey** *runs in from her parked car.*

Audrey Oi!

Andre *sees his mom and stops.*

Audrey There's a riot going on and you just feel to up and walk street? Like you have no home!

Andre I don't.

Audrey Even if you did you'd still be out here. Like some sort of street urchin! You know how many people have ended up in hospital tonight 'cause of it. They've smashed out next door's shop! You want to see the front of the house!

Andre And?

Audrey I dunno what is the matter with you.

Andre What you doing here?

Audrey They call me up as soon as they seen you never show. Threatening to kick you out.

Andre Is it?

Audrey And then what you gonna do? 'Cause I can't take you back.

Andre No one asked you to.

Audrey You don't see Andre. What you putting me through. I'm too old for this shit. I shouldn't be sat in my car in the middle of the night, waiting for you to stroll by.

Andre No one asked you to!

Audrey Actually darling they did. Saying if I never come down here and find you quick them a call the police. 'Cause you can't stick to no curfew? How hard is it?

Andre I had things doing?

Audrey I hate this estate – and yet I knows it's where you would be. What I don't understand is why you like it so much? It's ugly, and full of all sorts.

Andre It's home. Ain't full of nothing but family.

Audrey These people ain't your family. You think you're gonna be able to rely on them? Which of them would have noticed if you never reached your bed tonight?

Andre *shrugs.*

Andre They know I didn't rape no girl. Not 'cause they was with me all night just 'cause they know. The way family do.

Beat.

Audrey I wish I could know. I really do. But your dad had a gift for lying –

Andre I'm not my dad!

Audrey I know!

Andre I'm not like him.

Audrey Andre …

Andre I hate him!

Audrey I know.

Andre But then I hate you for seeing him in me!

Audrey I know.

Andre Mom. Go home!

Andre *gets on his bike and cycles off.*

Scene Eight

George *alone, drunk. The window is broken.* **Marcus** *enters.*

Marcus You know there's still people down there? (*Seeing the window.*) You OK?

George Fucking fantastic! You?

Marcus What happened to the window?

George You know I hadn't noticed!

Marcus Shit! Are you OK?

George I'm fine. I'm off to bed.

Marcus George. I'm so sorry. You weren't injured though right?

George No.

Marcus Cool. Go to bed. I'll have it all cleared up by morning.

George Don't be silly. It's not your fault. Just wanted to rant.

Marcus Honestly. It's the least I can do.

George I've arranged for someone to come out first thing tomorrow. It'll be fine tonight … so long as it doesn't rain again!

Marcus OK, well I'll at least clear up all this so you or Soriya don't end up cutting yourself.

George Where is Si?

Marcus Dad's.

George And why couldn't she call me?

Marcus *shrugs.*

George You needed to see how she stormed off earlier and just left me alone! Jumped in her car, drunk, and left me! I think she accused Andre of attacking that girl.

Marcus Andre? What?

George I know!

Marcus When did she see Andre?

George Oh he was passing, as usual.

Marcus And she accused him of the attack?

George Ah babes – I caught snippets of a heated convo from the balcony and filled large gaps myself.

Marcus Nah, nah, nah, wait! Si and Andre had a fight?

George Well, I dunno! He definitely was having a rant by the time I came down but whether it was at her I don't know. I asked him and he just shrugged it off.

Marcus Andre? Fuck! You know what … that's why his mom kicked him out! I'm so stupid! I knew something didn't seem right but I just put it to the back of my head! That fucking prick!

George Oi! Now we don't know that! God you're as bad as those boys out there!

Marcus No! I do know. It makes sense!

George Alright Sherlock! Quite a big accusation to throw at a sixteen-year-old boy that had the decency to stay with me this evening.

Marcus I need to speak to him.

George Well I'll be needing a strong word with your girlfriend.

Marcus I dunno what's going on with her … we just had a bit of a fight …

George Oh. Anything serious?

Marcus No! Yeah, maybe.

George Do we need wine? 'Cause I've been called a rapist and a 'paki lover' whilst attempts were made at my life.

Marcus What?!

George Shouted up from the street. I'm guessing it was meant for you.

Marcus Ah hun, I'm so …

George Don't you dare say you're sorry again!

Marcus Right!

George Pussy!

Marcus Yep!

George Wine!

Marcus Lets go for it! I've already had a spliff downstairs.

George And you're having a go at Soriya about cigarettes?

Marcus I know! It was stress relief ! Our secret?

George Well I have more …

Marcus I'll build, you get some glasses. Whoa! You necked this yourself already?

George What part of being called a rapist did you not understand?

Marcus Then you were clearly feeling guilty. (*Shakes the near empty bottle.*)

George Of raping a girl? Busted!

Marcus *and* **George** *laugh.*

George I shouldn't laugh. It may actually turn that way soon, anyway.

Marcus What way?

George Going for girls.

Marcus Shut up! A gorgeous girl like you! What happened to the banker?

George The white guy? Not really my type.

Marcus And what is your type?

George Well I've had the biggest crush on Si's brother since I was like thirteen but it didn't really work out, to Si's delight!

Marcus Really?

George I know! She's such a hater right?

Marcus And now he's married.

George Exactly! She could have ruined my life! If I'm still single when I hit thirty, I'll officially disown her! And put a curse on yours and hers relationship!

Marcus We're into witchery now?

George Oh yeah punk! And you two will be the first to get it!

Marcus That's providing we're still together!

George Stop being so wet! You guys have one little fight –

Marcus Little?

George You'll be fine. Do you feel to divulge?

Marcus Why not? Soriya has now decided to marry a Pakistani.

George What? Shut up! She doesn't even fancy Asian men.

Marcus Well, apparently fancying someone is 'too short- term'.

George What are you on about? Who has she met?

Marcus Oh there's no one in particular. She's thinking of an arrangement.

George Oh, hun. She's drunk and angry or something! You know how much stick she gave Ibi when he said he was gonna marry Umra?

Marcus Well, that's what she's talking –

George You have nothing to worry about. I know Soriya. She will never do that! Have you met Umra?

Marcus No. She wasn't there when we had dinner –

George Huh!

Marcus I didn't want to question it …

George You need to see her. Stunning girl. Young. They're first cousins, you know. No judgement, but seriously, she looks just like Soriya. Is that not wrong?

Marcus I don't know …

George Babes? Come on! It's like he's fucking his sister! It's wrong!

Marcus Whoa! George man!

George Someone has to say it. They think it's such a precious thing! It's not! And when I find someone and fall in love and live happily ever after, then Ibi will see what a mistake he made!

Marcus Well good luck to you.

George I hope so. I'm not looking for anything unrealistic. Just a nice guy.

Marcus Nice? Hmmm …

George Seriously! I hate guys that drive flash cars and am completely uninterested in pretentious jobs –

Marcus Pretentious?

George Jobs that they don't teach you in French …

Marcus What?!

George You know. 'My father is, my mom does …' Teachers, doctors, carpenters! Now they're normal jobs. Being the CEO of a blah blah blah that specialises in who gives a fuck …! Not interested!

Marcus Ha! Fair point. What exactly do you think I do?

George You're a business man.

Marcus Ha! That makes me sound like a pimp! Or even worse a used-car salesman.

George And what's so wrong with that?

Marcus I think I'd rather be a pimp.

George Yeah. Good point!

Marcus Well, the football player? Si mentioned something about a premiership football player.

George I don't know about premiership! He played for like the Gunners ... team ... or something. I wasn't really listening.

Marcus Right ... and ... ? Anything there?

George He was cute. Good arse.

Marcus Of course!

George Just ... I think. I want someone I have something in common with.

Marcus Have you been speaking to Soriya?

George What? Oh. Babes, common interests don't begin with matching skin tone! I have more chance of ending up with a black guy than a white guy if we're gonna base it on common interests!

Marcus And what do you have in common with them?

George *stands.*

George Babes! I'm from 'the junc'! Holiday in Tobago at least twice annually. LOVE curry goat and roti. Drive an X5 with a bigger engine size than yours, listen to grime, wear 'bling', from Links of London of course, and so am technically more street than you or any 'brear' from off that fucking Westbridge estate!

Marcus *laughs while* **George** *takes a bow.*

Marcus You're too good for everyone round here! Black, white, street –

George Posh?

Marcus Yeah!

George Thanks. Like I said. I know what I want. It's not unattainable and I have no intention of settling until I get it spot on.

Silence. **George** *leans towards* **Marcus**.

Marcus What are you doing?

George I don't know.

Marcus Look, no. Sorry if I misled you but … no.

George No, I'm sorry. Everything about this, us chilling here, is just reminding me of someone and it's confusing me.

Marcus OK. We cool?

George Our secret?

Marcus *nods. Lights fade to the sound of sirens and more havoc.*

Scene Nine

Saghir*'s house. The next morning. We hear a radio news bulletin reporting on last night's riots.*

Ibi Dad! Come on! Hurry up, eh? I promised chacha-ji we'd be two in the shop from open!

Saghir (*o/s*) They are not going to let us trade today! I promise you! There will be more police warnings after last night, there's no point.

Ibi Dad! Just hurry, yeah!

Saghir I can't find my phone! Where have you put it?

Ibi Try calling it!

Saghir I can't hear it!

Ibi Dad come on!

George *enters.*

George Hey.

Ibi Hey! Two mornings in a row?

George Yeah. I've just driven past the shop.

Ibi Yeah?

George Have you not been there yet?

Ibi No, on our way now, why?

George Look, it's all fixable. I took a couple of pictures. It didn't look like they'd managed to get inside so ...

George *hands* **Ibi** *her phone.*

Ibi Shit!

George You OK?

Ibi Yeah. Everything is covered but ... looks like we might just be out of action for a bit I guess.

George Well they'll be sorry when they have to go all the way to the high street for a bottle of milk.

Ibi Maybe.

George It's not just you guys. The entire street looks like ... well ... I'm sure you can gather. **Ibi** Bet the French deli looks fine.

George It'll be OK.

Ibi Yeah. Shit! Si's gone home if you're looking for her.

George I actually came to see you.

Ibi Oh, right. Look George, now's not the best time ...

George Yeah. Of course ... Well, no, I just came to share some good news.

Ibi Yeah?

George Just ended up emailing over a couple of pictures to that agency yesterday lunchtime and they've got me my first job!

Ibi That quick?

George I didn't even need to audition. They cast me straight from the photos!

Ibi Cool. What's it for?

George You are now looking at the new face of Pizza Hut.

Ibi Congratulations?

George I tried to get out of it.

Ibi Why?

George I told the agent it wasn't realistic for someone with my skin quality and physique to eat at the hut.

Ibi And what did they say to that?

George The commercial's worth eight grand and if I turn it down and lose their commission they'll have to strike me from their books.

Ibi Strict. What did you say to that?

George See you Monday.

Ibi *laughs.*

George Yeah ...

Ibi Look. I'm so sorry for the way I spoke to you yesterday. I have the utmost respect for you and I don't know ... I guess I was just angry and scared ...

George Scared?

Ibi Scared I'd not made the right decision.

George Ibi I want to tell you something –

Ibi No. Let me finish. Since the wedding I'd felt so distant to Umra. It's not what I imagined being married to be like and it's an adjustment.

George Of course ...

Ibi I mean I have tried so hard to please her, impress her even and the response was ... nothing.

George Ibi ...

Ibi So all those insecurities that were bugging me I just let them rip on you.

George If you can sense something's not right ...

Ibi But then, please don't say anything, but seeing how quickly Marcus and Si almost crumbled over the smallest thing? I mean come on, some old lady made a comment and their world's collapsed. That could never happen to us and that gives me confidence, strength even. Does that sound cocky?

George But you can't really compare –

Ibi I mean there's still a slight language barrier but my Punjabi's getting much better and her English is so much stronger and I think that's the reason for not feeling as close as we should.

George Ibi, I worry that ...

Ibi And I love her George! I really do!

George You do?

Ibi I mean I didn't even think it would be possible to feel like this about her so ... so soon I guess. But I've never felt like this about anyone.

George Anyone ...?

Ibi Ah! George! That came out wrong. This is just different, I guess, and feels so right. You understand yeah?

George Yes.

Ibi Sorry. What were you trying to say?

Saghir *enters.*

George Oh erm ... I can't even remember.

Saghir I give up! It's lost! Georgina?!

George Hello *Abba* !

Saghir Hello darling! You OK?! You hungry? You want tea?

George Oh I'm OK thank you. Trying this new diet thing.

Saghir Diet! There's nothing to you! This is why you are single! Men like meat!

George Love you too, *Abba*!

Saghir (*indicating the food tray*) Here!

George Thank you.

Ibi Look Dad. George just saw the shop.

Saghir They've trashed it?!

Ibi Here.

Ibi *passes* **Saghir** *the phone.*

Ibi Dad. Don't worry. We'll be covered.

Saghir What is that? (*Reads.*) 'Go Home Pak …' Ah!

Ibi Ah Dad. It's just kids.

Saghir Maybe. It's just sad that despite how long I've lived here. Despite having two British children. Despite learning their British fucking language – I will never be that.

Ibi What? British? Who cares?

Saghir I care. This is my home and I'm not going anywhere!

Ibi No one expects you to.

Saghir Someone does!

Ibi That's probably a couple of kids that couldn't give a toss either way they just enjoyed the chance to do a little vandalism. Excitement!

Saghir I need my phone!

Ibi Here. Use mine.

Ibi *passes* **Saghir** *his mobile.*

Saghir Come, we have to go down there!

Saghir *exits.*

Ibi We've got to …

George Yeah! Of course.

Ibi Are you gonna stay?

George No, no. I'm just gonna check my face but I'll let myself out.

Ibi OK, see you George.

George Bye.

Ibi *exits. Lights.*

Scene Ten

Outside the shop on the Westbridge. **Saghir** *on his mobile phone.*

Saghir Yes. I understand. So, what happens now? Well I'm outside the shop. Do I have to stay here?

But there's no way to secure it?

Oh, OK. And what time will that be?

But we don't need to be here?

I understand. Thank you.

Ibi *enters.*

Ibi That's all we're gonna get in the car.

Saghir Come, let's just go home.

Ibi *turns and exits in the direction he came.* **Audrey** *enters from the opposite side. She stops after noticing* **Saghir** *first and then the shop. She offers a half smile.* **Saghir** *returns it with a head nod.* **Audrey** *crosses in front of him in silence, continuing her journey.* **Saghir** *watches her pass.* **Audrey** *exits.* **Saghir** *takes one last look at his shop and then exits.*

Scene Eleven

Private garage on the Westbridge estate. As before.

Andre Tst! Oi!

Sara Hey mister!

Andre Sorry I'm late!

Sara You will be!

Andre Yeah yeah! What happened to your – (face).

She flinches and looks away

Andre Him?

Beat.

Andre I wish you'd tell someone!

Sara Like who? The police?

Andre What about your sister?

Sara She agrees with Dad.

Andre That's messed up! I wish … I wish –

Sara 'Low it! They'll get over it! Just sometimes you gotta ride things out.

Andre Why don't you come stay with me for a bit at the hostel?

Sara Andre the hero!

Andre Why not? I could sneak you in easy!

Sara You're not serious? That would give them ammunition to kill me!

Andre They wouldn't know where you were! It'd teach 'em a lesson.

Sara Nah! I've got no reason to act guilty. I work hard at school. Help out at home. They wouldn't have a problem with me having a boyfriend, except that it's you. That makes them wrong not me.

Andre And what? They're just gonna keep punching you in the face until you stop?

Sara They're pissed. They'll calm down.

Andre They've tried to call me a fucking rapist.

Sara We got caught dude. By Dad's friend. What else could he say? That was mortifying! I would never have lived that down.

Andre Sounds like you're glad he did that.

Sara Well in a way I am. I'm a young girl. My reputation would have been ruined …

Andre What reputation? You're telling me you're gonna be with me the rest of your life so only what I think of you matters.

Sara I know. And I love you, but let's be realistic. I'd love to be with you forever but if it don't work …

Andre Why wouldn't it work?

Sara Just saying innit, if it don't work, I'm screwed. I'm the one with the damaged rep. Not you. No one would want to touch me.

Andre I want to touch you.

Sara I want you to touch me. **Andre** Where? There?

Sara Maybe …

Andre *kisses her.*

Andre There?

Andre *and* **Sara** *kiss again. It quickly turns into more.* **Marcus** *enters talking into his mobile.*

Marcus I'll be at my mom's. Please, Si, just call me back.

Marcus *instantly notices* **Andre** *and* **Sara***.*

Marcus Ah, are you serious?

Andre You don't know about knocking?

Marcus For who?

The Westbridge 443

Andre This ain't your space fam! Ain't you got a yard to be chilling in?

Marcus Same way you have a hostel to be getting back to innit? Who's she?

Andre It's my bredrin from school.

Marcus Oh you two are *friends*?

Sara Yes.

Marcus You live on Westbridge too?

Sara No, erm ...

Andre She lives across the way.

Marcus And yet you're such good friends.

Andre No –

Marcus Course not 'cause you don't even really go school do you?

Andre Differently, we were trying to have a private convo so if you don't mind ...

Marcus Convo? I think that's where it's all going wrong for you Andre. If that's how you insist on talking to girls.

Andre Look. What do you want?

Marcus Who you stepping to, you fucking prick?!

Andre Dickhead!

Marcus What did you just say?!

Marcus *drags up* **Andre** *viciously and acts as though he's going to hit him.* **Andre** *is very shocked by this reaction.*

Andre Nothing. I didn't say nothing.

Marcus *lets him go.*

Marcus I can't believe I just caught little Andre having sex! I mean don't get me wrong, I was definitely boning girls by the time I was your age but still it's odd to see. I proper think of you as a rugrat!

Andre Yeah well I'm not!

Marcus Having sex ay? In the estate where that girl got raped. You got a proper little thing for Indian girls don't you?

Andre What are you on about? I'm sixteen! I've a thing for all girls!

Marcus And yet you only seem to get caught fucking the Asian ones.

Andre Ones? The only 'one' I've been fucking is her? That's my wife you prick!

Marcus Well that's a lie ain't it? I mean you fucked some next girl last week. (*Whispers.*) Against her will. (*Turning to* **Sara**.) Did you know about that? The girl that got attacked? It was your boyfriend that 'attacked' her.

Andre Oh my days! SHUT UP! What girl? What fucking girl? Will people just drop it! If you can't name her or point her out how can you be so protective of her!

Marcus (*grabs him again*) 'Cause she was a youte. Family friends with Si that you put your grubby hands on! And I can't even get into the dramz that's causing me.

Andre I didn't touch no one! There was no one to touch!

Marcus You fucking perverted liar! What?

Marcus *lays into* **Andre**, *slapping him repeatedly in the face. It's more to humiliate than to injure.*

Sara Oi! Stop it! Stop it!

Marcus What part of your man's a rapist did you not hear?

Through struggle **Andre** *falls to the floor.*

You make me sick! After everything your mom's done for you.

Marcus *kicks him out of anger. Throughout the rest of his rant he continuously kicks* **Andre**.

Marcus   And I swear to god you ever try talk to Soriya in a way again! Nah, you ever try to talk to her! I'll fucking kill you! Think you're a badman? Huh? Huh?!

Sara   Help! Help! Please! Somebody help us!

Marcus *then steps back, having shocked himself.*

Sara   Andre! Andre! I'm so sorry! Please be OK. I didn't know. I swear. I had no idea people knew it was you. I had know idea people knew my name! Please, please be OK! Andre! Please! I love you! I want to be with you. If you get through this I promise I will tell everyone the truth about us! I don't care anymore. I just want to be with you. Andre. Andre!

Marcus *hears* **Sara**'*s mumblings and is confused.*

Soriya (*from off*)   Marcus!

Soriya *enters.*

Soriya   Marcus!

On hearing **Soriya**'*s voice* **Sara** *panics, backs away and exits.*

Marcus   Si!

Soriya (*seeing* **Andre**)   What's going on?

Andre *begins to stand, visibly hurt.*

Marcus   Well here you are. The perfect excuse to leave me. Take it!

Soriya   Is that what you think I'm doing? Looking for excuses? Andre? Are you OK?!

Andre   Don't touch me! What you even doing here?

Soriya   I just saw Marcus's car … are you OK?

Andre   Why act like you care?

Andre *stands and touches his face for damage. His nose is bleeding.*

Soriya   You're hurt.

Andre   I'm fine. And I'll be fine.

Soriya   Marcus!

Marcus   What?

Soriya   Don't talk to me like that.

Marcus   Like what? What?! This is just how I talk, ennit?!

Soriya   Stop it!

Andre   Where's Sara?

Marcus   You blind? She dipped! Soon as she heard Si. Loyal!

Soriya   What?

Andre   What did you say to her?

Soriya   How do you know Sara, Andre?

Marcus   I didn't say anything.

Soriya   Andre?

Andre   If you scared her?

Marcus   How? She ducked off. She don't care about you.

Andre   Nah, she's just probably scared. And I'm not surprised. Your girl's a snake!

Soriya   Answer my question!

Andre   I'm sorry, but really who are you to me? Ain't it obvious?

Marcus   Watch it.

Soriya   Isn't what obvious?

Marcus   Si just leave it

Andre   Yeah, Si, leave it!

Marcus   I ain't warning you again!

Soriya   Will someone explain?

Andre   She's my girl! Sara's my girl.

Soriya   But when she was raped …

Andre   Are you really that dumb? No one was raped! She was with me and her dad's friend didn't like it!

Soriya   They said you raped her.

Andre   Bit more entertaining, innit?

Andre *sits down to make a phone call. No one answers. He redials.*

Soriya (*to* **Marcus**)   Did you know, before?

Marcus   Why the fuck would I know?

Soriya   What is with you?

Marcus   Are you serious? You wanna know what's with me?

Soriya   We'll talk when we get home, OK?

Marcus   Why? You might as well just say what you're saying, here! Who cares anymore? Fucking talk.

Soriya   Stop swearing at me!

Marcus   Talk! Soriya! You're telling me you don't want to be with me. I'm too different! Too mixed up for you! So what am I risking? Huh? TALK!

Soriya   I have doubts! I'm sorry.

Marcus   Well as long as you're sorry …

Soriya   I can't believe you hit him.

Marcus   Really?! I'm a black man from Westbridge. Is that not just what we do?!

Andre   You ain't black fam.

Marcus   You what?

Andre You heard. And you ain't from round here neither. Not really. Not the Westbridge. We don't churn out dickheads like you.

Marcus Well I'm sorry to disappoint.

Andre Mock all you want. But you're the one arguing on street with gal and for what? Nothing's really wrong. Nothing tragic has happened. Has it? You're not homeless, say, with a mom who don't trust you. You've not got the entire neighbourhood where you live putting a question mark above your head. And on top of all that. The thing that would have made it all worthwhile …

Andre *breaks*.

Marcus Andre …

Andre What?! I'm fine.

Marcus Go home.

Andre Is that a joke?

Marcus You just gonna stay here?

Andre She might come back.

Marcus You're gonna wait for her?

Andre Well I can hardly go to hers, can I?

Marcus I don't get it! Is she worth all this?

Andre I've got no choice. I love her.

Marcus Andre. It don't have to be this hard. I love Si, but –

Andre Nah soz fam. You don't. And she don't love you. You both just enjoy fucking each other 'cause it's exciting. You're not really supposed to be together, so it's dangerous. But at the end of the day, that's all it is – a good bang! That's why you don't get it. You know what, 'low it. I'll wait outside.

Andre *has been calling someone throughout. They're not answering. He exits.*

Soriya   He didn't do anything.

Marcus   As you said, that's not even the issue anymore.

The End.